Pharmacological Enhancements in the Military: Legal and Ethical Aspects

Wie sollte die informierte Zustimmung im Militär in Bezug auf pharmakologisches Enhancement aussehen?

Quel consentement éclairé dans les Armées pour l'augmentation des capacités par voie pharmacologique ?

International Studies on Military Ethics

THE SERIES IS EDITED UNDER THE AUSPICES OF THE INTERNATIONAL SOCIETY FOR MILITARY ETHICS IN EUROPE (EUROISME)

VOLUME 12

EURO ISME
International Society for Military Ethics in Europe

The titles published in this series are listed at *brill.com/isme*

Pharmacological Enhancements in the Military: Legal and Ethical Aspects

Wie sollte die informierte Zustimmung im Militär in Bezug auf pharmakologisches Enhancement aussehen?

Quel consentement éclairé dans les Armées pour l'augmentation des capacités par voie pharmacologique ?

By

Richard M. Heames

BRILL | NIJHOFF

LEIDEN | BOSTON

The views expressed in this paper are those of the author and do not necessarily represent the official thinking or policy of the UK Ministry of Defence or any other Department of Her Britannic Majesty's Government of the United Kingdom. Furthermore, such views should not be considered as constituting an official endorsement of factual accuracy, opinion, conclusion or recommendation of the UK Ministry of Defence or any other Department of Her Britannic Majesty's Government of the United Kingdom.

Die in dieser Abhandlung ausgesprochenen Ansichten sind die des Autors und stellen nicht unbedingt die des britischen Verteidigungsministeriums oder irgendeines anderen Ministeriums Ihrer Britannischen Majestät des Vereinigten Königreiches dar. Außerdem sollten solche Ansichten nicht als konstituierend für eine offizielle Billigung sachlicher Richtigkeit, Meinung, Fazit oder Empfehlung des britischen Verteidigungsministeriums oder irgendeines anderen Ministeriums der Regierung Ihrer Britannischen Majestät des Vereinigten Königreichs angesehen werden.

Les vues exprimées dans ce mémoire sont celles de l'auteur et ne représentent pas nécessairement la pensée officielle de la politique du ministère de la Défense du Royaume-Uni ni de tout autre ministère du gouvernement de Sa Majesté Britannique. De plus, ces vues ne doivent pas être considérées comme reflétant avec précision la réalité, l'opinion, les conclusions ou les recommandations du gouvernement du Royaume-Uni de Sa Majesté Britannique.

German translation of the text by Gerta K. Badde-Valentine, French translation by Jean-François Palard.

The Library of Congress Cataloging-in-Publication Data is available online at https://catalog.loc.gov

Typeface for the Latin, Greek, and Cyrillic scripts: "Brill". See and download: brill.com/brill-typeface.

ISSN 2214-7926
ISBN 978-90-04-67772-2 (paperback)
ISBN 978-90-04-67774-6 (e-book)

This book is printed on acid-free paper and produced in a sustainable manner.

The jury of EuroISME's annual prize for the best student's thesis on military ethics consists of

1. Colonel Rev. Prof. Dr. P.J. McCormack, MBE, (chairman, United Kingdom)
2. Brigadier General (ret.) Benoît Royal (France)
3. Senior Chaplain Lt.Col. Dr. Janne Aalto (Finland)
4. Dr. Veronika Bock (Germany)
5. Mil Superior MMag. Stefan Gugerel (Austria)
6. Dr. Asta Maskaliūnaitė (Estonia)
7. Maj.Gen. (res) Dr. Juan Moliner Gonzalez (Spain)
8. Ms. Ivana Gošić (Serbia, Secretary)

Enquiries: secretariat.ethicsprize@euroisme.eu
www.euroisme.eu

The prize is financially supported by

Contents/Inhalt/Table

Pharmacological Enhancements in the Military: Legal and Ethical Aspects

Introduction

Humans are a frail species that have survived and dominated the land due to intellect, resourcefulness and ability to adapt. This survivability and adaptability hold true for armed conflict, where a soldier[1] still needs to overcome emotions such as fear and respond to the physical demands of hunger, thirst and fatigue. Training can help mitigate these potential weaknesses but an ability to use the latest advances in science and technology to upgrade the performance of a soldier could give the desired advantage to defeat an adversary. This becomes even more important when other states and non-state actors may also gain access to this technology.

Human enhancement is a rapidly advancing field with Allhoff convinced *"we are near the start of the Human Enhancement Revolution."*[2] The speed of advance of technology from being available to being used, results in a delay to the ethic surrounding it. This is true of pharmacological enhancement (PCE) as much as exoskeletons and human-machine interfacing. Several militaries and other organisations have invested heavily in human enhancement, capitalising on scientific advances in neurosciences, biotechnology, robotics and the ability to miniaturise technology.[3] Enhancing drugs are already available with up to 20% improvement in ability in those that take them in specific tests.[4] It is therefore better to have a policy for PCE use in place with time for deliberation, rather than be forced into a sudden decision.

Ethical issues arising from human enhancement include autonomy, safety and dignity.[5] The first two are the cornerstones of the ethics surrounding informed consent (IC) which emanated from the necessity to protect human subjects against the risks of research. IC is now the standard currency for ethical medical practice based on autonomy and the maintenance of health and well-being. The military currently follow civilian IC guidance but this may not

1 The word soldier is used as a term to encapsulate all members in all services of the UK Armed Forces.

2 Fritz Allhoff *et al.*, "Ethics of Human Enhancement: 25 Questions & Answers," *Studies in Ethics, Law, and Technology* 4, no. 1 (2010), 1.

3 Maxwell J. Mehlman, Patrick Lin, and Keith Abney, "Enhanced Warfighters: A Policy Framework," in *Military Medical Ethics for the 21st Century*, ed. M. L. Gross and D. Carrick, Military and Defence Ethics (Farnham: Ashgate Publishing Limited, 2013), 113.

4 Anders Sandberg and Nick Bostrom, "Converging Cognitive Enhancements," *Annals New York Academy of Sciences* 1093 (2006): 205.

5 Maxwell Mehlman, Patrick Lin, and Keith Abney, "Enhanced Warfighters: Risk, Ethics, and Policy," *Case Legal Studies Research Paper* No. 2013–2, (2013), 4.

 | DOI:10.1163/9789004677746_002

be appropriate, as the military have to balance the protection of individuals from any risks at the expense of overriding their autonomy. What remains unclear is how those risks are quantified, who decides whether the risk is an acceptable one and whether IC is required? For civilians, a competent, autonomous individual would decide whether the risk is acceptable under an IC process but for the military the partial loss of autonomy on joining an organisation where lawful orders have to be followed, creates challenges in gaining IC.

This paper will define human enhancements, explain what PCEs are and why an individual or the military might use them. It will give a brief outline of specific issues surrounding PCE use in the military including the laws and regulations applicable to the licensing and the issuing of prescription-only medications, the effect PCE use might exert on both military careers and the chain of command, and how PCE users might be perceived by their colleagues and society. An important part of military life is the duty of care by all those responsible for subordinates and this should be factored in to those authorising missions where the requirement for PCEs are considered vital for mission success. Arguments for and against the requirement for IC in the military will be presented.

IC will be examined in detail from its theory and history, touching on where the military have succeeded and failed with IC in the past. Any drug must be thoroughly researched before being fit for human consumption and this requires a greater level of IC following established ethical principles and if conducted by the military or on military personnel as research subjects, approval has to be sought from a dedicated ethics committee. This paper will detail what is required for consent to be 'informed' and demonstrate that full information is never known with doctors often masking their lack of knowledge. The same critical analysis will be done for how 'consensual' consent is in the military, whose personnel must follow orders and are therefore susceptible to coercion.

The final section of the essay will focus on the role of military doctors in the IC process and the unique duality of their position acting as both a doctor and military officer, arguing that the ethical duty as a doctor takes primacy. The evidence presented in the paper will be drawn together to suggest a template for gaining IC for PCE use in the Armed Services, paying attention to the method, style and timing of communication. The template will contain a combination of broad and informed consent for PCE use during service that would provide a theoretical effective balance of maximising the information provided and ensuring that wherever possible, the provision of PCEs are consensual with few exceptions. In order to best protect the individuals themselves and wider society from soldiers who have taken PCEs, the military must ensure they have comprehensive and supporting policies and regulations surrounding their use.

CHAPTER 1

Pharmacological Enhancements

What Are Human and Pharmacological Enhancements?

The definition of human enhancements according to Juengst are "interventions designed to improve human form or functioning beyond what is necessary to sustain or restore health."[1] Mehlman's interpretation of that definition excludes vaccinations which improve immune systems to sustain health and furthermore groups all medical treatments as either sustaining or restoring health.[2] There is an important difference between a drug for treatment and one for enhancement, with society generally accepting a treatment which is intended to alleviate a disease. A grey area for medicine with Juengst's definition is undertaking a treatment to prevent a future disease which may or may not occur, such as undergoing total colectomy surgery for familial polyposis coli, a condition which has a high chance of causing bowel cancer.[3] This is hard to categorize as an enhancement or treatment as it only potentially improves human functioning and is not strictly necessary to sustain health.

Consider treatments that may be required for a medical condition but also have beneficial effects on those disease-free and considered 'normal'. Erythropoietin is used to treat anaemia but has been taken by a Tour de France cyclist with a normal haemoglobin level to boost sport performance.[4] The former has been treated whereas the cyclist would be judged enhanced. The difference draws attention to the term normal, described by Mehlman as the typical range of functioning for humans as a species and compared relative to one's own baseline and trajectory of health.[5] For haemoglobin

1 Eric T. Juengst, "What Does Enhancement Mean?," in: *Enhancing Human Traits: Ethical and Social Implications*, ed. Eric Parens, Hastings Center Studies in Ethics Series (Washington DC: Georgetown University Press, 2000), 29.

2 Maxwell Mehlman, "Bioethics of Military Performance Enhancement," *Journal of the Royal Army Medical Corps* 165, no. 4 (2019): 226.

3 Macmillan Cancer Support, "Familial Adenomatous Polyposis (FAP)," <https://www.macmillan.org.uk/cancer-information-and-support/worried-about-cancer/causes-and-risk-factors/familial-adenomatous-polyposis-fap>, (accessed April 6, 2020).

4 Jacque Wilson, "Lance Armstrong's Doping Drugs—CNN," *CNN*, January 18, 2013, <https://edition.cnn.com/2013/01/15/health/armstrong-ped-explainer/index.html>, (accessed April 12, 2020).

5 Maxwell Mehlman, Patrick Lin, and Keith Abney, "Enhanced Warfighters: Risk, Ethics, and Policy," *Case Legal Studies Research Paper* No. 2013–2, (2013), 14.

 DOI:10.1163/9789004677746_003

concentration, the normal range captures 95% or 97.5% of a normal distribution curve generated by a section of the population.[6] However, standards of normality change with time like height and weight over the last century and will no doubt change with use of enhancements.[7]

Mohamed highlighted the difficulty in separating a treatment from enhancement effect in his example of taking a PCE for jet lag or insomnia.[8] Is the drug used treating symptoms already present, or enhancing the brain to prevent the condition? This could be regarded as the same for soldiers taking a PCE when fatigued on operational deployment and whether the PCEs have returned them to normal or enhanced them above normal. Further difficulties in understanding enhancement is that over the last few decades, the line differentiating health states and diseases has blurred and more interventions are considered treatments.[9] The ongoing implication is that some PCEs could be argued as therapy or enhancement, although fundamentally the issue with IC remains the same for both groups.

Equally, it is possible that some enhancements could be negative or 'disenhancements', with a military example of using a PCE to remove memories that would result in soldiers developing post-traumatic stress disorder.[10] Again is this treating the brain or enhancing it? If a distinction is not made between therapy and enhancement, it might result in all forms of human enhancement being morally permissible.[11] This paper will follow the definition of enhancement as something which improves a person and lifts them above the normal baseline. It will focus on pharmacological drugs as one aspect of human enhancement, excluding the range of other possible enhancements such as transcranial magnetic stimulation, genetic modification and human-computer interaction.

Pharmacological enhancements (PCEs) for this paper are defined as drugs which are prescription-only medicines (POM) and not those acquired either by illicit means or purchased over-the-counter. Regulatory control for PCEs like all drugs in the UK, is undertaken by the Medicine and Healthcare Products

6 Ernest Beutler and Jill Waalen, "The Definition of Anemia: What Is the Lower Limit of Normal of the Blood Hemoglobin Concentration?," *Blood* 107, no. 5 (2006): 1747.

7 S. Rosenbaum, "100 Years of Heights and Weights," *Journal of the Royal Statistical Society. Series A (Statistics in Society)* 151, no. 2 (1988): 276–309.

8 Ahmed Dahir Mohamed, "Neuroethical Issues in Pharmacological Cognitive Enhancement," *WIREs Cognitive Science* 5, no. 5 (2014): 538.

9 Mehlman (n 2)., 226.

10 Mehlman, Lin and Abney (n 5)., 15.

11 Fritz Allhoff *et al.*, "Ethics of Human Enhancement: 25 Questions & Answers," *Studies in Ethics, Law, and Technology* 4, no. 1 (2010), 8.

Regulatory Agency (MHRA). The MHRA accept drugs as safe and approved for use, classifying certain drugs as 'controlled' with specific regulations for their use and potential misuse.[12] A POM can only be prescribed by a licensed doctor, although there is a military exemption to this regulation, described later. A drug can be prescribed for a non-licensed indication, termed 'off-label', but the recipient should be informed when that is the case.[13] The majority of PCEs were not originally licensed for their enhanced capabilities, therefore, their use would be off-label, raising the necessity to inform the recipient of that fact. It is assumed that any future drugs developed would fall under the same regulatory controls.

PCEs can be divided into two broad categories, those affecting cognition and those affecting the body's physical attributes. Cognition can be defined as the processes a human utilises to organise information.[14] General health, a balanced diet and long-term exercise can improve cognition by itself and there are a range of drugs affecting the brain chemistry with positive and negative effects.[15] Those positive effects could be termed cognitive enhancement, defined by Sandberg as "*the amplification or extension of core capacities of the mind through improvement or augmentation of internal or external information processing systems*."[16] Drugs that change brain chemistry could exert negative effects by altering soldiers' perceptions of their actions and consequences of their behaviour. Loss of emotional connection could deny the armed forces the social bonding and trust that is currently instilled by its values and ethos.

Well known drugs that affect cognition include nicotine which increases alertness and cognitive processing,[17] and caffeine which increases the arousal

---

12 United Kingdom. HM Government, "About Us—Medicines and Healthcare Products Regulatory Agency," https://www.gov.uk/government/organisations/medicines-and-healthcare-products-regulatory-agency/about#our-responsibilities, *Misuse of Drugs Act 1971* (London: HMSO, 1971), <http://www.legislation.gov.uk/ukpga/1971/38/contents>, "The Controlled Drugs (Supervision of Management and Use) Regulations 2013. Information about the Regulations," 2013, <https://assets.publishing.service.gov.uk/government/uploads/system/uploads/attachment_data/file/214915/15-02-2013-controlled-drugs-regulation-information.pdf> (accessed March 26, 2020).

13 United Kingdom. HM Government, "Off-Label or Unlicensed Use of Medicines: Prescribers' Responsibilities," 2014, <https://www.gov.uk/drug-safety-update/off-label-or-unlicensed-use-of-medicines-prescribers-responsibilities>, (accessed May 4, 2020).

14 Nick Bostrom and Anders Sandberg, "Cognitive Enhancement: Methods, Ethics, Regulatory Challenges," *Science and Engineering Ethics* 15, no. 3 (2009): 312.

15 *ibid.*, 314.

16 Anders Sandberg and Nick Bostrom, "Converging Cognitive Enhancements," *Annals New York Academy of Sciences* 1093 (2006): 201.

17 Carol S. Myers *et al.*, "Dose-Related Enhancement of Mood and Cognition in Smokers Administered Nicotine Nasal Spray," *Neuropsychopharmacology* 33, no. 3 (2008): 594.

level, particularly when fatigued.[18] However, this paper is using the term PCEs to include only those drugs that are prescribed and as both nicotine and caffeine are widely available over-the-counter, they will not be discussed in further detail. An example of a cognitive PCE is modafinil, a drug licensed for narcolepsy and discovered to maintain alertness and improve cognition.[19] As modafinil can increase wakefulness with minimal side effects, it has potential to enhance soldiers for an off-label indication.[20] Amphetamines are another group of drugs that act as stimulants and have been approved for use in the US Air Force for lengthy missions.[21] There are drugs which affect cognition and used in the treatment of mental health such as propranolol which has had some success in treating the memory effects of post-traumatic stress disorder (PTSD). PTSD is a condition highly familiar to the military but as propranolol has been used in this case as a treatment rather than enhancement, it is not applicable to this paper's discussion.[22]

From the physical perspective, there are a number of PCEs which could be used to build up a soldier including anabolic steroids, erythropoietin (blood doping) and growth hormones.[23] Currently, these substances are banned by the military unless they are prescribed by a doctor for a specific indication.[24] It seems intuitive to want a 'stronger' soldier for close combat and the British Army has recently increased the level of fitness required.[25] On the other hand, the importance of absolute strength for military personnel in combat is perhaps perceived as less critical, as women have been allowed in front line

18 Tom M. McLellan, John A. Caldwell, and Harris R Lieberman, "A Review of Caffeine's Effects on Cognitive, Physical and Occupational Performance," *Neuroscience & Biobehavioral Reviews*, 71 (2016): 297.

19 Kelli J. Westcott, "Modafinil, Sleep Deprivation, and Cognitive Function in Military and Medical Settings," *Military Medicine* 170, no. 4 (2005): 334.

20 *ibid.*

21 John A. Caldwell and J. Lynn Caldwell, "Fatigue in Military Aviation: An Overview of U.S. Military-Approved Pharmacological Countermeasures," *Aviation, Space, and Environmental Medicine* 76, no. 7 (2005): C45.

22 Alain Brunet *et al.*, "Reduction of PTSD Symptoms With Pre-Reactivation Propranolol Therapy: A Randomized Controlled Trial," *American Journal of Psychiatry* 175, no. 5 (2018): 427–33.

23 Karl E. Friedl, "U.S. Army Research on Pharmacological Enhancement of Soldier Performance: Stimulants, Anabolic Hormones, and Blood Doping," *The Journal of Strength & Conditioning Research* 29 (2015): S72.

24 British Army, "People. Drugs and Supplements," <https://www.army.mod.uk/people/join-well/drugs-and-supplements/>, (accessed March 30, 2020).

25 British Army, "New Physical Employment Standards for the Army," <https://www.army.mod.uk/physical-employment-standards/> (accessed May 6, 2020).

infantry units since 2018.[26] Undoubtedly, a real benefit of PCEs on physical attributes would be to increase stamina and endurance whilst reducing the need for food, but this remains elusive as additional nutritional supplementation is required to achieve these beneficial effects.[27]

The success of PCEs affecting physical attributes will be discussed below, but despite many healthy individuals taking PCEs to improve their memories or level of alertness, Maslen's review of the literature shows that the evidence of their effectiveness is inconclusive, with limited enhancement for specific tasks, at particular dosages, for a proportion of people.[28] Interestingly, research has not established if the benefits of PCEs increase the performance of manned weapons systems and the quality of life of those manning them.[29] Further questions to consider are whether PCEs should be used routinely or just for specific missions, where failure to use them could lead to disastrous consequences?

Why Are PCEs Relevant Now?

The relevance of discussing PCEs for the military now is not just to align the ethical discussions with the rapid technological advance, but also to compare it to where sport currently sits in the debate, where there are some similar issues with safety and policy. Despite attempts to eliminate drugs from sport, use remains widespread due to the lure of success and high earnings, with low risk of getting caught and minimal penalties.[30] The World Anti-Doping Agency

26 Lizzie Dearden, "Women Now Allowed to Apply for Royal Marines and All Other Frontline Military Roles, Defence Secretary Announces," *The Independent*, October 25, 2018, <https://www.independent.co.uk/news/uk/home-news/women-soldiers-army-military-sas-defence-government-infantry-frontline-gavin-williamson-female-a8601371.html> (accessed April 2, 2020).

27 Joaquín Pérez-Guisado and Philip M Jakeman, "Citrulline Malate Enhances Athletic Anaerobic Performance and Relieves Muscle Soreness," *The Journal of Strength & Conditioning Research* 24, no. 5 (2010), 1222.

28 Hannah Maslen, Nadira Faulmüller, and Julian Savulescu, "Pharmacological Cognitive Enhancement—How Neuroscientific Research Could Advance Ethical Debate," *Frontiers in Systems Neuroscience* 8 (2014): 3.

29 Marten Meijer, "A Human Performance Perspective on the Ethical Use of Cogniceuticals: Commentary on 'Recommendations for the Ethical Use of Pharmacologic Fatigue Countermeasures in the U.S. Military,'" *Aviation, Space, and Environmental Medicine* 78, no. 5 (2007): B133.

30 J. Savulescu, B. Foddy, and M. Clayton, "Why We Should Allow Performance Enhancing Drugs in Sport," *British Journal of Sports Medicine* 38, no. 6 (2004): 666.

(WDA) declared drug use for sport illegal due to a lack of fairness and equality, if it either enhanced performance, posed a health risk, or violated the 'spirit of sport'.[31] The PCEs banned by the WDA broadly fall into two categories, those that increase power and those that increase stamina.[32] Many sports competitors have experienced dramatic positive effects when taking PCEs for a competitive edge, the exact same effect that is desired by the military.[33]

Savulescu argues that sport discriminates against the 'genetically unfit' and a winner is one who has the combination of genetic potential and the ideal balance of their psychology, training and judgement. For this reason, he advocates that competitors should be permitted PCE use to level the playing field, remove genetic inequality and the financial differential between rich and poor countries.[34] The arguments either for or against doping in sport revolve around fairness and equality which contrast with the military that aims to avoid fairness and equality by seeking a competitive advantage to win. A further argument by Mehlman is that an enhanced sportsperson does not benefit society, whereas enhancing military personnel to increase the likelihood of success of a nationally-tasked mission, could decrease the overall risk of harm to wider society.[35] Where both sides of the doping debate in sport agree, is that the health and safety of the individual is paramount.[36] In contrast, for the military it may be that the health and safety of the unit, or even society takes primacy over that of the individual.

Why Would Individuals and the Military Want PCEs?

The military might want PCEs for three reasons: to gain a competitive edge, match an opponent's capability and when working with other nations as a

---

31 World Anti-Doping Agency, "World Anti-Doping Code" (Montreal: World Anti-Doping Agency, 2015), 14, 30, <https://www.wada-ama.org/sites/default/files/resources/files/wada_anti-doping_code_2019_english_final_revised_v1_linked.pdf> (accessed March 12, 2020).

32 Lincoln Allison, "Faster, Stronger, Higher," *The Guardian*, August 9, 2004, <https://www.theguardian.com/sport/2004/aug/09/athensolympics2004.olympicgames> (accessed January 1, 2020).

33 Kate Harvey, "Sports Science and Medicine," *The Nuffield Council on Bioethics*, 2014, 5, <https://nuffieldbioethics.org/publications/sports-science-and-medicine> (accessed January 6, 2020).

34 Savulescu, Foddy and Clayton (n 30)., 667–8.

35 Mehlman, Lin and Abney (n 5)., 114.

36 Julian Savulescu, Leon Creaney, and Anna Vondy, "Should Athletes Be Allowed to Use Performance Enhancing Drugs?," *BMJ* (*Clinical Research Ed.*) 347 (2013): f6150.

coalition. The ability to enhance human performance and gain a competitive edge over the enemy is not new. War over the centuries has involved face-to-face combat and even with modern technology, it is still a human endeavour as seen in the war against terrorism and the UK involvement in the conflicts in Iraq and Afghanistan. The Incas chewed coca leaves in the 15th Century which contained cocaine, reducing hunger, thirst and fatigue, improving the Incas stamina and endurance.[37] Rum was issued to soldiers and sailors in the 17th Century because it was believed the alcohol made them better fighters.[38] There was mixed success using opium, with the Indian military gaining enhanced fighting spirit and combat performance, whereas the Chinese suffered significant opium abuse, severely impacting the ability of their troops.[39]

In modern times, amphetamines were used to improve stamina and maintain alertness such as German tank crews taking Panzerschokolade (tank chocolate) and the RAF using Benzedrine.[40] The US war in Vietnam saw unprecedented consumption by troops of both prescribed and self-prescribed psychoactive drugs including amphetamines, marijuana, LSD and heroin.[41] Irregular armed groups such as ISIS, Taliban and Al Qaeda have used psychoactive drugs to make up for shortfalls in military ability and distributed for rewards and recruitment, as well as to enhance their human capability.[42] The 'Jihadi Pill', predominantly made in Syria was used by Daesh fighters to become fearless and euphoric.[43]

All militaries strive to have a performance edge to increase the chance of mission success whether it is via technology, training or doctrine and a cognitive advantage is no different.[44] This has become even more important since the UK military has reduced the number of serving personnel over the last decade yet maintained similar outputs. Although modern warfare platforms need fewer operators and maintainers, the resulting effect remains an overburdened and stressed system. The impact is greater with reduced personnel resilience

37 L. Kamienski, *Shooting Up: A History of Drugs in Warfare* (Oxford: Hurst, 2017), 46–47.

38 *ibid.*, 9.

39 *ibid.*, 63.

40 *ibid.*, 111, 117.

41 *ibid.*, 188.

42 *ibid.*, 233–235.

43 Mirren Gidda, "Drugs in War: What Is Captagon, the 'Jihad Pill' Used by Islamic State Militants?," *Newsweek*, May 12, 2017, <https://www.newsweek.com/drugs-captagon-islamic-state-jihad-war-amphetamines-saudi-arabia-608233> (accessed March 26, 2020).

44 Michael B. Russo, "Recommendations for the Ethical Use of Pharmacologic Fatigue Countermeasures in the U.S. Military," *Aviation, Space, and Environmental Medicine* 78, no. 5 (2007): B125.

as highlighted by the media pointing out that one in thirteen troops were prescribed anti-depressants for mental health since 2018, with an increased suicide rate.[45] Sleep deprivation is also a problem for troops whether operational or not and reduces their cognitive functioning, exacerbated by caffeine and alcohol consumption.[46] If sleep deprivation impairs judgement, increases the risk of human error and reduces innovation, there might be an ethical imperative to provide PCEs to soldiers to prevent poor-decision making when under the inevitable fatigue from combat.[47]

Secondly, all advanced militaries are now facing each other with increasing technological parity in a world of increased fragility.[48] The expectation that future adversaries will provide their military with PCEs to alleviate fatigue, increase muscular strength, or create other winning advantages must be accepted.[49] The US Army has approved use of dextroamphetamine and the US Air Force has approved modafinil for select crews and personnel.[50] The US has its own military medical cognitive research collaboration to establish and deliver cutting-edge capabilities.[51] It is already investigating PCEs that increase pain tolerance and encapsulated oxygen that can be stored in the body to increase survival for injured warfighters.[52] The likelihood that other state and

45 Sean Rayment, "Thousands of Soldiers on Antidepressants as They Battle Mental Health Issues, New Figures Reveal," *The Mirror*, July 28, 2018, <https://www.mirror.co.uk/news/uk-news/thousands-soldiers-antidepressants-battle-mental-12996613>, Ministry of Defence., "FOI2017/13417," 2018, <https://assets.publishing.service.gov.uk/government/uploads/system/uploads/attachment_data/file/691866/2017-13417.pdf> (accessed March 31, 2020).

46 Paul Scharre and Lauren Fish, "Human Performance Enhancement," *Center for a New American Security*, 2018, 7, <https://www.cnas.org/publications/reports/human-performance-enhancement-1> (accessed January 6, 2020).

47 Olav Kjellevold Olsen, Ståle Pallesen, and Eid Jarle, "The Impact of Partial Sleep Deprivation on Moral Reasoning in Military Officers," *Sleep* 33, no. 8 (2010): 1086.

48 Kenneth Ford and Clark Glymour, "The Enhanced Warfighter," *Bulletin of the Atomic Scientists* 70, no. 1 (2014): 43.

49 *ibid.*, 47.

50 Mary A. Kautz, Maria L. Thomas, and J. Lynn Caldwell, "Considerations of Pharmacology on Fitness for Duty in the Operational Environment," *Aviation, Space, and Environmental Medicine* 78, no. 5 (2007): B109.

51 Eric B. Schoomaker, "Military Medical Research on Cognitive Performance: The Warfighters Competitive Edge," *Aviation, Space, and Environmental Medicine* 78, no. 5 (2007): B4.

52 James Patrey *et al.*, "Human Performance Enhancement for NATO Military Operations (Science, Technology, and Ethics)," in *NATO Research and Technology Organisation* (Virginia, USA: Office of Naval Research Warfighter Performance Department, 2009), 1, <https://apps.dtic.mil/dtic/tr/fulltext/u2/a562561.pdf> (accessed January 6, 2020).

non-state actors are doing the same must be high and therefore, the UK must follow suit to level the playing field.[53]

Thirdly, the UK military might need PCEs to work with NATO, UN and other coalition forces in the event that some or all of the other nations are using PCEs. There are inevitable risks from a mismatch when what is ethically acceptable to one nation may be unacceptable to another. Consider the example of Fijians who were banned from drinking alcohol by a Western coalition commander yet allowed to make and drink kava, a substance containing psychoactive compounds and affecting night vision.[54] What happens if a coalition soldier who has taken PCEs to promote alertness, is responding to an emergency situation and needs the support of an unenhanced UK soldier who is drowsy and not fit to respond?

There are a broad range of reasons why a soldier might take a PCE. Schelle considered that peer pressure is an important factor in influencing whether someone takes a PCE.[55] This is usually a positive mechanism, with a person more likely to take a PCE if their friends and colleagues are taking them, but the converse is also true when strong disapproval by others may lower willingness to use PCEs. The effect of this can be multiplied by social pressure extending outside of the immediate friendship group. A German survey of university students discovered the willingness to take PCEs depended on personal attitude to risk, peer prevalence, cost and side effects.[56]

The media can influence whether an individual might take PCEs by raising their profile and general public awareness. The Cambridge University rag, Varsity, stated that 10% of students took substances such as modafinil and Ritalin to improve their academic performance, which highlighted the benefits and normality of use.[57] Despite awareness of side effects, BBC News even gave coverage of the rough cost a student might be expected to pay for "smart pills," although they did point out the illegality of selling them.[58] Society can

53 President's Council on Bioethics, *Beyond Therapy: Biotechnology and the Pursuit of Happiness* (New York: Regan Books, 2003), 136.

54 Russo (n 44)., B121.

55 Kimberly J. Schelle *et al.*, "Attitudes toward Pharmacological Cognitive Enhancement—a Review," *Frontiers in Systems Neuroscience* 8 (2014): 8.

56 Sebastian Sattler *et al.*, "Evaluating the Drivers of and Obstacles to the Willingness to Use Cognitive Enhancement Drugs: The Influence of Drug Characteristics, Social Environment, and Personal Characteristics," *Substance Abuse Treatment, Prevention, and Policy* 9, no. 1 (2014): 5.

57 Natasha Lennard, "One in Ten Takes Drugs to Study," *Varsity*, March 6, 2009, <https://www.varsity.co.uk/news/1307> (accessed March 31, 2020).

58 BBC News, "Sussex University Students Illegally Buying 'Smart Pills,'" *BBC News*, March 13, 2018, <https://www.bbc.co.uk/news/uk-england-43383717> (accessed March 31, 2020).

change its perspective and attitude quickly, normalising PCEs just by exposure to them and therefore, PCE use could get adopted rapidly with plenty of media coverage.[59]

Another reason to take PCEs is via self-medication as part of a lifestyle choice, to aid recovery from training or physical activity, or to improve physical performance. Many military personnel already use supplements ranging from dietary to banned substances, with up to 38% of UK recruits in training taking them according to one study.[60] It is surprising that soldiers continue to take banned substances despite a zero tolerance policy.[61] There are some specific reasons why soldiers would willingly take PCEs relating to the military values and ethos that are firmly instilled on joining up. These include if they considered it as part of a moral code, a belief that it is an honourable thing to do or even guilt over colleagues who are already deployed. A soldier could take a PCE seeking enhanced aggression on a subsequent mission to avenge the death of a colleague killed in action.

Lastly, there are some occupations where individuals must comply with certain actions, for example hand washing by surgeons before operating and compulsory rest periods for long distance truck drivers.[62] This occupational accord where an individual consents to specific actions on accepting certain employments, is primarily based on preserving their health and safety. The military therefore, could establish an occupational reason for their personnel to take a PCE in a similar manner to when the US directed their pilots to take stimulants for prolonged missions. However, this is unlikely to be the case for the majority of PCEs where the balance of risk and benefits is not as clear cut.

What Are the Military Concerns Surrounding PCE Use?

There are a number of issues around PCE use in the military including law, policy, operational, civil-military relations and IC. UK forces have to uphold both Service and civil law noting that "*In order that the Armed Forces can operate effectively a necessary reliance is placed on the maintenance of both personal*

59 Adam Bear and Joshua Knobe, "Normality: Part Descriptive, Part Prescriptive," *Cognition* 167 (2017): 25.

60 Anna Casey *et al.*, "Supplement Use by UK-Based British Army Soldiers in Training," *The British Journal of Nutrition* 112, no. 7 (2014): 1178–1180.

61 British Army, 'People. Drugs and Supplements.' (n. 29).

62 Maslen, Faulmüller and Savulescu (n. 28)., 6.

and imposed discipline."[63] If PCEs are illegal in civilian life or banned by the military, then they cannot be self-prescribed and if legally allowed, there must be a policy to support their use.

Banning PCEs or limiting their access could result in an expanding black market of supply leading to a reduction in safety. This occurred with Viagra, forcing the MHRA to change its category from being a POM to being available over-the-counter.[64] More studies to determine safety and efficacy will provide consumers' confidence to use PCEs and legalising them will promote their development, ultimately making them cheaper and safer.[65] The military should replicate Scharre's recommendation of having a high level policy review, examining each PCE on a case-by-case basis, investigating its efficacy, safety and utility.[66] Furthermore, PCE use in research or on operations should be voluntary.

Schedule 17 of UK medicine regulations authorises the Armed Forces to supply and administer medicines for soldiers, bypassing a licensed doctor's prescription.[67] This exemption was designed to cover troops in environments without immediate access to doctors. Any treatments prescribed should ideally be by trained 'medics',[68] who have been signed off as competent by a doctor, or if there are no personnel with medical skills, permission should be obtained via communication to a doctor if at all possible. What stops those commanding a deployed unit from ordering their medics to prescribe PCEs and ordering the soldiers to take them, or even getting the soldiers to self-administer in a similar way to fentanyl lozenges?[69] Although legal, there has to

---

63 United Kingdom. Ministry of Defence, *JSP 830: The Manual of Service Law* (London: HMSO, 2016), 1-1-3.

64 Sabrina Barr, "Viagra Now Available over the Counter without Prescription in UK," *The Independent*, March 27, 2018, <https://www.independent.co.uk/life-style/health-and-families/viagra-buy-without-prescription-over-counter-uk-pharmacies-male-impotence-erectile-dysfunction-a8275461.html> (accessed April 3, 2020).

65 Bostrom and Sandberg (n. 14)., 333.

66 Scharre and Fish (n. 46)., 3.

67 United Kingdom, "The Human Medicines Regulations 2012," Pub. L. No. 1916, Schedule 17 (2012), Pt 2, 10, Pt 5, 17, <http://www.legislation.gov.uk/uksi/2012/1916/schedule/17/made> (accessed April 6, 2020).

68 Medic is a term used to cover a combat medical technician of the British Army and its sister service equivalents. They are trained to diagnose, prescribe and manage medical emergencies but do not come under a National regulatory body.

69 CBRN Delivery Team, *2017DIN04–165. Fentanyl Lozenge 800 Micrograms (OTFC) Single—Introduction into Service as Self Administered Operational Analgesia.* (Bristol: Ministry of Defence, 2017).

remain authority and accountability in this instance to ensure the safety and protection of the soldier.

From an operational and command perspective, elements of coercion or insubordination will be discussed in the section on IC, but PCE use has other potential employment impacts. Would a soldier's career be accelerated if by taking PCEs, it meant they would be sent on more critical missions? This same factor could affect their remuneration, promotion and recognition by the award of medals. Unit cohesion and morale is vital for mission success via communication, teamwork and shared ethos. Would this remain the same between those who are enhanced and those not? Could it motivate those not being enhanced into a 'them and us' scenario leading to a sense of feeling second class or missing out. More importantly, a mission could be called off if those undertaking it were not enhanced.

Soldiers represent society and its values and are relied upon to protect society whilst respecting human rights and international humanitarian law.[70] The UK has a moral contract known as the Armed Forces Covenant (AFC), which recognises that soldiers put the needs of the Service above their own, potentially involving the sacrifice of life and the duty that society has by ensuring they are treated fairly, thus establishing a mutual benefit for both the military and society.[71] This AFC frames a duty of care for military personnel who have accepted imposed discipline and thus reduced autonomy, and means the public would be unsupportive of PCE use if it was considered unsafe or unfair. This duty of care was considered so important that the government directed all single services to update their legal and moral responsibilities beyond reiterating their values, standards and ethos.[72]

70 British Army, *Values and Standards of the British Army, AC 64649* (Andover: Army Headquarters, 2018), 25.

71 Helen McCartney, "The Military Covenant and the Civil–Military Contract in Britain," *International Affairs* 86, no. 2 (2010): 413.

72 House of Commons Defence Committee, *Duty of Care. Third Report of Session 2004–05. Volume I. HC 63-I* (London: The Stationery Office Limited, 2005), 5.

CHAPTER 2

Informed Consent

Theory of Informed Consent

Before detailing the issues around IC in the military, it is relevant to understand its evolution. The 20th Century had a number of fundamental events which shaped the development of IC, the first of which was during the Second World War when Nazis used prisoners arriving at the concentration camps for research and cruel experimentation against their will. From the trials afterwards, where doctors were held to account for their actions, the Nuremberg Code was established in 1947 and listed ten explicit principles for doctors experimenting on humans and forbade experiments on prisoners.[1] The first principle was gaining voluntary, IC of the subject.[2] The following year, the United Nations made a Universal Declaration of Human Rights in response to the extensive Nazi inhumanities, which contained Article 5 stating no-one should be subjected to cruel or inhuman treatment.[3]

The Declaration of Helsinki (1964), produced by the World Medical Association (WMA) created the ethical principles for conducting research on humans or identifiable human material and data, distinguishing therapeutic from non-therapeutic procedures.[4] It placed the primary duty of physicians as promoting health and protecting patients' rights in research and being held accountable for both. The guidance stated any study's risks must not outweigh the benefits, it should be approved by a Research Ethics Committee (REC) and voluntary IC of a participant is essential, being mindful of a dependency relationship between the physician and subject. The declaration noted that if an intervention was not proven effective, it could still be used, providing there

1 British Medical Journal, "The Nuremberg Code (1947)," *British Medical Journal* 313, no. 7070 (1996): 1448.

2 Michael Gross, *Military Medical Research Ethics: Investigational Drugs, Clinical Trials and Enhancement* (Oxford: Oxford University Press, 2019), 2.

3 United Nations, "Universal Declaration of Human Rights," 1948, <https://www.un.org/en/universal-declaration-human-rights/> (accessed January 9, 2020).

4 World Medical Association, "Ethical Principles for Medical Research Involving Human Subjects," *WMA Declaration of Helsinki*, 2018, <https://www.wma.net/policies-post/wma-declaration-of-helsinki-ethical-principles-for-medical-research-involving-human-subjects/>, (accessed April 7, 2020).

 | DOI:10.1163/9789004677746_004

was adequate IC and the doctor's judgement believed it would save life, restore health or alleviate suffering.

The Belmont Report released in 1979 was produced as an attempt to summarise the ethics up to that time point.[5] The report set out three basic principles as respect for persons, beneficence and justice.[6] The respect for persons was about treating individuals as autonomous and capable of self-determination whilst protecting those considered vulnerable. Beneficence fundamentally related to avoidance of doing harm and maximising the benefits whilst minimising possible harms when treating a person. Lastly, justice directed a fairness so that all of society shared the benefits of research along with its burdens.

Nuremberg, Helsinki and Belmont were all aimed at research ethics and the requirement for voluntary consent. The concept of IC for healthcare emerged in the 1950s, moving away from simple disclosure by physicians towards an emphasis on the subject's understanding. Prior to the 1950s, any consent involved minimising any disclosures which might upset the patient.[7] The 1957 Salgo court case originated the term IC, stating there was a duty to disclose treatment risks and options after a man suffered paralysis from a routine procedure, with the case considered as battery.[8] A few years later the Natanson court case moved the physician's failure to undertake IC from battery to an act of negligence, a position where it has remained since.[9] In 1972, three separate USA courts produced decisions supporting a more patient-oriented standard of disclosure which meant the patient had to be given sufficient information to enable them to make an intelligent choice.[10] This was not popular with physicians, who felt that the demands placed on them to deliver that information was too onerous and even inconsistent with good patient care.

Drawing together the history, IC is based on a respect for patient autonomy and self-determination. The word autonomy came from Greek origins, with auto meaning self and nomos meaning rule.[11] IC is an autonomous

5 The National Commission for the Protection of Human Subjects of Biomedical and Behavioural Research, "The Belmont Report: Ethical Principles and Guidelines for the Protection of Human Subjects of Research," 1979, <https://www.hhs.gov/ohrp/sites/default/files/the-belmont-report-508c_FINAL.pdf>, (accessed January 8, 2020).

6 *ibid.*, 4.

7 Tom L. Beauchamp, "Informed Consent: Its History, Meaning, and Present Challenges," *Cambridge Quarterly of Healthcare Ethics* 20, no. 4 (2011): 515.

8 R. R. Faden, T. L. Beauchamp, and N. M. P. King, *A History and Theory of Informed Consent* (New York: Oxford University Press, 1986), 125.

9 *ibid.*, 129.

10 *ibid.*, 132.

11 J. W. Berg *et al.*, *Informed Consent: Legal Theory and Clinical Practice*, Second (New York: Oxford University Press, 2001), 15.

authorisation by the individual to allow a healthcare professional to perform a medical action to them, only if the individual is competent and free from being under the control of others. Berg has defined IC as something that "refers to legal rules that prescribe behaviours for physicians and other healthcare professionals in their interactions with patients."[12] Both parties have to be involved with the patient having IC as a right and a doctor having it as a duty or obligation.[13] IC can also be viewed in terms of the institutional and policy rules, so in the case of healthcare, if the NHS rules of consent are followed, it is considered valid and informed.[14]

Over the last 50 years, IC has been the ethically acceptable medical practice based on the values of autonomy and individual well-being, now with a greater focus on shared decision-making between patient and doctor. As Berg described, IC implies formal actions with legal connotations, often involving documentation such as for surgery. In these formal actions, it is expected that both parties have full understanding of the benefits of the transaction and potential adverse outcomes, with the patient trusting the healthcare professional. Many aspects outside of medicine are gaining increased formality and are frequently seen with consumer protection and the detailed small print that accompanies a product or service. Ultimately, it seems the driver of formality and written IC is the protection of those doing the action from accusation, litigation and compensation.[15]

In summary, for IC to be valid for healthcare, an individual must fulfil four criteria:

1. Be mentally competent—this potentially excludes those who are vulnerable, at the extremes of age or unconscious.
2. Understand the risks, benefits and alternative options including that of doing nothing, with the opportunity to ask questions.
3. Have the ability to withdraw consent at any time.
4. Not be under duress.

This appears to be simple and straightforward but Corrigan discusses an "empty ethics" model where any autonomous individual, if provided with sufficient information and the time to process that information, will make the decision to accept a treatment or not. This implies a universal standard and ignores cultural differences.[16] The ability of any individual to understand will

---

12 *ibid.*, 3.

13 *ibid.*, 14.

14 Beauchamp (n. 7)., 518.

15 O. O'Neill, "Some Limits of Informed Consent," *Journal of Medical Ethics* 29, no. 1 (2003): 4.

16 Oonagh Corrigan, "Empty Ethics: The Problem with Informed Consent," *Sociology of Health & Illness* 25, no. 3 (2003): 770.

require a variable amount of information and time, implying that the process of IC should be tailored to the individual.

Military Issues with Informed Consent

In the past, the military has aligned its IC process to that of the civilian world and bypassed it under certain circumstances, causing harm and foregoing the duty of care to its soldiers. The Nuremberg declaration has the first principle as voluntary, informed consent of the subject being absolutely essential.[17] Despite that principle, both the UK and US experimented on unconsented service personnel during the Cold War, exposing them to radiation, chemical agents and LSD.[18] More recently, the US Department of Defense (DOD) obtained a Food and Drug Administration (FDA) waiver of informed consent to administer pyridostigmine and botulinum toxin vaccine to troops for Operation Desert Storm.[19] Grounds cited for the waiver were that it was impossible to obtain IC from over 500,000 troops and some might refuse placing them in danger.[20] The vaccine, but not pyridostigmine, was eventually given on a voluntary basis, basing the reasoning on 'experimentation' versus 'protection' of troops. Pyridostigmine was believed to be safe after decades of experience with larger doses treating myasthenia gravis, whereas the vaccine was under investigation for its effectiveness.[21]

There is a dangerous precedent if IC can be waived for Defence. However, for a DOD waiver to be valid, stringent conditions must be met:

> in order to facilitate the accomplishment of the military mission, preservation of the health of the individual and the safety of other personnel require that a particular treatment be provided to a specified group of

---

17 Gross, *Military Medical Research Ethics: Investigational Drugs, Clinical Trials and Enhancement*, 2.

18 George J. Annas, "Changing the Consent Rules for Desert Storm," *New England Journal of Medicine* 326, no. 11 (March 12, 1992): 771, Adam Lusher, "The Bizarre True Story of When the UK Military Tested LSD on Royal Marines," *The Independent*, May 24, 2018, <https://www.independent.co.uk/news/uk/home-news/lsd-video-porton-down-chemical-weapons-experiments-trials-uk-military-army-marines-sixties-acid-a8366906.html> (accessed April 29, 2020).

19 Joel Martin Schofer, "Violations of Informed Consent During War," *JAMA* 281, no. 17 (1999): 1657.

20 Annas, 'Changing the Consent Rules for Desert Storm' (n 18)., 770.

21 *ibid.*, 772.

> military personnel, without regard to what might be any individual's personal preference for no treatment or for some alternative treatment.[22]

Those refusing the drugs would either have to leave the operational theatre and not fulfil their military obligations, or remain unprotected, which would put them at risk, increase the danger to their unit colleagues and reduce the chance of mission success.[23] The US case of forced administration of unapproved drugs was taken to court and lost, including the appeals, with none of the court cases mentioning the Nuremberg Code and all supporting the use of pyridostigmine as it was used as a treatment.[24]

In 2002, two pilots returning to Kuwait from a long-range training exercise in Afghanistan, mistook live gunfire for enemy insurgent activity and killed four Canadian pilots in a friendly-fire tragedy. In the ensuing court case, the defence argued that the pilots were coerced into taking Dexedrine which impaired their ability and resulted in the accidental bombing. Charges were dropped and although no blame was ever attributed to the drug, it highlighted the issue of lack of IC for a prescribed medication.[25] Did the Dexedrine affect their mental capacity or influence their ability to control their behaviour, or was it just pilot error as the board of inquiry concluded?[26] The US military have no right to refuse medical treatment that makes them fit for combat or returns them to active duty.[27] Therefore, was the Dexedrine used as a 'treatment' and was it required to make them fit for combat? US Army regulations state that "An Army member on active duty or active duty for training will usually be required to submit to medical care considered necessary to preserve his life,

22 Richard A. Rettig, *Military Use of Drugs Not Yet Approved by the FDA for CW/BW Defense: Lessons from the Gulf War* (Santa Monica: RAND Corporation, 1999), XII.

23 Richard A. Rettig, *Waiving Informed Consent: Military Use of Non-FDA-Approved Drugs in Combat* (Santa Monica: RAND Corporation, 2000), <https://www.rand.org/pubs/research_briefs/RB7534.html> (accessed April 30, 2020).

24 George J. Annas, "Protecting Soldiers from Friendly Fire: The Consent Requirement for Using Investigational Drugs and Vaccines in Combat," *American Journal of Law & Medicine* 24, no. 2/3 (1998): 249.

25 Lauren R. Robbins, "Refusing to Be All That You Can Be: Regulating against Forced Cognitive Enhancement in the Military," in *Military Medical Ethics for the 21st Century*, ed. M. L. Gross and D. Carrick, Military and Defence Ethics (Farnham: Ashgate Publishing Limited, 2013), 127.

26 Oliver Burkeman and Richard Norton-Taylor, "US Pilots Blame Drug for Friendly Fire Deaths," *The Guardian*, January 4, 2003, <https://www.theguardian.com/world/2003/jan/04/afghanistan.richardnortontaylor> (accessed March 27, 2020).

27 Annas, 'Protecting Soldiers from Friendly Fire: The Consent Requirement for Using Investigational Drugs and Vaccines in Combat' (n 24)., 250.

alleviate undue suffering, or protect or maintain the health of others."[28] The key question is whether taking PCEs are a standard of 'medical care' to 'protect or maintain the health of others'?

Following the past violation of the rights and ethics of service personnel and the dangers of Defence gaining legal waivers to avoid IC, Mehlman adapted the Belmont principles for the military. Beneficence, respect for persons and justice changed to proportionality, paternalism and fairness.[29] Firstly, proportionality covers imposing a biomedical risk on troops only if necessary for a legitimate operation, where that risk is proportional to the military advantage gained. Secondly, paternalism is required due to reduced autonomy and the duty to obey which restricts a soldier's ability to withhold consent. Therefore, a commander must ensure the biomedical risks imposed are proportionate and maintain privacy, dignity and confidentiality.[30] Lastly, fairness is a difficult area for commanders who may have to manage imposing a biomedical risk on a section of their subordinates, yet ensure it is done in a non-discriminatory manner and not used as a punishment.[31]

Although the Belmont principles were designed to guide research, Mehlman's adapted military principles in combination, encapsulate what is meant by duty of care, a term which covers all moral and legal responsibilities, ranging from being wounded to safety at work. Duty of care is an important concept that is a responsibility of all military personnel above the lowest rank, who will be in charge of, or supervising those subordinates more junior than them.[32] When new recruits join the military they forfeit a degree of autonomy and understand that they may be ordered into a life-threatening situation.[33] The new recruit implicitly consents to a range of activities to achieve legitimate military ends, on the understanding and trust that the military will minimise the risks as part of its duty of care. A soldier accepts new weapons and training which are always evolving, so could this be compared to new medicines with

---

28 Stephen E. Deardorff, "Informed Consent, Termination of Medical Treatment, and the Federal Tort Claims Act--A New Proposal for the Military Health Care System," *Military Law Review* 115, no. Winter (1987): 68.

29 Maxwell J. Mehlman and Stephanie Corley, "A Framework for Military Bioethics," *Journal of Military Ethics* 13, no. 4 (2014): 337.

30 Michael L. Gross, *Bioethics and Armed Conflict. Moral Dilemmas of Medicine and War* (Cambridge: MIT Press, 2006), 45.

31 Mehlman and Corley (n 29)., 339–340.

32 House of Commons Defence Committee, *Duty of Care. Third Report of Session 2004–05. Volume I. HC 63-I*, 29.

33 William J. FitzPatrick and Lee L. Zwanziger, "Defending Against Biochemical Warfare," *The Journal of Philosophy, Science & Law* 3, no. 2 (2003): 9.

an implied consent for the taking of PCEs? It is accepted that military personnel may go to war with potential loss of life, but at present it is not widely known that PCEs are available. However, what is known always varies with time and if PCE use became commonplace, implied consent could be valid.

The military chain of command holds the responsibility for any risk being minimised and responsible for upholding the duty of care, of which one part for the UK is the Competent Medical Authority (CMA). The CMA is a senior military physician, who has signed off the medical aspects of a deployment plan and held accountable. However, who is ultimately accountable and is this body independent and empowered to prevent the military compromising itself in order to achieve its goal?[34] As PCEs are classed as medicines, the Defence Medical Services (DMS) would be the military authority and its three-star Director General holds full accountability.[35] Fortunately, there are external, independent inspections completed by the Care Quality Commission who can prosecute the DMS if medical standards are breached, including if people are harmed or placed in danger of harm?[36]

Is it acceptable for the military to violate the consent process and take a paternalistic view if it believes it is upholding the duty of care? Paternalism has been defined as "the interference of a state or an individual with another person, against their will, and defended or motivated by a claim that the person interfered with will be better off or protected from harm."[37] Paternalistic policies limit individual choices but are allowed if the authority considers there is overriding benefit to the individual.[38] Although medicine has moved away from paternalism, it remains dominant in the military today and the IC process could be waived, if an individual putting their own preferences first, risks their own life and those of others,[39] noting a soldier's personal health can affect those around them.[40] If consent is waived for PCEs, does it make

34 Jessica Wolfendale and Steve Clarke, "Paternalism, Consent, and the Use of Experimental Drugs in the Military," *The Journal of Medicine and Philosophy: A Forum for Bioethics and Philosophy of Medicine* 33, no. 4 (2008): 347.

35 United Kingdom. HM Government, "Defence Medical Services," <https://www.gov.uk/government/groups/defence-medical-services> (accessed May 18, 2020).

36 Care Quality Commission, "Defence Medical Services," 2019, <https://www.cqc.org.uk/what-we-do/services-we-regulate/defence-medical-services>, (accessed April 9, 2020).

37 Gerald Dworkin, "Paternalism," ed. Edward N. Zalta, *The Stanford Encyclopedia of Philosophy* (Stanford: Metaphysics Research Lab, Stanford University, 2019), <https://plato.stanford.edu/entries/paternalism/>, (accessed January 8, 2020).

38 Wolfendale and Clarke (n. 34)., 339.

39 *ibid.*, 341.

40 Edmund G. Howe and Edward D. Martin, "Treating the Troops," *Hastings Center Report* 21, no. 2 (1991): 23.

the individual a guinea pig and move the drug into an experimental or investigational category, with the resulting necessity for a greater level of IC? Trust in those accountable must be maintained, with duty of care at the forefront of decision-making if the consent process gets waived, as was the case of pyridostigmine and for the use of experimental drugs in combat.[41]

The notion of 'anticipatory consent' is one where the person cannot consent due to temporarily lacking full capacity such as injecting a soldier with a ComboPen, the antidote required when incapacitated by a nerve agent.[42] This could be coherent with PCEs, for example, the provision of drugs to combat fatigue at a critical moment when there is no time for detailed discussion. However, this veers towards a treatment rather than enhancement. Areas of service life which might need a future anticipatory consent could be incorporated into a broader consent which is more generalised and less specific,[43] outlining themes of what soldiers might have to agree to, allowing flexibility and a baseline of information. This consent could be started at recruitment, renewed annually and when there are new developments or scientific understanding.[44] The benefit of an annual broad consent is that repetition and building of information gains greater understanding but the danger is it becomes yet another form to sign with limited understanding of its significance.[45]

For PCE use, from the issues highlighted, it would seem logical that waivers should be avoided and where possible use both broad and IC. However, O'Neill disagrees with IC, believing those promoting it have poor arguments and exaggerated claims, citing too many exceptions for IC in medical practice, such as those who are mentally impaired, unconscious or under constraint such as prisoners.[46] He also described an *"opacity of consent"* when an individual consents to a certain action, without understanding that it might entail another necessary action.[47] This opacity was highlighted by the Alder Hey Children's Hospital retaining children's organs after death. The parents had consented to tissue being used for research but would not have consented to organs being

41 Wolfendale and Clarke (n. 34)., 345.

42 iMedi.co.uk, "Autoject (Combopen) Nerve Agent Antidote L4a1," 2009, <https://imedi.co.uk/autoject-combopen-nerve-agent-antidote-l4a1> (accessed April 30, 2020).

43 Gert Helgesson, "In Defense of Broad Consent," *Cambridge Quarterly of Healthcare Ethics* 21, no. 1 (2012): 40.

44 Rettig (n. 22)., ch. 4.

45 FitzPatrick and Zwanziger (n. 33)., 15.

46 O'Neill (n. 15)., 4.

47 *ibid.*, 6.

removed, even though organs are made up of tissues.[48] This results in policy makers introducing or tightening IC procedures, to increase the protection of patients' welfare and the opportunity for them to make an informed choice.[49]

Importance of Informed Consent for Military Research

Gaining IC for biomedical research requires an elevated level of IC to protect patients and healthy volunteers from exploitation and harm as described by the Helsinki declaration and Belmont principles. The only civilian exceptions when IC is not required for research are for retrospective and emergency studies.[50] For the US, the 2002 Defense Appropriations Act can waive consent if the research directly benefits subjects, advances the development of a medical product necessary to the military and abides by all normal laws and regulations.[51] Since 2002, no waivers have been given but Gross believes that to improve military medical research, the current regulations need to be exploited by waivers and broadening the scope of civilian medical research for military purposes.[52]

To protect UK troops from exploitation, the MOD have their own ethics research committee (MODREC) composed of experts and independents.[53] The independents' role is vital as an advocate outside of military influence to protect the safety of those participating in research and to avoid a "command culture."[54] MODREC has published its principles that "protect and promote the interests of participants by describing robust scientific and ethical conduct and proportionate, assurance-based management of human participant research."[55] These are aligned with national and international ethical

48 Clare Dyer, "Consent Needed For Organ Retention, BMA Says," *British Medical Journal* 321, no. 7269 (2000): 1098.

49 Corrigan (n. 16)., 769.

50 Gross, *Military Medical Research Ethics: Investigational Drugs, Clinical Trials and Enhancement*, 6.

51 John McManus *et al.*, "Informed Consent and Ethical Issues in Military Medical Research," *Academic Emergency Medicine* 12, no. 11 (2005): 1123.

52 Gross (n. 50)., 7.

53 United Kingdom. Ministry of Defence, "Ministry of Defence Research Ethics Committee," <https://www.gov.uk/government/groups/ministry-of-defence-research-ethics-committees#guidance-documents> (accessed January 9, 2020).

54 United Kingdom. Ministry of Defence, *JSP 536. Governance of Research Involving Human Participants. Part 1: Directive*, 3rd ed. (London: HMSO, 2020), 5–5, Mehlman, Lin and Abney (n 3)., 115.

55 United Kingdom. Ministry of Defence, *JSP 536. Governance of Research Involving Human Participants. Part 1: Directive, 1–1.*

principles where the rights of trial subjects "*prevail over interests of science and society.*"[56] On IC, MODREC explicitly states that a soldier can refuse to partake in any research project and that the study information provided must be in a suitable format and proportional to the anticipated risk-benefit analysis.[57] Proportionality means that if risks are high or the study treatment deviates from standard practice, far more information should be provided and supports the proportionality described by Mehlman's adapted Belmont principles.

The individual must have "reasonable time" to decide whether to be involved which should not be the same day as receiving the information.[58] Corrigan discovered from her own research that trial subjects did not understand all the information given, what was being tested or if it involved active treatment.[59] Reasons given were trust in medical experts and the expectation that doctors would put their best interests first and foremost.[60] Individuals' perceptions of medical research vary according to their background and cultural norms.[61] Even the research title affects perceptions which when containing the word 'experiment' was least favourable and 'study' being most popular.[62] Worryingly is why people consent to research and Corrigan's small study had over 96% consent to the study for financial reward, with some doing so to please their doctor.[63] Her conclusion was that the IC process in isolation resulted in an "*empty ethics*" where the principles of IC did not take account of the social context.[64]

Faden argued that not all research requires IC, particularly for comparative-effectiveness research, believing it over-protects patients when the research has minimal effect on what matters to them and under-protects them from errors and management when the research needed to reduce those problems

56 United Kingdom, "The Medicines for Human Use (Clinical Trials) Regulations," Pub. L. No. 1031, Schedule 1, pt. 2, para. 3, (2004), <http://www.legislation.gov.uk/uksi/2004/1031/schedule/1/part/2/paragraph/3/made#text%3Dinformed consent> (accessed January 1, 2020).

57 United Kingdom. Ministry of Defence, *JSP 536. Governance of Research Involving Human Participants. Part 1: Directive*, 3–4.

58 *ibid.*

59 Corrigan (n. 16)., 774–775.

60 *ibid.*, 778–780.

61 *ibid.*, 777.

62 Ruth R. Faden, *Advisory Committee on Human Radiation Experiments. Final Report.* (Washington DC: U.S. Government Printing Office, 1995), 734.

63 Corrigan (n. 16)., 782–784.

64 *ibid.*, 787.

becomes too burdensome.[65] If an institution had a shared vision of continuous learning to enhance patient care with absolute transparency, then just simply informing patients of a study, allowing an opportunity to decline would be ethically acceptable. This only works if there are comparable options of treatment and not if there is higher risk, uncertainty, or the informational need is higher.[66] The determination of what constitutes low risk for randomised-controlled trials is described as having clinical equipoise and falling within a current standard of care.[67]

The dilemma of the overriding role of military necessity and maintaining patient autonomy is also relevant to research. Mission success of a military objective may take precedence over an individual soldier's rights and in the words of Gross, "Military medicine is not exclusively patient centered. Rather its mission is to maintain force preparedness."[68] As PCEs would be used off-label in healthy military volunteers, any trial is unlikely to get through an ethics committee according to a Dutch author.[69] PCEs are not yet a standard of care and potentially high risk, necessitating full IC for research. The UK should not pursue the US in allowing waivers of IC but follow established research ethics to gain knowledge, that might better protect soldiers on operations as a duty of care. In doing so, the military should follow Mehlman's advice that a lengthy period of rigorous testing is required for any PCE which should only be introduced gradually.[70]

---

65 Ruth R. Faden, Tom L. Beauchamp, and Nancy E. Kass, "Informed Consent, Comparative Effectiveness, and Learning Health Care," *New England Journal of Medicine* 370, no. 8 (2014): 766.

66 *ibid.*, 767.

67 Marilyn C. Morris and Robert M. Nelson, "Randomized, Controlled Trials as Minimal Risk: An Ethical Analysis*," *Critical Care Medicine* 35, no. 3 (2007): 943.

68 Gross (n. 49)., 4.

69 D. O. E. Gebhardt, "Off-Label Administration of Drugs to Healthy Military Personnel. Dubious Ethics of Preventive Measures," *Journal of Medical Ethics* 31, no. 5 (2005): 268.

70 Maxwell Mehlman, Patrick Lin, and Keith Abney, "Enhanced Warfighters: Risk, Ethics, and Policy," *Case Legal Studies Research Paper* No. 2013–2, (2013), 65.

CHAPTER 3

Future of Informed Consent

How Informed and How Consensual Is Informed Consent?

To ensure a soldier is truly informed, the desired benefits, unwanted effects and risks must be known and articulated to the soldier in a way that can be understood. The main risk with PCEs are their side effects which vary from drug to drug. PCEs affecting physical attributes such as anabolic steroids can cause permanent liver damage and growth hormones can lead to loss of vision and diabetes.[1] Stimulants such as amphetamines cause agitation, nervousness, sleeplessness, irritability and nausea.[2] Modafinil can cause headaches, gastrointestinal upset, sleep disturbance, depression and a drive to commit suicide, considered so significant, that the European Medicines Agency concluded it should not be prescribed for many disorders, including shift-work sleep disorder.[3]

The risks and benefits should be quantitative where possible to aid decision-making, for example, drug A may have 20% of users gaining cognitive enhancement but 1% commit suicide. This leads to the quandary of who decides if the risk-to-benefit ratio is too high: the CMA, the operational commander or the warfighter? Add this to the unknown risk of death or injury from a mission, comparing whether a soldier was enhanced or not makes the analysis difficult. What is known is that an increased likelihood of side effects decreases the willingness to use PCEs,[4] and although the tolerability of any side effects is an individual concern, collectively they could impact on mission success. There is consensus that individual autonomy can override minor medical risks and the

1 U.S. Anti-Doping Agency, "Effects of Performance-Enhancing Drugs," <https://www.usada.org/athletes/substances/effects-of-performance-enhancing-drugs/> (accessed May 8, 2020).

2 Paul Scharre and Lauren Fish, "Human Performance Enhancement," *Center for a New American Security*, 2018, 8, <https://www.cnas.org/publications/reports/human-performance-enhancement-1> (accessed January 6, 2020).

3 European Medicines Agency, 'Modafinil' (2010) <https://www.ema.europa.eu/en/medicines/human/referrals/modafinil> accessed 31 March 2020.

4 Sebastian Sattler *et al.*, "Evaluating the Drivers of and Obstacles to the Willingness to Use Cognitive Enhancement Drugs: The Influence of Drug Characteristics, Social Environment, and Personal Characteristics," *Substance Abuse Treatment, Prevention, and Policy* 9, no. 1 (2014): 9.

 | DOI:10.1163/9789004677746_005

correct person to judge whether the benefits are worth the risks is not necessarily the medical experts, according to Bostrom.[5]

The understanding of the information is a vital part of IC, with all individuals having differing perceptions and comprehension, especially of statistical risk. The level of a soldier's comprehension may be limited due to their literacy, with the Army recently taking new recruits with a reading age as low as aged five and almost 40% having the literacy and numeracy level of an eleven-year-old.[6] Therefore, a young soldier could not be considered informed if the limits of comprehension mean they do not fundamentally understand what they are consenting to.

PCEs should be reversible so that the enhanced effects and associated risks are removed when the need is no longer required, such as returning from deployment or discharge from the Service. However, PCEs that affect cognitive processing would likely have irreversible effects due to the complexity of neural processing and adaptation of brain cells to altered neurochemistry. This raises concerns if military personnel are compelled to take medications without choice. If the PCE is not reversible, there will be an impact on society having an enhanced person amongst them.[7] Over half the public believe that PCEs provide an unfair advantage to users, irrespective of whether it is considered cheating or not.[8] Nonetheless, wider use of PCEs could bring gains to society, with increased productivity leading to a reduction in poverty.[9] Buchanan takes it a step further, perceiving a dramatic positive benefit to society and the wider economy from enhancements.[10]

Other concerns revolve around the risk of dependence and abuse, with a national US survey published in 2006 finding that 13% of people taking

5 Nick Bostrom and Anders Sandberg, "Cognitive Enhancement: Methods, Ethics, Regulatory Challenges," *Science and Engineering Ethics* 15, no. 3 (2009): 323.

6 Neil Sears, "Army Signs up Recruits with a Reading Age as Young as FIVE in Desperate Bid to Boost Troop Numbers," *The Daily Mail*, April 5, 2020, <https://www.dailymail.co.uk/news/article-8190009/Army-signs-recruits-reading-age-young-FIVE-desperate-bid-boost-troop-numbers.html>, Katherine Sellgren, "Almost 40% of Army Recruits Have Reading Age of 11, MPs Warn," *BBC News*, July 18, 2013, <https://www.bbc.co.uk/news/education-23346693> (accessed May 1, 2020).

7 Fritz Allhoff *et al.*, "Ethics of Human Enhancement: 25 Questions & Answers," *Studies in Ethics, Law, and Technology* 4, no. 1 (2010), 15.

8 Kimberly J. Schelle *et al.*, "Attitudes toward Pharmacological Cognitive Enhancement—a Review," *Frontiers in Systems Neuroscience* 8 (2014): 10.

9 Ahmed Dahir Mohamed, "Neuroethical Issues in Pharmacological Cognitive Enhancement," *WIREs Cognitive Science* 5, no. 5 (2014): 537.

10 A. E. Buchanan, *Beyond Humanity?: The Ethics of Biomedical Enhancement*, (Oxford: OUP Oxford, 2011), 45.

stimulants such as amphetamines met the criteria for dependence or abuse which could have an impact on society.[11] Unintended consequences of PCEs could affect individuals, with a reduction in performance for those already high performing in a particular area as seen with amphetamines and creativity.[12] What if designer PCEs became a "*black ball*" technology that brought an end to civilisation?[13] Consider a cognitive PCE that fundamentally changed behaviour so its user was more prone to violence and destruction after several years of use. If the full mechanism of action and side effects are not understood, is it truly informed consent? However, despite advances in science, complete understanding of how PCEs work and their long-term effects may never be known and therefore, information imparted can only be what is known at the time, acknowledging any gaps and limitations.

Katz believes physicians place greater value on longevity rather than on quality of life and that it is medicine and not law that should formulate the doctrine on IC, with greater emphasis on disclosure rather than consent.[14] The reality is doctors undertake their disclosure with a view to avoid legal liability for alleged non-disclosure.[15] How can soldiers be informed about PCEs when doctors are uncomfortable to admit ignorance over benefits and risks, the alternatives to treatment and presenting that information in an easily-digestible format for patients?[16] Katz judged the highest value on autonomy as the ultimate safeguard, whereas beneficence could reduce the person to a disease or label, be less caring and increase the chance of the doctor making the decision on behalf of the patient.[17] His conclusion was that physicians must acknowledge the extent of their scientific knowledge and ignorance, embrace joint decision-making and allow the patient to have the deciding vote.[18]

With a degree of autonomy forfeited when joining the military, there is a danger that soldiers could be 'informed' of PCE requirement with the 'consent' part being bypassed.[19] To ensure that the use of PCEs is consensual for

11 Larry A. Kroutil *et al.*, "Nonmedical Use of Prescription Stimulants in the United States," *Drug and Alcohol Dependence* 84, no. 2 (2006): 140.

12 Martha J. Farah *et al.*, "When We Enhance Cognition with Adderall, Do We Sacrifice Creativity? A Preliminary Study," *Psychopharmacology* 202, no. 1 (2009): 541.

13 Nick Bostrom, "The Vulnerable World Hypothesis," *Global Policy* 10, no. 4 (2019): 455.

14 Jay Katz, "Informed Consent—Must It Remain a Fairy Tale," *Journal of Contemporary Health Law and Policy* 10 (1994): 71.

15 *ibid.*, 77.

16 *ibid.*, 80–83.

17 *ibid.*, 85.

18 *ibid.*, 90–91.

19 Lauren R. Robbins, "Refusing to Be All That You Can Be: Regulating against Forced Cognitive Enhancement in the Military," in *Military Medical Ethics for the 21st Century*,

a soldier, the Belmont principle of respecting persons is core when military recruits could be considered a vulnerable group and prone to being under duress to following instructions by the chain of command. As described earlier, the camaraderie from a unit facilitates peer pressure on individuals into conforming to a set of common values and might incite the taking of PCEs against 'better judgement'. If a soldier was directly ordered to take a PCE, they would have to obey if it was a lawful order. However, obeying all lawful orders is not always the case because sometimes they can be superseded by the necessity to conform to other regulations such as the Geneva Convention or Law of Armed Conflict.[20]

Intelligent humans are capable of making their own autonomous choices but what if a particular measure benefits the entire military unit? Is there any circumstance when the sacrifice of personal autonomy is acceptable to promote the safety and therefore health of the wider group? Pellegrino argues that there is for preventative health, where the social construct means individuals "*give up autonomy to receive certain benefits*" and absolute "*self-interest is incompatible with life in a civilized community.*"[21] Examples are the compulsory wearing of motorcycle helmets to reduce head injury from motorbike crashes and wearing seat belts in cars to reduce polytrauma in a crash. Of note is that the most effective preventive measures have been those imposed by law rather than by restraining choice.[22] There is similarity here in relinquishing some autonomy by joining the military and the directed wearing of preventative measures such as body armour or fire-retardant uniform.

Following the line of preventative health, if the taking of PCEs increased the individual and collective health and survivability, it should be compelled and not require consent. Annas disagrees, believing that prescription medications should not be forced on soldiers and military doctors should not be forced to prescribe them.[23] If a soldier refused a PCE, would that make them unfit for operational duty and potentially limit future career options? If a soldier refuses medical care that preserves their health or that of others on active

ed. M. L. Gross and D. Carrick, Military and Defence Ethics (Farnham: Ashgate Publishing Limited, 2013), 148.

20 United Kingdom. Development Concepts and Doctrine Centre, *JSP 383. The Joint Service Manual of the Law of Armed Conflict* (Shrivenham: DCDC, 2004), 13–14, 21–26.

21 Edmund D. Pellegrino, "Autonomy and Coercion in Disease Prevention and Health Promotion," *Theoretical Medicine* 5, no. 1 (1984): 88.

22 *ibid.*, 90.

23 Catherine L. Annas and George J. Annas, "Enhancing the Fighting Force: Medical Research on American Soldiers," *Journal of Contemporary Health Law and Policy* 25, no. 2 (2009): 308.

duty, it could be considered a disciplinary offence.[24] Refusal of other types of medical care results in referral to a medical board to determine whether the refusal is reasonable or not.[25] The board determines if the medical care is needed to protect the soldier's health, that of others, or enables him to perform his duty properly. If the outcome is that the medical treatment is required, the soldier undergoes a disciplinary process or is administratively discharged from service.[26] Robbins considers the onus should be on the soldier, who should have the right to refuse without it affecting their liberty.[27] If a soldier refused before deployment, an alternative person could take their place but refusal on the battlefield would put others in danger. Clearly, there must be policy setting out the regulations and guidance covering PCEs, which should incorporate a consensual approach where possible and avoid an acute situation of refusal during conflict.

As PCEs are drugs that must be prescribed by a licensed physician, could a military doctor decide that the benefit of PCE use for the individual or team undertaking a mission would avoid the need for gaining consent, irrespective of the informed component? This focuses attention on whether military doctors are physicians, officers, or both and which takes primacy? The answer is clear to Annas, judging that the military doctor should be a *"physician first, last and always."*[28] Medical ethics should not change for a doctor whether military or civilian, during peacetime or in war, but there have been historical circumstances which seemingly justified variation from normal medical ethical obligations. Penicillin was given in priority to WW2 troops with sexually-transmitted diseases rather than those wounded, because the former would return to the front line faster and more recently was the suggestion of prescribing mood-stabiliser medications to ensure that soldiers remain in, or return them to, the theatres of Iraq and Afghanistan.[29]

The conflicting roles of being both a physician and soldier cause a dilemma of dual loyalty to each profession. This can be easily resolved if international

24 George J. Annas, "Changing the Consent Rules for Desert Storm," *New England Journal of Medicine* 326, no. 11 (March 12, 1992): 772.

25 Lauren R. Robbins, "Refusing to Be All That You Can Be: Regulating against Forced Cognitive Enhancement in the Military," in *Military Medical Ethics for the 21st Century*, ed. M. L. Gross and D. Carrick, Military and Defence Ethics (Farnham: Ashgate Publishing Limited, 2013), 129.

26 *ibid.*, 130.

27 Robbins (n. 25), 134.

28 George J. Annas, "Military Medical Ethics—Physician First, Last, Always," *New England Journal of Medicine* 359, no. 11 (2008): 1090.

29 *ibid.*, 1088.

guidance is followed like those from the World Medical Association stating that during armed conflict, physicians have a primary obligation to the patient and from the Geneva Convention stating that medical treatment should be administered for medical reasons and conform to medical ethics.[30] Both sets of guidance have potential flaws; PCEs are not treatments for medical reasons and the primary obligation to the patient might be enforced use of PCEs for their own protection. However, there are concerns if military necessity enforces the use of PCEs, that override the principles and ethics of doctors, with potential for abuse.[31]

A doctor's professional responsibility is to the society it serves and that responsibility is determined by both the profession and independent regulatory bodies.[32] For a military doctor, this includes regulations set out by the General Medical Council, the medical specialty professional college and the respective Service.[33] There is no defined mechanism to resolve any conflict between these various regulatory bodies.[34] Is the military doctor a military officer first who must obey and give lawful orders, or a doctor whose primary concern is that of the patient? Cantor proposed that doctors should do their duty no matter their convictions, but this was aimed at conscientious objection and implied that the duty of a doctor overrides all else.[35] The Nuremberg trials proved that doing something you were ordered to do, against your moral code, was no defence.[36] In contrast, Mehlman does not think that military

30 Daniel Messelken and Hans Ulrich Baer, "Hovering Between Roles: Military Medical Ethics," in: *Military Medical Ethics for the 21st Century*, M. L. Gross and D. Carrick (eds)., Military and Defence Ethics (Farnham: Ashgate Publishing Limited, 2013), 268.

31 *ibid.*, 270.

32 Dan W. Brock, "Conscientious Refusal by Physicians and Pharmacists: Who Is Obligated to Do What, and Why?," *Theoretical Medicine and Bioethics* 29, no. 3 (2008): 193.

33 Examples of these regulations are General Medical Council, "Good Medical Practice," 2019, <https://www.gmc-uk.org/ethical-guidance/ethical-guidance-for-doctors/good-medical-practice>, The Royal College of Anaesthetists, "Guidelines for the Provision of Anaesthetic Services," 2020, <https://www.rcoa.ac.uk/safety-standards-quality/guidance-resources/guidelines-provision-anaesthetic-services>, United Kingdom. Ministry of Defence, *The Queen's Regulations for the Army 1975. AC13206*, (London: Ministry of Defence, 2019), <https://assets.publishing.service.gov.uk/government/uploads/system/uploads/attachment_data/file/826092/The_Queen_s_Regulations_for_the_Army_1975.pdf> (accessed April 6, 2020).

34 Nathan K. Gamble and Michal Pruski, "Medical Acts and Conscientious Objection: What Can a Physician Be Compelled to Do?," *The New Bioethics* 25, no. 3 (2019): 263.

35 Julie D. Cantor, "Conscientious Objection Gone Awry — Restoring Selfless Professionalism in Medicine," *New England Journal of Medicine* 360, no. 15 (2009): 1485.

36 Harvard Law School Library, "Nuremberg—Transcript Viewer—Transcript for NMT 1: Medical Case," *Nuremberg Trials Project*, 2016, <http://nuremberg.law.harvard.edu/transcripts/1-transcript-for-nmt-1-medical-case?seq=2586> (accessed March 11, 2020).

doctors following medical ethics and moral duties can override their military obligations and believes they should articulate the biomedical risk to decision-makers and be robust in challenging their commanders' intent.[37]

Physicians can only be expected to support medical acts which promote and restore health and are not obliged to provide non-medical services. The latter is fully supported by Gamble pointing out that "Soldiers who voluntarily join the military cannot simply be compelled to do everything that lies within their skillset, and neither should physicians be so compelled."[38] If prescribing a PCE brings about a health benefit, it would constitute a medical act but if prescribed in the absence of symptoms or pathology and driven by military need, it would constitute a socio-clinical act, as described by Gamble for social desires like aesthetic surgery.[39] This paper has described PCEs as an enhancement and not treatment, therefore prescribing them is a socio-clinical act and Gamble believes military doctors should not be 'obliged' to support it.

Currently, there is no written policy addressing the issue of whether a military physician can be legally ordered to administer a drug if it was considered medically unethical. An exception might be if it was believed to be therapeutic for emergencies in combat. This ethical deviation can result in patient harm as exampled by the administration of a clotting agent to save lives from polytrauma, effectively ordered by medical superiors despite not having completed research on its effects. Later studies proved its use led to unnecessary deaths and even at the time caused doctors concern at the Baghdad combat hospital in 2006, "I worry that some soldiers were hurt by the overzealous use of unproven therapies."[40] The impact of this is magnified, when despite the fact that a soldier must accept standard medical treatment or face disciplinary action, they are not obliged to accept interventions that are not recognized by the medical profession as standard procedures.[41] Similar to the situation with PCEs, the use of the clotting agent was not standard procedure and should only have been given under IC or if given unconsented in emergency, should have a known, generally accepted risk-benefit analysis.

37 Maxwell J. Mehlman and Stephanie Corley, "A Framework for Military Bioethics," *Journal of Military Ethics* 13, no. 4 (2014): 345.

38 Gamble and Pruski (n. 34)., 268.

39 *ibid.*, 275.

40 Robert Little, "Army Medicine: Untested in Battle," *The Baltimore Sun*, March 29, 2009, <https://www.baltimoresun.com/news/nation-world/bal-te.militarymed29mar29-story.html> (accessed March 30, 2020).

41 George J. Annas, "Protecting Soldiers from Friendly Fire: The Consent Requirement for Using Investigational Drugs and Vaccines in Combat," *American Journal of Law & Medicine* 24, no. 2/3 (1998): 257.

Delivering Effective Military Informed Consent

The final section of this paper will examine the practical aspects of military IC, covering how and when it should be done to maximise the informed and consensual components and the policy framework to support PCE use. IC must be underpinned by effective communication between the person informing and the person consenting. In the 1991 Gulf War, anthrax vaccination was not compulsory but given under implied consent.[42] Veterans later reported increased ill-health which many blamed on the anthrax vaccination, leading to fear and distrust of the military institution. To counter this for the 2003 Iraq war, explicit consent was used, coupled with an information programme by written, verbal and video means. A cooling off period was allowed before signing a consent form to strengthen the IC process.[43] Despite this, more than half of the British military refused the anthrax vaccination.[44] A survey of those deployed in the 2003 Iraq war discovered their vaccination concerns revolved around its safety, effectiveness and IC.[45] Regardless of all the information and communication, it failed to provide a perceived balanced view and address the unease that the vaccination might be ineffective and cause future illness.[46] Apprehension over why the vaccination was now voluntary and requiring IC when it had previously been compulsory, resulted in the loss of trust and confidence in the MOD, who were believed to be covering up harmful effects. The conclusion was that IC may be desirable on ethical or legal grounds but it may not lead to the expected positive effect.[47] Therefore, an IC policy for PCEs that increases anxiety and reduces uptake will fail to achieve its goal.

The method of communicating IC is vital to confirm that the individual is both informed, especially understanding the risks, and has consented freely. Lessons can be drawn from how Public Health authorities disseminate risk information, where communication has the broad aim of presenting information in such a way that it is understood and usable, allowing the individual to make a judgement on the risk and be actively supported by the informer.[48]

42 Dominic Murphy *et al.*, "UK Armed Forces Responses to an Informed Consent Policy for Anthrax Vaccination: A Paradoxical Effect?," *Vaccine* 24, no. 16 (2006): 3109.

43 *ibid.*, 3110.

44 Cathel Kerr, "Anthrax Vaccine Gets Cold Shoulder from Troops," *Canadian Medical Association Journal* 168, no. 10 (2003): 1308.

45 Murphy and others (n. 42)., 3111.

46 Dominic Murphy, Neil Greenberg, and Duncan Bland, "Health Concerns in UK Armed Forces Personnel," *Journal of the Royal Society of Medicine* 102, no. 4 (2009): 144.

47 Murphy and others (n. 42)., 3113.

48 P. J. Nicholson, "Communicating Health Risk," *Occupational Medicine* 49, no. 4 (1999): 253.

Nicholson highlighted that risks need to be discussed verbally, using a common language, an empathetic style, with the right amount of competence and openness.[49] He also noted that dressing more informally than expected supported effective communication. This would be an important point for the military with the obvious differential in rank structure when wearing uniform and the potential coercion it brings.

The World Health Organisation has noted shifts in public perception of information, with decreased trust in what experts and authorities say and a move towards the use of online sources and social media for obtaining advice, preferring opinion-based stories rather than those referenced.[50] The key is establishing trust and it is fortunate that doctors are amongst the most trusted by the public,[51] so it is they who should deliver the information, as opposed to non-medical MOD officials. Overloading information can fail to establish understanding, therefore, information should be delivered over multiple occasions, each delivering a few central messages and facts that build on what has been said previously. As time progresses, new information will inevitably arise and this should be disclosed as soon as possible to maintain the IC.[52]

For soldiers embarking on a military career, there should be both broad consent and IC for future PCE use. Broad consent alone could be prone to exploitation as occurred with the Havasupai Indian tribe who signed a broad consent for diabetic research that was expanded for wider purposes, for which if known, they would have refused consent.[53] The tribe were considered a vulnerable population, perhaps not dissimilar to new military recruits. Broad consent would be improved if there were approximate limits as to what could be covered by it, but this shifts the responsibility for duty of care to the chain of command. However, as a baseline, broad consent of potential future PCE use should be undertaken for every military recruit, providing an opportunity for opting out and leaving the Service at that point. This broad consent should be repeated at each promotion and on any change or extension to length of service. This repetition provides a balance of frequency and avoiding it becoming a tick-box process, also allowing for updated information as it becomes

49 *ibid.*, 254.

50 World Health Organisation, "An Introduction to Risk Communication," 1, <https://www.who.int/risk-communication/introduction-to-risk-communication.pdf?ua=1>, (accessed March 12, 2020).

51 Nicholson (n. 48)., 254.

52 Mahmood Adil, "Risk Communication in Healthcare: An Overview," *Journal of Communication in Healthcare* 1, no. 4 (2008): 365.

53 Tom L. Beauchamp, "Informed Consent: Its History, Meaning, and Present Challenges," *Cambridge Quarterly of Healthcare Ethics* 20, no. 4 (2011): 521.

available. Most importantly, it allows for the fact that as an individual matures from new recruit to trained soldier and through career progression, they gain life and military experience which alters their understanding and attitude to risk.[54]

Full IC containing all the specific detail should be undertaken when the soldier joins a unit that requires PCEs for its missions to succeed and repeated as part of pre-deployment training (PDT). Both allow timely points at which to opt out of PCE use, with PDT being the final moment at which refusal could occur. Once deployed in an operational environment where PCEs have been identified as critical to mission success, one team member that has not been enhanced may increase the risk to themselves and the unit, becoming a liability. In that case, consent could be bypassed and the soldier compelled to take the PCE. If soldiers are recruited for research, to avoid exploitation, a greater depth of IC remains mandated in accordance with the Belmont Report and MODREC approval.

To avoid any aspects of coercion and to maintain trust, IC information should be given in a conducive environment by a doctor trained in risk communication, current in knowledge of PCEs, ideally not in uniform and without superiors present.[55] Questions should be encouraged and background information should be provided via all forms of media, with a repository of frequently asked questions and answers being easily accessible on the internet and defence intranet. By engaging with the chain of command, soldiers could even regain partial autonomy by having control over the timings and method of delivery of the PCE.

Should there be a signed consent form for PCEs, even though implied consent is used for other drug prescriptions?[56] A signed consent does not necessarily imply IC and whether there has been full disclosure of every risk and benefit known, or minimal imparted knowledge. Whatever information is communicated by the physician must be truthful in accordance with their professional guidelines. However, as discussed earlier, doctors often gloss over areas where their knowledge is limited or the facts unknown and this must be overcome. Nonetheless, a signed consent form does provide a documented record of a meeting, it could highlight areas of information covered and it does protect the military doctor by forming the basis of a legal defence in the

54 Thomas Dohmen *et al.*, "Risk Attitudes across the Life Course," *The Economic Journal* 127, no. 605 (2017): F114.

55 John McManus *et al.*, "Informed Consent and Ethical Issues in Military Medical Research," *Academic Emergency Medicine* 12, no. 11 (2005): 1122.

56 Beauchamp (n. 53)., 517.

event of complaint.[57] On balance, a signed IC form should be used for soldiers accepting PCEs for transparency and accountability, and be stored securely as part of their medical documents.

Undoubtedly, policies must be implemented regarding PCE use, including any legal connotations such as who is responsible if the wrong dose is delivered. Is it the doctor, individual, command or manufacturer? Maslen pointed out that only when the personal benefits and full risks of enhancement are known can policy be truly informed and ethical.[58]

As this complete information may never be known, the starting basis of any policy should encapsulate the four components to ethical decision-making when using PCEs as described by the US Army Aeromedical Research Laboratory:[59]

i. Use is voluntary.
ii. The drug is safe for its intended use.
iii. Dosage and use are consistent with its function.
iv. Alternative non-pharmacological agents have been fully explored first.

This is aligned to Mehlman's adapted Belmont principles of proportionality, paternalism and fairness and his earlier published hybrid framework, addressing the broader issues of transparency with the public and accountability for those in command making the decisions of necessity.[60]

57 *ibid.*, 519.

58 Hannah Maslen, Nadira Faulmüller, and Julian Savulescu, "Pharmacological Cognitive Enhancement—How Neuroscientific Research Could Advance Ethical Debate," *Frontiers in Systems Neuroscience* 8 (2014): 8.

59 Scharre and Fish (n. 2)., 10.

60 Maxwell Mehlman, Patrick Lin, and Keith Abney, "Enhanced Warfighters: Risk, Ethics, and Policy," *Case Legal Studies Research Paper* No. 2013–2, (2013), 75–76.

Conclusion

The capability for human enhancement is already present and the UK will have to consider use of PCEs, either by a positive move to invest in that technology, or whether forced to consider it, in order to match opponents in a conflict. This issue deserves critical attention now during relative peace, because during wartime or conflict, it is much harder to give it the same rational and rigorous debate. Whichever direction the UK takes, it seems sensible to follow Annas' advice for military doctors and strive for an unequivocal policy based around traditional ethics where medical care of the individual takes primacy.[1] PCEs should not be considered a medical treatment but a group of drugs, only available by prescription from a licensed doctor, which increase a soldier's ability above the normal range.

This paper agrees with Gross stating, "Military medical ethics only *permits* informed consent."[2] Therefore, use of PCEs in the military will require an IC process to protect the individual, who unlike their civilian counterparts, has given up part of their autonomy on joining the military and who is vulnerable to peer pressure, unintended and intended coercion by those in command. The military has failed with IC in the past and exploited soldiers causing actual and potential harm and therefore a revised IC process, adapted from current civilian procedures is required.

Consent can only be considered informed once there is sufficient understanding of the risks, benefits and duration of effects, which are communicated in a manner commensurate with the recipient's intellectual capacity that ensures understanding. Much of this knowledge will come from new studies and as the likely research population would be military, enhanced IC as described by the Belmont Report should be followed, along with the established MODREC approval that protects the rights of personnel. Where knowledge is lacking, doctors must maintain trust by being honest and admitting any gaps or limitations.

To ensure the use of PCEs remains consensual, opting out must be allowed without the threat of discipline and any impact on career progression must be minimised with advanced disclosure. Even if previously consented, refusal to take PCEs at any stage prior to a deployment should be accepted without

1 Annas, 'Protecting Soldiers from Friendly Fire: The Consent Requirement for Using Investigational Drugs and Vaccines in Combat' (n. 101)., 275.

2 Michael L. Gross, *Bioethics and Armed Conflict. Moral Dilemmas of Medicine and War* (Cambridge: MIT Press, 2006), 107.

 | DOI:10.1163/9789004677746_006

prejudice. However, once the mission has commenced, PCE use could be ordered. The justification for this non-consensual use would be that the interests of the unit, mission or state override that of the individual.[3] Difficulty remains in the area of unintended consequences of PCEs, which may remain unknown for many years and who decides that the risks of PCEs are deemed essential for mission success and outweigh the benefits?

The IC process for military PCE use should be underpinned by policy and an accepted mindset that IC is an ongoing process and not a one-stop shop. The process should commence with broad consent on first joining the Services and reiterated at every promotion and career extension, or when new key knowledge becomes known. This consent should be augmented by full IC as defined in this paper, when joining a military unit whose likely missions require PCEs and again during PDT. IC but not broad consent should require a signature and the delivery of the information should be via a military doctor who has been trained in communicating risk, in an environment designed to minimise any sense of rank differential and therefore facilitating the consensual approach and avoidance of coercion. Background information needs to be made freely accessible online and via all forms of media communication. If this method of IC is followed by the military, it will best protect those individuals taking PCEs by ensuring a balance of proportionality, paternalism and fairness. It will also protect the prescribing military doctors from negligence and protect those in command by transparency and accountability.

---

3 Maxwell Mehlman, Patrick Lin, and Keith Abney, "Enhanced Warfighters: Risk, Ethics, and Policy," *Case Legal Studies Research Paper* No. 2013–2, (2013), 58.

Bibliography

Adil, Mahmood. "Risk Communication in Healthcare: An Overview." *Journal of Communication in Healthcare* 1, no. 4 (2008): 363–72. DOI: 10.1179/cih.2008.1.4.363.

Advisory Committee on Human Radiation Experiments. "Executive Summary and Guide to Final Report," 1995. <https://www.osti.gov/opennet/servlets/purl/120931/120931.pdf> (accessed January 9, 2020).

Allhoff, Fritz, Lin Patrick, Moor James, and Weckert John. "Ethics of Human Enhancement: 25 Questions & Answers." *Studies in Ethics, Law, and Technology* 4, no. 1 (2010) 1–39. DOI: 10.2202/1941-6008.1110.

Allison, Lincoln. "Faster, Stronger, Higher." *The Guardian*, August 9, 2004. <https://www.theguardian.com/sport/2004/aug/09/athensolympics2004.olympicgames> (accessed April 1, 2020).

Annas, Catherine L., and George J. Annas. "Enhancing the Fighting Force: Medical Research on American Soldiers." *Journal of Contemporary Health Law and Policy* 25, no. 2 (2009): 283–308.

Annas, George J. "Changing the Consent Rules for Desert Storm." *New England Journal of Medicine* 326, no. 11 (1992): 770–73. DOI: 10.1056/NEJM199203123261117.

Annas, George J. "Military Medical Ethics—Physician First, Last, Always." *New England Journal of Medicine* 359, no. 11 (2008): 1087–90. DOI: 10.1056/NEJMp0805975.

Annas, George J. "Protecting Soldiers from Friendly Fire: The Consent Requirement for Using Investigational Drugs and Vaccines in Combat." *American Journal of Law & Medicine* 24, no. 2/3 (1998): 245–60.

Barr, Sabrina. "Viagra Now Available over the Counter without Prescription in UK." *The Independent*, March 27, 2018; <https://www.independent.co.uk/life-style/health-and-families/viagra-buy-without-prescription-over-counter-uk-pharmacies-male-impotence-erectile-dysfunction-a8275461.html> (accessed April 3, 2020).

BBC News. "Sussex University Students Illegally Buying 'Smart Pills.'" *BBC News*, March 13, 2018; <https://www.bbc.co.uk/news/uk-england-43383717> (accessed March 31, 2020).

Bear, Adam, and Joshua Knobe. "Normality: Part Descriptive, Part Prescriptive." *Cognition* 167 (2017): 25–37. DOI: https://doi.org/10.1016/j.cognition.2016.10.024.

Beauchamp, Tom L. "Informed Consent: Its History, Meaning, and Present Challenges." *Cambridge Quarterly of Healthcare Ethics* 20, no. 4 (2011): 515–523. DOI: 10.1017/S0963180111000259.

Berg, J. W., P. S. Appelbaum, C. W. Lidz, and L. S. Parker. *Informed Consent: Legal Theory and Clinical Practice*. Second. New York: Oxford University Press, 2001.

Beutler, Ernest, and Jill Waalen. "The Definition of Anemia: What Is the Lower Limit of Normal of the Blood Hemoglobin Concentration?" *Blood* 107, no. 5 (March 2006): 1747–50. DOI: 10.1182/blood-2005-07-3046.

Bostrom, Nick. "The Vulnerable World Hypothesis," *Global Policy* 10, no. 4 (2019): 455–76. DOI: 10.1111/1758-5899.12718.

Bostrom, Nick, and Anders Sandberg. "Cognitive Enhancement: Methods, Ethics, Regulatory Challenges," *Science and Engineering Ethics* 15, no. 3 (2009): 311–41. DOI: 10.1007/s11948-009-9142-5.

British Army. "New Physical Employment Standards for the Army," <https://www.army.mod.uk/physical-employment-standards/> (accessed May 6, 2020).

British Army. "People. Drugs and Supplements," <https://www.army.mod.uk/people/join-well/drugs-and-supplements/> (accessed March 30, 2020).

British Army. *Values and Standards of the British Army. AC 64649*. Andover: Army Headquarters, 2018, <https://www.army.mod.uk/media/5219/20180910-values_standards_2018_final.pdf> (accessed March 26, 2020).

British Medical Journal. "The Nuremberg Code (1947)," *British Medical Journal* 313, no. 7070 (1996): 1448. DOI: 10.1136/bmj.313.7070.1448.

Brock, Dan W. "Conscientious Refusal by Physicians and Pharmacists: Who Is Obligated to Do What, and Why?" *Theoretical Medicine and Bioethics* 29, no. 3 (2008): 187–200. DOI: 10.1007/s11017-008-9076-y.

Brunet, Alain, Daniel Saumier, Aihua Liu, David L Streiner, Jacques Tremblay, and Roger K Pitman. "Reduction of PTSD Symptoms With Pre-Reactivation Propranolol Therapy: A Randomized Controlled Trial." *American Journal of Psychiatry* 175, no. 5 (January 12, 2018): 427–33. DOI: 10.1176/appi.ajp.2017.17050481.

Buchanan, A. E. *Beyond Humanity?: The Ethics of Biomedical Enhancement*. Oxford: OUP Oxford, 2011.

Burkeman, Oliver, and Richard Norton-Taylor, "US Pilots Blame Drug for Friendly Fire Deaths." *The Guardian*, January 4, 2003. <https://www.theguardian.com/world/2003/jan/04/afghanistan.richardnortontaylor> (accessed March 27, 2020).

Caldwell, John A., and J. Lynn Caldwell. "Fatigue in Military Aviation: An Overview of U.S. Military-Approved Pharmacological Countermeasures." *Aviation, Space, and Environmental Medicine* 76, no. 7 (2005): C39–51.

Cantor, Julie D. "Conscientious Objection Gone Awry—Restoring Selfless Professionalism in Medicine." *New England Journal of Medicine* 360, no. 15 (2009): 1484–85. DOI: 10.1056/NEJMp0902019.

Care Quality Commission. "Defence Medical Services," 2019, <https://www.cqc.org.uk/what-we-do/services-we-regulate/defence-medical-services> (accessed April 9, 2020).

Carrick, D., P. M. L. Gross, P. J. Connelly, P. G. Lucas, and P. P. Robinson. *Military Medical Ethics for the 21st Century*, Military and Defence Ethics. Ashgate Publishing Limited, 2013.

Casey, Anna, Jason Hughes, Rachel M Izard, and Julie P Greeves. "Supplement Use by UK-Based British Army Soldiers in Training." *The British Journal of Nutrition* 112, no. 7 (2014): 1175–84. DOI: 10.1017/S0007114514001597.

CBRN Delivery Team. *2017DIN04–165. Fentanyl Lozenge 800 Micrograms (OTFC) Single—Introduction into Service as Self Administered Operational Analgesia.* Bristol: Ministry of Defence, 2017.

Corrigan, Oonagh. "Empty Ethics: The Problem with Informed Consent." *Sociology of Health & Illness* 25, no. 3 (2003): 768–92.

Dearden, Lizzie. "Women Now Allowed to Apply for Royal Marines and All Other Frontline Military Roles, Defence Secretary Announces." *The Independent*, October 25, 2018. <https://www.independent.co.uk/news/uk/home-news/women-soldiers-army-military-sas-defence-government-infantry-frontline-gavin-williamson-female-a8601371.html> (accessed April 2, 2020).

Deardorff, Stephen E. "Informed Consent, Termination of Medical Treatment, and the Federal Tort Claims Act--A New Proposal for the Military Health Care System." *Military Law Review* 115, no. Winter (1987): 1–120.

Dohmen, Thomas, Armin Falk, Bart H H Golsteyn, David Huffman, and Uwe Sunde. "Risk Attitudes across the Life Course." *The Economic Journal* 127, no. 605 (2017): F95–116. DOI: 10.1111/ecoj.12322.

Drabiak-Syed, Katherine. "Reining In the Pharmacological Enhancement Train: We Should Remain Vigilant about Regulatory Standards for Prescribing Controlled Substances." *The Journal of Law, Medicine & Ethics* 39, no. 2 (2011): 272–79. DOI: 10.1111/j.1748-720X.2011.00596.x.

Dunne, T. "Liberalism." In *The Globalisation of World Politics. An Introduction to World Politics*, edited by John Baylis, Steve Smith, and Patricia Owens, 102–13. Oxford: Oxford University Press, 2011.

Dworkin, Gerald. "Paternalism." Edited by Edward N. Zalta. *The Stanford Encyclopedia of Philosophy*. Stanford: Metaphysics Research Lab, Stanford University, 2019. <https://plato.stanford.edu/entries/paternalism/> (accessed January 8, 2020).

Dyer, Clare. "Consent Needed For Organ Retention, BMA Says." *British Medical Journal* 321, no. 7269 (2000): 1098.

European Medicines Agency. "Modafinil," 2010. <https://www.ema.europa.eu/en/medicines/human/referrals/modafinil> (accessed March 31, 2020).

Faden, R. R., T. L. Beauchamp, and N. M. P. King. *A History and Theory of Informed Consent*. New York: Oxford University Press, 1986.

Faden, Ruth R. *Advisory Committee on Human Radiation Experiments. Final Report.* Washington DC: U.S. Government Printing Office, 1995.

Faden, Ruth R., Tom L. Beauchamp, and Nancy E. Kass. "Informed Consent, Comparative Effectiveness, and Learning Health Care." *New England Journal of Medicine* 370, no. 8 (2014): 766–68. DOI: 10.1056/NEJMhle1313674.

Farah, Martha J., Caroline Haimm, Geena Sankoorikal, and Anjan Chatterjee. "When We Enhance Cognition with Adderall, Do We Sacrifice Creativity? A Preliminary Study." *Psychopharmacology* 202, no. 1 (2009): 541–47. DOI: 10.1007/s00213-008-1369-3.

FitzPatrick, William J., and Lee L. Zwanziger. "Defending Against Biochemical Warfare." *The Journal of Philosophy, Science & Law* 3, no. 2 (2003): 1–19. DOI: 10.5840/jpsl2003323.

Ford, Kenneth, and Clark Glymour. "The Enhanced Warfighter." *Bulletin of the Atomic Scientists* 70, no. 1 (2014): 43–53.

Friedl, Karl E. "U.S. Army Research on Pharmacological Enhancement of Soldier Performance: Stimulants, Anabolic Hormones, and Blood Doping." *The Journal of Strength & Conditioning Research* 29 (2015): S71–76.

Galliott, J., and M Lotz. *Super Soldiers: The Ethical, Legal and Social Implications*. Emerging Technologies, Ethics and International Affairs. Farnham: Taylor & Francis, 2016.

Gamble, Nathan K., and Michal Pruski. "Medical Acts and Conscientious Objection: What Can a Physician Be Compelled to Do?" *The New Bioethics* 25, no. 3 (2019): 262–82. DOI: 10.1080/20502877.2019.1649871.

Gebhardt, D. O. E. "Off-Label Administration of Drugs to Healthy Military Personnel. Dubious Ethics of Preventive Measures." *Journal of Medical Ethics* 31, no. 5 (2005): 268. DOI: 10.1136/jme.2004.008821.

General Medical Council. "Good Medical Practice," 2019, <https://www.gmc-uk.org/ethical-guidance/ethical-guidance-for-doctors/good-medical-practice> (accessed April 6, 2020).

Gidda, Mirren. "Drugs in War: What Is Captagon, the 'Jihad Pill' Used by Islamic State Militants?" *Newsweek*, May 12, 2017, <https://www.newsweek.com/drugs-captagon-islamic-state-jihad-war-amphetamines-saudi-arabia-608233> (accessed March 26, 2020).

Gross, Michael. *Military Medical Research Ethics: Investigational Drugs, Clinical Trials and Enhancement*. Oxford: Oxford University Press, 2019.

Gross, Michael L. *Bioethics and Armed Conflict. Moral Dilemmas of Medicine and War*. Cambridge: MIT Press, 2006.

Harvard Law School Library. "Nuremberg—Transcript Viewer—Transcript for NMT 1: Medical Case." *Nuremberg Trials Project*, 2016, <http://nuremberg.law.harvard.edu/transcripts/1-transcript-for-nmt-1-medical-case?seq=2586> (accessed March 11, 2020).

Harvey, Kate. "Sports Science and Medicine." *The Nuffield Council on Bioethics*, 2014. <https://nuffieldbioethics.org/publications/sports-science-and-medicine> (accessed January 6, 2020).

Helgesson, Gert. "In Defense of Broad Consent." *Cambridge Quarterly of Healthcare Ethics* 21, no. 1 (2012): 40–50. DOI: 10.1017/S096318011100048X.

House of Commons Defence Committee. *Duty of Care. Third Report of Session 2004–05. Volume I. HC 63-I*. London: The Stationery Office Limited, 2005.

Howe, Edmund G., and Edward D. Martin. "Treating the Troops." *Hastings Center Report* 21, no. 2 (1991): 21–24. DOI: 10.2307/3562332.

iMedi.co.uk. "Autoject (Combopen) Nerve Agent Antidote L4a1," 2009. <https://imedi.co.uk/autoject-combopen-nerve-agent-antidote-l4a1> (accessed April 30, 2020).

JASON. JSR-07-625. "Human Performance." Virginia, USA, 2008. <https://fas.org/irp/agency/dod/jason/human.pdf> (accessed April 9, 2020).

Juengst, Eric T. "What Does Enhancement Mean?" in: *Enhancing Human Traits: Ethical and Social Implications*, edited by Eric Parens, 29–47. Hastings Center Studies in Ethics Series. Washington DC: Georgetown University Press, 2000.

Kamienski, L. *Shooting Up: A History of Drugs in Warfare*. Oxford: Hurst, 2017.

Kamm, Frances M. "Is There a Problem With Enhancement?" *The American Journal of Bioethics* 5, no. 3 (2005): 5–14. DOI: 10.1080/15265160590945101.

Katz, Jay. "Informed Consent—Must It Remain a Fairy Tale." *Journal of Contemporary Health Law and Policy* 10 (1994): 69–92.

Katz, J., and A. M. Capron. *The Silent World of Doctor and Patient*. Baltimore: Johns Hopkins University Press, 2002.

Kautz, Mary A., Maria L. Thomas, and J. Lynn Caldwell. "Considerations of Pharmacology on Fitness for Duty in the Operational Environment." *Aviation, Space, and Environmental Medicine* 78, no. 5 (2007): B107–12.

Kerr, Cathel. "Anthrax Vaccine Gets Cold Shoulder from Troops." *Canadian Medical Association Journal* 168, no. 10 (2003): 1308.

Kroutil, Larry A., David L. Van Brunt, Mindy A. Herman-Stahl, David C. Heller, Robert M. Bray, and Michael A. Penne. "Nonmedical Use of Prescription Stimulants in the United States." *Drug and Alcohol Dependence* 84, no. 2 (2006): 135–43.

Lennard, Natasha. "One in Ten Takes Drugs to Study." *Varsity*. March 6, 2009. <https://www.varsity.co.uk/news/1307> (accessed March 31, 2020).

Little, Robert. "Army Medicine: Untested in Battle." *The Baltimore Sun*, March 29, 2009. <https://www.baltimoresun.com/news/nation-world/bal-te.militarymed29mar29-story.html> (accessed March 30, 2020).

Lusher, Adam. "The Bizarre True Story of When the UK Military Tested LSD on Royal Marines." *The Independent*. May 24, 2018. <https://www.independent.co.uk/news/uk/home-news/lsd-video-porton-down-chemical-weapons-experiments-trials-uk-military-army-marines-sixties-acid-a8366906.html> (accessed April 29, 2020).

Maheshwari, Nidhi, and Vineeth V Kumar. *Military Psychology: Concepts, Trends and Interventions*. New Delhi, India: Sage Publications Pvt. Ltd, 2016.

Maslen, Hannah, Nadira Faulmüller, and Julian Savulescu. "Pharmacological Cognitive Enhancement—How Neuroscientific Research Could Advance Ethical Debate." *Frontiers in Systems Neuroscience* 8 (2014): 1–12. DOI: 10.3389/fnsys.2014.00107.

McCartney, Helen. "The Military Covenant and the Civil–Military Contract in Britain." *International Affairs* 86, no. 2 (2010): 411–28. DOI: 10.1111/j.1468-2346.2010.00889.x.

McLellan, Tom M., John A. Caldwell, and Harris R. Lieberman. "A Review of Caffeine's Effects on Cognitive, Physical and Occupational Performance." *Neuroscience & Biobehavioral Reviews* 71 (2016): 294–312. DOI: https://doi.org/10.1016/j.neubiorev.2016.09.001.

McManus, John, Sumeru G. Mehta, Annette R. McClinton, Robert A. De Lorenzo, and Toney W. Baskin. "Informed Consent and Ethical Issues in Military Medical Research." *Academic Emergency Medicine* 12, no. 11 (2005): 1120–26. DOI: 10.1197/j.aem.2005.05.037.

Mehlman, Maxwell. "Bioethics of Military Performance Enhancement." *Journal of the Royal Army Medical Corps* 165, no. 4 (2019): 226–231. DOI: 10.1136/jramc-2018-001130.

Mehlman, Maxwell J., and Stephanie Corley. "A Framework for Military Bioethics." *Journal of Military Ethics* 13, no. 4 (2014): 331–49. DOI: 10.1080/15027570.2014.992214.

Mehlman, Maxwell J., Patrick Lin, and Keith Abney. "Enhanced Warfighters: A Policy Framework." In *Military Medical Ethics for the 21st Century*, edited by M. L. Gross and D. Carrick, 113–26. Military and Defence Ethics. Farnham: Ashgate Publishing Limited, 2013.

Mehlman, Maxwell, Patrick Lin, and Keith Abney. "Enhanced Warfighters: Risk, Ethics, and Policy." *Case Legal Studies Research Paper No. 2013–2*. Elsevier BV, January 18, 2013. DOI: 10.2139/ssrn.2202982.

Meijer, Marten. "A Human Performance Perspective on the Ethical Use of Cogniceuticals: Commentary on 'Recommendations for the Ethical Use of Pharmacologic Fatigue Countermeasures in the U.S. Military.'" *Aviation, Space, and Environmental Medicine* 78, no. 5 (2007): B131–33.

Messelken, Daniel, and Hans Ulrich Baer. "Hovering Between Roles: Military Medical Ethics." In *Military Medical Ethics for the 21st Century*, edited by M. L. Gross and D. Carrick, 261–77. Military and Defence Ethics. Farnham: Ashgate Publishing Limited, 2013.

Mohamed, Ahmed Dahir. "Neuroethical Issues in Pharmacological Cognitive Enhancement." *WIREs Cognitive Science* 5, no. 5 (2014): 533–49. DOI: 10.1002/wcs.1306.

Morris, Marilyn C., and Robert M. Nelson. "Randomized, Controlled Trials as Minimal Risk: An Ethical Analysis*." *Critical Care Medicine* 35, no. 3 (2007): 940–44.

Murphy, Dominic, Christopher Dandeker, Oded Horn, Matthew Hotopf, Lisa Hull, Margaret Jones, Theresa Marteau, Roberto Rona, and Simon Wessely. "UK

Armed Forces Responses to an Informed Consent Policy for Anthrax Vaccination: A Paradoxical Effect?" *Vaccine* 24, no. 16 (2006): 3109–14. DOI: 10.1016/j.vaccine.2006.01.043.

Murphy, Dominic, Neil Greenberg, and Duncan Bland. "Health Concerns in UK Armed Forces Personnel." *Journal of the Royal Society of Medicine* 102, no. 4 (2009): 143–47. DOI: 10.1258/jrsm.2009.080387.

Myers, Carol S., Richard C. Taylor, Eric T. Moolchan, and Stephen J. Heishman. "Dose-Related Enhancement of Mood and Cognition in Smokers Administered Nicotine Nasal Spray." *Neuropsychopharmacology* 33, no. 3 (2008): 588–98. DOI: 10.1038/sj.npp.1301425.

Newlands, Emma. "'They Even Gave Us Oranges on One Occasion': Human Experimentation in the British Army During the Second World War." *War & Society* 32, no. 1 (2013): 19–63. DOI: 10.1179/0729247312Z.00000000016.

Nicholson, P. J. "Communicating Health Risk." *Occupational Medicine* 49, no. 4 (1999): 253–56. DOI: 10.1093/occmed/49.4.253.

O'Neill, O. "Some Limits of Informed Consent." *Journal of Medical Ethics* 29, no. 1 (2003): 4–7. DOI: 10.1136/jme.29.1.4.

Olsen, Olav Kjellevold, Ståle Pallesen, and Eid Jarle. "The Impact of Partial Sleep Deprivation on Moral Reasoning in Military Officers." *Sleep* 33, no. 8 (2010): 1086–90. DOI: 10.1093/sleep/33.8.1086.

Parens, E. *Enhancing Human Traits: Ethical and Social Implications*. Hastings Center Studies in Ethics Series. Washington DC: Georgetown University Press, 2000.

Patrey, James, Judith Lytle, William Sobotka, GeorgiAnna Sheppard, and Susan R. Kayar. "Human Performance Enhancement for NATO Military Operations (Science, Technology, and Ethics)." In *NATO Research and Technology Organisation*, 1–7. Virginia, USA: Office of Naval Research Warfighter Performance Department, 2009 https://apps.dtic.mil/dtic/tr/fulltext/u2/a562561.pdf (accessed January 6, 2020).

Pellegrino, Edmund D. "Autonomy and Coercion in Disease Prevention and Health Promotion." *Theoretical Medicine* 5, no. 1 (1984): 83–91. DOI: 10.1007/BF00489248.

Pérez-Guisado, Joaquín, and Philip M Jakeman. "Citrulline Malate Enhances Athletic Anaerobic Performance and Relieves Muscle Soreness." *The Journal of Strength & Conditioning Research* 24, no. 5 (2010): 1215–22.

President's Council on Bioethics. *Beyond Therapy: Biotechnology and the Pursuit of Happiness*. New York: Regan Books, 2003.

Rayment, Sean. "Thousands of Soldiers on Antidepressants as They Battle Mental Health Issues, New Figures Reveal." *The Mirror*, July 28, 2018. <https://www.mirror.co.uk/news/uk-news/thousands-soldiers-antidepressants-battle-mental-12996613> (accessed March 31, 2020).

Rettig, Richard. *Waiving Informed Consent: Military Use of Non-FDA-Approved Drugs in Combat*. Santa Monica: RAND Corporation, 2000. DOI: 10.7249/rb7534 (accessed April 30, 2020).

Rettig, Richard A. "Military Use of Drugs Not Yet Approved by the FDA for CW/BW Defense: Lessons from the Gulf War." Santa Monica: RAND Corporation, 1999. <https://www.rand.org/pubs/monograph_reports/MR1018z9.html> (accessed March 11, 2020).

Robbins, Lauren R. "Refusing to Be All That You Can Be: Regulating against Forced Cognitive Enhancement in the Military." In *Military Medical Ethics for the 21st Century*, edited by M. L. Gross and D. Carrick, 127–38. Military and Defence Ethics. Farnham: Ashgate Publishing Limited, 2013.

Rosenbaum, S. "100 Years of Heights and Weights." *Journal of the Royal Statistical Society. Series A (Statistics in Society)* 151, no. 2 (1988): 276–309. DOI: 10.2307/2982758.

Russo, Michael B. "Recommendations for the Ethical Use of Pharmacologic Fatigue Countermeasures in the U.S. Military." *Aviation, Space, and Environmental Medicine* 78, no. 5 (2007): B119–27.

Sandberg, Anders, and Nick Bostrom. "Converging Cognitive Enhancements." *Annals New York Academy of Sciences* 1093 (2006): 201–27. DOI: 10.1196/annals.1382.015.

Sattler, Sebastian, Guido Mehlkop, Peter Graeff, and Carsten Sauer. "Evaluating the Drivers of and Obstacles to the Willingness to Use Cognitive Enhancement Drugs: The Influence of Drug Characteristics, Social Environment, and Personal Characteristics." *Substance Abuse Treatment, Prevention, and Policy* 9, no. 1 (2014): 1–14. DOI: 10.1186/1747-597X-9-8.

Savulescu, Julian. "Conscientious Objection in Medicine." *BMJ* 332, no. 7536 (2006): 294–97. DOI: 10.1136/bmj.332.7536.294.

Savulescu, J., and N Bostrom. *Human Enhancement*. Oxford: OUP Oxford, 2009.

Savulescu, J., B. Foddy, and M. Clayton. "Why We Should Allow Performance Enhancing Drugs in Sport." *British Journal of Sports Medicine* 38, no. 6 (2004): 666–670. DOI: 10.1136/bjsm.2003.005249.

Savulescu, Julian, Leon Creaney, and Anna Vondy. "Should Athletes Be Allowed to Use Performance Enhancing Drugs?" *BMJ (Clinical Research Ed.)* 347 (2013): f6150. DOI: 10.1136/bmj.f6150.

Scharre, Paul, and Lauren Fish. "Human Performance Enhancement." *Center for a New American Security*, 2018. <https://www.cnas.org/publications/reports/human-performance-enhancement-1> (accessed January 6, 2020).

Schelle, Kimberly J., Nadira Faulmüller, Lucius Caviola, and Miles Hewstone. "Attitudes toward Pharmacological Cognitive Enhancement—a Review." *Frontiers in Systems Neuroscience* 8 (2014): 1–14. DOI: 10.3389/fnsys.2014.00053.

Schofer, Joel Martin. "Violations of Informed Consent During War." *JAMA* 281, no. 17 (May 5, 1999): 1657.

Schoomaker, Eric B. "Military Medical Research on Cognitive Performance: The Warfighters Competitive Edge." *Aviation, Space, and Environmental Medicine* 78, no. 5 (2007): B4–6.

Sears, Neil. "Army Signs up Recruits with a Reading Age as Young as FIVE in Desperate Bid to Boost Troop Numbers." *The Daily Mail.* April 5, 2020. <https://www.dailymail.co.uk/news/article-8190009/Army-signs-recruits-reading-age-young-FIVE-desperate-bid-boost-troop-numbers.html> (accessed May 1, 2020).

Sellgren, Katherine. "Almost 40% of Army Recruits Have Reading Age of 11, MPs Warn." *BBC News*, July 18, 2013, <https://www.bbc.co.uk/news/education-23346693> (accessed May 1, 2020).

Support, Macmillan Cancer. "Familial Adenomatous Polyposis (FAP)." <https://www.macmillan.org.uk/cancer-information-and-support/worried-about-cancer/causes-and-risk-factors/familial-adenomatous-polyposis-fap> (accessed April 6, 2020).

The National Commission for the Protection of Human Subjects of Biomedical and Behavioural Research. "The Belmont Report: Ethical Principles and Guidelines for the Protection of Human Subjects of Research," 1979. <https://www.hhs.gov/ohrp/sites/default/files/the-belmont-report-508c_FINAL.pdf> (accessed January 8, 2020).

The Royal College of Anaesthetists. "Guidelines for the Provision of Anaesthetic Services," 2020, <https://www.rcoa.ac.uk/safety-standards-quality/guidance-resources/guidelines-provision-anaesthetic-services> (accessed April 6, 2020).

U.S. Anti-Doping Agency. "Effects of Performance-Enhancing Drugs." <https://www.usada.org/athletes/substances/effects-of-performance-enhancing-drugs/> (accessed May 8, 2020).

United Kingdom. Department of Health. "About Us—Medicines and Healthcare Products Regulatory Agency," <https://www.gov.uk/government/organisations/medicines-and-healthcare-products-regulatory-agency/about#our-responsibilities> (accessed March 26, 2020).

United Kingdom. Department of Health. "The Controlled Drugs (Supervision of Management and Use) Regulations 2013. Information about the Regulations," 2013. <https://assets.publishing.service.gov.uk/government/uploads/system/uploads/attachment_data/file/214915/15-02-2013-controlled-drugs-regulation-information.pdf> (accessed March 26, 2020).

United Kingdom. Development Concepts and Doctrine Centre. *JSP 383. The Joint Service Manual of the Law of Armed Conflict.* Shrivenham: DCDC, 2004.

United Kingdom. HM Government. "Defence Medical Services." <https://www.gov.uk/government/groups/defence-medical-services> (accessed May 18, 2020).

United Kingdom. HM Government. "Off-Label or Unlicensed Use of Medicines: Prescribers' Responsibilities," 2014, <https://www.gov.uk/drug-safety-update/off-label-or-unlicensed-use-of-medicines-prescribers-responsibilities> (accessed May 4, 2020).

United Kingdom. HM Government. "Misuse of Drugs Act 1971," 1971. <http://www.legislation.gov.uk/ukpga/1971/38/contents> (accessed March 26, 2020).

United Kingdom. Ministry of Defence. "FOI2017/13417," 2018. <https://assets.publishing.service.gov.uk/government/uploads/system/uploads/attachment_data/file/691866/2017-13417.pdf> (accessed March 31, 2020).

United Kingdom. Ministry of Defence. *JSP 536. Governance of Research Involving Human Participants. Part 1: Directive*. 3rd ed. London: HMSO, 2020.

United Kingdom. Ministry of Defence. *JSP 830: The Manual of Service Law*. London: HMSO, 2016.

United Kingdom. Ministry of Defence. *The Queen's Regulations for the Army 1975. AC13206*. London: Ministry of Defence, 2019.

United Kingdom. Ministry of Defence. "Ministry of Defence Research Ethics Committee." <https://www.gov.uk/government/groups/ministry-of-defence-research-ethics-committees#guidance-documents> (accessed January 9, 2020).

United Kingdom. The Human Medicines Regulations 2012, Pub. L. No. 1916, Schedule 17 (2012), <http://www.legislation.gov.uk/uksi/2012/1916/schedule/17/made> (accessed April 6, 2020).

United Kingdom. The Medicines for Human Use (Clinical Trials) Regulations, Pub. L. No. 1031, Schedule 1 (2004). <http://www.legislation.gov.uk/uksi/2004/1031/schedule/1/part/2/paragraph/3/made#text%3Dinformed%consent> (accessed January 1, 2020).

United Nations. "Universal Declaration of Human Rights," 1948. <https://www.un.org/en/universal-declaration-human-rights/ (accessed January 9, 2020)>.

Wamberg, Jacob, Mads Rosendahl Thomsen, and Kasper Lippert-Rasmussen. *The Posthuman Condition : Ethics, Aesthetics and Politics of Biotechnological Challenges*. Aarhus, Denmark: Aarhus University Press, 2012.

Westcott, Kelli J. "Modafinil, Sleep Deprivation, and Cognitive Function in Military and Medical Settings." *Military Medicine* 170, no. 4 (2005): 333–35. DOI: 10.7205/MILMED.170.4.333.

Wilson, Jacque. "Lance Armstrong's Doping Drugs—CNN." *CNN*, January 18, 2013. <https://edition.cnn.com/2013/01/15/health/armstrong-ped-explainer/index.html> (accessed April 12, 2020).

Wolfendale, Jessica. "Performance-Enhancing Technologies and Moral Responsibility in the Military." *The American Journal of Bioethics* 8, no. 2 (2008): 28–38. DOI: 10.1080/15265160802014969.

Wolfendale, Jessica, and Steve Clarke. "Paternalism, Consent, and the Use of Experimental Drugs in the Military." *The Journal of Medicine and Philosophy: A Forum for Bioethics and Philosophy of Medicine* 33, no. 4 (2008): 337–55. DOI: 10.1093/jmp/jhn014.

World Anti-Doping Agency. "World Anti-Doping Code." Montreal: World Anti-Doping Agency, 2015, <https://www.wada-ama.org/sites/default/files/resources/files/wada_anti-doping_code_2019_english_final_revised_v1_linked.pdf> (accessed March 12, 2020).

World Health Organisation. "An Introduction to Risk Communication." Accessed March 12, 2020, <https://www.who.int/risk-communication/introduction-to-risk-communication.pdf?ua=1> (accessed March 12, 2020).

World Medical Association. "Ethical Principles for Medical Research Involving Human Subjects." *WMA Declaration of Helsinki*, 2018 <https://www.wma.net/policies-post/wma-declaration-of-helsinki-ethical-principles-for-medical-research-involving-human-subjects/> (accessed January 9, 2020).

Wie sollte die informierte Zustimmung im Militär in Bezug auf pharmakologisches Enhancement aussehen?

Einführung

Die Menschheit ist eine schwache Gattung, die aufgrund ihres Intellekts, ihres Einfallreichtums und ihrer Anpassungsfähigkeit überlebt und das Land beherrscht hat. Dieser Einfallsreichtum und diese Anpassungsfähigkeit gelten auch für bewaffnete Konflikte, in denen ein Soldat[1] doch noch Gefühle wie Furcht überwinden und mit physischen Herausforderungen wie Hunger, Durst und Erschöpfung umgehen muss. Die militärische Ausbildung kann diese potenziellen Schwächen mildern, aber eine Fähigkeit, die neuesten Fortschritte in Wissenschaft und Technologie einzusetzen, um die Leistungsfähigkeit eines Soldaten zu steigern, könnte den erwünschten Vorteil, einen Feind zu besiegen, mit sich bringen. Dies wird ganz besonders wichtig, wenn andere staatlichen und nicht-staatlichen Beteiligten auch Zugang zu dieser Technologie erhalten könnten.

Human Enhancement ist ein sich rapide entwickelnder Bereich, von dem Allhoff überzeugt ist, dass *„wir uns sehr nahe am Beginn der Revolution des Human Enhancement befinden."*[2] Die Schnelligkeit, mit der der Fortschritt der Technologie zur Gebrauchsfertigkeit schreitet, führt zu einer Verlangsamung der damit verbundenen Ethik. Dies trifft sowohl auf pharmakologische Leistungssteigerung (im folgenden PCE genannt), als auch auf Exoskelette und die Mensch-Maschine-Schnittstelle zu. Verschiedene Militärs und andere Organisationen haben sehr stark in Human Enhancement investiert. Sie haben auf wissenschaftliche Fortschritte in Neurowissenschaft, Biotechnologie, Robotik und die Fähigkeit, Technologie zu miniaturisieren, gesetzt.[3] Leistungserhöhende Arzneistoffe stehen bereits zur Verfügung, mit einer bis zu 20% Steigerung der Leistungsfähigkeit bei solchen, die sie für bestimmte Tests einnehmen.[4] Deshalb ist es vorzuziehen, eine Strategie für den Einsatz

1 Die Bezeichnung "Soldat" wird als ein Begriff benutzt, der alle Mitglieder im militärischen Dienst der britischen Streitkräfte einschließt.

2 Fritz Allhoff *et al.*, "Ethics of Human Enhancement: 25 Questions and Answers" (Die Ethik des Human Enhancements: 25 Fragen & Antworten), *Studies in Ethics, Law and Technology* 4, Nr. 1 (2010), 1.

3 Maxwell J. Mehlman, Patrick Lin und Keith Abney, "Enhanced Warfighters: A Policy Framework," (Enhancement für Streitkräfte: ein Strategierahmen) in: *Military Medical Ethics for the 21. Century*, Hsg. M. L. Gross und D. Carrick, Military and Defence Ethics (Farnham: Ashgate Publishing Limited, 2013), 113.

4 Anders Sandberg und Nick Bostrom, "Converging Cognitive Enhancements," (Konvergierende Kognitive Enhancements) – Annals *New York Academy of Sciences* 1093 (2006): 205.

 | DOI:10.1163/9789004677746_007

von PCEs einzuplanen, um Zeit für Überlegungen zu gewinnen, statt gezwungen zu sein, ganz plötzlich eine Entscheidung zu treffen.

Human Enhancement wirft ethische Fragen auf, wie Autonomie, Sicherheit und Menschenwürde.[5] Die ersten beiden sind der Eckstein der Ethik im Umfeld der informierten Einwilligungserklärung (IC), die aus der Notwendigkeit, menschliche Probanden vor den Risiken der Forschung zu schützen, hervorgeht. Heutzutage ist IC die Standardpraxis für ethische medizinische Behandlungsmethoden und fußt auf der Notwendigkeit von Autonomie und der Erhaltung von Gesundheit und leiblichem Wohlbefinden. Derzeit befolgt das Militär die IC-Richtlinien für die Zivilbevölkerung, aber das ist wahrscheinlich nicht wirklich geeignet, da das Militär den Schutz des Einzelnen vor jeglichen Risiken abwägen muss und das ist der individuellen Autonomie übergeordnet. Es bleibt ungewiss, wie weit diese Risiken quantifiziert sind, wer darüber entscheidet, ob es akzeptabel ist das Risiko einzugehen und ob dabei IC erforderlich ist. Für die Zivilbevölkerung würde eine befugte, autonome Fachkraft entscheiden, ob das Risiko im Rahmen eines IC-Prozesses akzeptabel ist, aber für das Militär erstellt der teilweise Verlust von Autonomie beim Beitritt in eine Organisation, in der gesetzliche Befehle ausgeführt werden müssen, für die Erwerbung von IC eine Herausforderung dar.

Diese Arbeit definiert Human Enhancement, erklärt, was pharmakologische Wirkstoffe sind und warum ein Einzelner oder das Militär sie benutzen könnten. Sie erstellt eine kurze Beschreibung spezifischer Themen zum Einsatz pharmakologischer Wirkstoffe im Militär, einschließlich der Gesetze und Regelungen, die für die Lizensierung und Ausgabe von rezeptpflichtigen Arzneistoffen anwendbar sind, die Auswirkung, die der Gebrauch von diesen Wirkstoffen auf sowohl militärische Karrieren als auch die Kommandostruktur ausübt, und wie Benutzer von pharmakologischen Wirkstoffen von ihren Kollegen und der Gesellschaft wahrgenommen werden. Ein wichtiger Teil des militärischen Lebens ist die Sorgfaltspflicht all jener, die für Untergeordnete verantwortlich sind, und dies muss von denen, die Einsätze autorisieren, in denen die Notwendigkeit für pharmakologische Wirkstoffe für den Erfolg der Einsätze als äußerst wichtig erachtet wird, berücksichtigt werden. Es werden Argumente für und gegen die Anforderung von IC im Militär vorgestellt.

IC wird im Detail mit Hinsicht auf Theorie und Geschichte untersucht. Die Arbeit spricht die militärischen Fallstudien zu den Erfolgen und Fehlschlägen des IC in der Vergangenheit an. Jeder Arzneistoff muss gründlich auf Eignung

5 Maxwell Mehlman, Patrick Lin und Keith Abney, "Enhanced Warfighters: Risk, Ethics, and Policy,"(Enhancement für Streitkräfte: Risiko, Ethik und Strategie), *Case Legal Studies Research Paper* Nr. 2013–2, (2013), 4.

für den menschlichen Verzehr untersucht werden, und dies erfordert eine Einwilligungserklärung auf höherer Ebene im Einklang mit etablierten ethischen Prinzipien, und wenn es vom Militär ausgeführt oder am Militärpersonal als Probanden benutzt wird, muss es von einem dedizierten Ethik-Komitee genehmigt werden. Diese Arbeit setzt sich zum Ziel im Detail aufzuzeigen, inwiefern eine Einwilligung auf informierter Kenntnisnahme beruht und nachzuweisen, dass eine vollständige Kenntnisnahme nicht möglich ist, da Ärzte oft ihr Mangel an Fachwissen verbergen. Die gleiche kritische Analyse wird durchgeführt, inwiefern ein beiderseitiges Einverständnis im militärischen Bereich möglich ist, dessen Personal Befehle befolgen muss und somit manipulierbar ist.

Der letzte Abschnitt dieses Essays konzentriert sich auf die Rolle der Militärärzte im IC-Prozess und die besondere Dualität ihrer Position, da sie als Arzt und zugleich als militärischer Offizier handeln. Darin wird angeführt, dass die ethische Pflicht als Arzt vorrangig ist. Die in dieser Arbeit vorgelegten Nachweise werden zusammengebracht, um eine Vorlage für die Erhaltung von IC für pharmakologische Leistungssteigerungsmittel (PCE) im Militär vorzuschlagen, unter Beachtung von Methode, Stil und Kommunikationsplanung. Die Vorlage verfügt über eine Kombination von weitgehendem Konsens und informiertem Konsens für den Gebrauch von PCE während des Dienstes, um die angebotenen Informationen theoretisch effektiv auszugleichen und so weit wie möglich sicherzustellen, dass die Vergabe von PCEs, von einigen Ausnahmen abgesehen, von einer Einwilligungserklärung begleitet wird. Um die Einzelnen selbst und die Gesellschaft vor Streitkräften, die PCEs eingenommen haben zu schützen, muss das Militär sicherstellen, dass sie über umfassende und unterstützende Strategien und Regulierungen für ihre Benutzung verfügen.

KAPITEL 1

Pharmakologische Leistungs-steigerungsmittel

Was sind Human Enhancement und pharmakologische Leistungs-steigerungsmittel?

Die Definition von Human Enhancement sind nach Juengst „Interventionen, die geschaffen wurden, um den menschlichen Körper bzw. seine Funktionen über das Erforderliche hinaus zu steigern, um Gesundheit zu erhalten oder wiederherzustellen".[1] Mehlmans Deutung dieser Definition schließt Impfungen aus, die Immunsysteme aus gesundheitlichen Gründen verbessern, sowie alle Gruppen ärztlicher Behandlungen, die die Gesundheit erhalten bzw. wiederherstellen.[2] Es besteht ein wichtiger Unterschied zwischen einem Medikament zur Behandlung und einem für Leistungssteigerung, wobei die Gesellschaft im Allgemeinen eine Behandlung akzeptiert, die zur Linderung einer Krankheit verschrieben wird. Eine Grauzone oder ein Medikament im Einklang mit Juengsts Definierung ist eine Behandlung um eine zukünftige Krankheit, die eintreten könnte, aber es nicht unbedingt zu tun braucht, zu verhindern, z. B. ein Dickdarmresektion aufgrund einer familiären Polypenbildung des Dickdarms, die, wenn unbehandelt, mit höchster Wahrscheinlichkeit zu einem Darmkrebs führt.[3] Dies lässt sich schwer als Enhancement oder Behandlung einstufen, da es nur potenziell die menschliche Funktionsfähigkeit verbessert und es nicht zwingend erforderlich ist, um die Gesundheit zu erhalten.

Schauen wir uns Behandlungen an, die für eine Krankheit erforderlich sind, aber auch gesunden Menschen zugutekommen. Erythropoietin wird zur Behandlung von Anämie benutzt, aber es wurde auch von einem Tour de France-Radler mit einem normalen Hämoglobinspiegel eingenommen,

1 Eric T. Juengst, "What does Enhancement mean?" (Was bedeutet "Enhancement"?), in: *Enhancing Human Traits: Ethical and Social Implications*, Hsg. Eric Parens, Hastings Center Studies in Ethics Series (Washington DC: Georgetown University Press, 2000), 29.

2 Maxwell Mehlman, "Bioethics of Military Performance Enhancement," (Bioethik militärischen Enhancements) *Journal of the Royal Army Medical Corps* 165, Nr. 4 (2019): 226.

3 Macmillan Cancer Support, "Familial Adenomatous Polyposis (FAP)" (Familiäre adenomatöse Polyposis), <https://www.macmillan.org.uk/cancer-information-and-support/worried-about-cancer/causes-and-risk-factors/familial-adenomatous-polyposis-fap,> (Zugriff 6. April, 2020).

 | DOI:10.1163/9789004677746_008

um seine sportliche Leistung zu erhöhen.[4] Der ärztliche Gebrauch spricht von Behandlung, während man dies beim Radler als Leistungssteigerung einstuft. Der Unterschied betont den Begriff „normal," der von Mehlman für den typischen Bereich der Funktionsfähigkeit für Menschen als Gattung benutzt und als relativ für die Grundlinie und Kurve der eigenen Gesundheit verglichen wird.[5] Für eine Hämoglobinkonzentration erfasst der normale Bereich 95% oder 97.5% einer normalen Verteilungskurve, die aus einem Anteil der Bevölkerung errechnet wird.[6] Allerdings ändern sich die Normen mit der Zeit, wie zum Beispiel Größe und Gewicht im Zuge des letzten Jahrhunderts, und sie werden sich zweifelsohne mit der Benutzung von Enhancements ändern.[7]

In seinem Beispiel von der Einnahme eines PCE für Jetlag oder Schlaflosigkeit hebt Mohamed die Schwierigkeit hervor, ärztliche Behandlung und die Wirkung von Enhancement voneinander zu trennen.[8] Wird das Mittel zur Behandlung bereits vorhandener Symptome eingesetzt, oder steigert es die Leistung des Gehirns, um diesen Zustand zu verhindern? Dies könnte man auch von Soldaten sagen, die bei Müdigkeit in einem Einsatz ein PCE anwenden, sowie sich die Frage stellen, ob die PCEs sie in den Normalzustand zurückversetzten oder sie darüber hinaus steigerten. Das Verständnis von Enhancement wird noch schwieriger, wenn man bedenkt, dass während der letzten Jahrzehnte die Linien zwischen verschiedenen Gesundheitszuständen und Krankheiten verwischt wurden und mehr Interventionen als Behandlung gelten.[9] Die anhaltende Folgerung ist, dass man einige PCEs als Therapie oder Enhancement betrachten kann, obwohl im Grunde das Problem des IC für beide Gruppen derselbe bleibt.

Ebenso ist es möglich, dass einige Enhancements negativ sein könnten, oder auch als „Disenhancements" (Verringerungen) gelten; ein militärisches Beispiel ist die Einnahme eines PCE zum Auslöschen von Erinnerungen, die

---

4 Jacque Wilson, "Lance Armstrong's Doping Drugs – CNN," (Lance Armstrongs Doping-Drogen) *CNN*, 18. Januar, 2013, <https://edition.cnn.com/2013/01/15/health/armstrong-ped-explainer/index.html,> (Zugriff 12. April, 2020).

5 Mehlman, Lin und Abney, "Enhanced Warfighters: Risk, Ethics, and Policy,"(Enhancement für Streitkräfte: Risiken, Ethik und Strategie), 14.

6 Ernest Beutler und Jill Waalen, "The Definition of Anemia: What Is the Lower Limit of Normal of the Blood Hemoglobin Concentration?,"(Die Definition von Anämie: Was ist die niedrigere Grenze für die Hämoglobinkonzentration im Blut?) *Blood* 107, Nr. 5 (2006): 1747.

7 S. Rosenbaum, "100 Years of Heights and Weights," (100 Jahre der Körpergröße und -gewichte), *Journal of the Royal Statistical Society. Serie A* (*Statistics in Society*) 151, Nr. 2 (1988): 276–309.

8 Ahmed Dahir Mohamed, "Neuroethical Issues in Pharmacological Cognitive Enhancement," (Neuroethische Probleme mit pharmakologischen, kognitiven Enhancements) *WIREs Cognitive Science* 5, Nr. 5 (2014): 538.

9 Mehlman, "Bioethics of Military Performance Enhancement." (Bioethik der militärischen Leistungssteigerung), 226.

bei Soldaten zu posttraumatischen Belastungsstörungen führen könnten.[10] Fragen wir uns noch einmal, ist dies eine Behandlung des Gehirns oder steigert es seine Leistungsfähigkeit? Wenn zwischen Therapie und Enhancement kein Unterschied gemacht wird, kann dies zur Folge haben, dass alle Formen von Human Enhancement moralisch zulässig sind.[11] Diese Arbeit verfolgt die Definition von Enhancement als etwas, das eine Person verbessert und sie über die Normalbedingungen hebt. Sie konzentriert sich auf pharmakologische Wirkstoffe als ein Aspekt von Human Enhancement, mit Ausnahme einer Reihe von anderen möglichen Enhancements, wie transkranielle Magnetstimulation, genetische Modifizierung und Mensch-Computer-Schnittstelle.

Pharmakologische Enhancements (PCEs) werden in dieser Arbeit als rezeptpflichtige Medikamente (POM) bezeichnet und nicht als solche, die illegal beschafft wurden oder die rezeptfrei sind. Wie für alle Medikamente im Vereinigten Königreich untersteht die gesetzliche Kontrolle der Behörde „Medicine and Healthcare Products Regulatory Agency (MHRA)" (Aufsichtsbehörde für Arzneimittel und Gesundheitsprodukte). Die MHRA genehmigt Medikamente und Gesundheitsprodukte für eine Verschreibung, die sicher und zugelassen ist, wobei einige Medikamente mit bestimmten Vorschriften für ihre Benutzung und potenziellen Missbrauch, als „geregelt" kategorisiert werden.[12] Ein rezeptpflichtiges Mittel kann nur von einem zugelassenen Arzt verschrieben werden, obwohl es hier eine Ausnahmeregelung für das Militär gibt, die an anderer Stelle beschrieben wird. Ein Medikament kann für eine nicht zugelassene Indikation verschrieben werden, mit Off-Label-Use bezeichnet, aber in einem solchen Fall ist der Empfänger darüber zu informieren.[13] Die meisten PCEs wurden ursprünglich nicht für ihre

10 Mehlman, Lin, und Abney, "Enhanced Warfighters: Risk, Ethics, and Policy."(Enhancement für Streitkräfte: Risiken, Ethik und Strategie), 15.

11 Allhoff *et al.*, "Ethics of Human Enhancement: 25 Questions & Answers."(Die Ethik des Human Enhancements: 25 Fragen und Antworten), 8.

12 United Kingdom. HM Government, "About Us – Medicines and Healthcare Products Regulatory Agency," (Über uns – Regulierungsbehörde für Medikamente und Gesundheitsprodukte), <https://www.gov.uk/government/organisations/medicines-and-healthcare-products-regulatory-agency/about#our-responsibilities>, *Misuse of Drugs Act 1971* (London: HMSO, 1971), <http://www.legislation.gov.uk/ukpga/1971/38/contents>, "The Controlled Drugs (Supervision of Management and Use) Regulations 2013. Information about the Regulations," (Kontrollierte Substanzen (Überwachung von Management und Benutzung) 2013, <https://assets.publishing.service.gov.uk/government/uploads/system/uploads/attachment_data/file/214915/15-02-2013-controlled-drugs-regulation-information.pdf> (Zugriff: 26. März, 2020).

13 United Kingdom. HM Government, "Off.label or Unlicensed Use of Medicines: Prescriber's Responsibilities" (Off-Label oder nicht verschriebene Benutzung von Medikamenten: Die Verantwortungen des Verschreibers,) 2014,

leistungssteigernden Fähigkeiten zugelassen, ihr Gebrauch wäre somit für Off-Label-Use, und es ist erforderlich, den Empfänger darüber zu informieren. Es ist anzunehmen, dass zukünftig entwickelte Medikamente den gleichen gesetzlichen Kontrollen unterstehen.

PCEs lassen sich in zwei breite Kategorien aufteilen: Jene die sich auf das Wahrnehmungsvermögen auswirken und jene die die physischen Eigenschaften des Körpers beeinflussen. Das Wahrnehmungsvermögen ist als die Prozesse zu definieren, die ein Mensch benutzt, um Informationen einzuordnen.[14] Die allgemeine Gesundheit, eine gut ausgewogene Diät und langfristig betriebener Sport selbst können das Wahrnehmungsvermögen verbessern, und es gibt eine Reihe von Medikamenten, die die Hirnchemie positiv oder auch negativ beeinflussen.[15] Für diese positiven Auswirkungen könnte man den Begriff „Wahrnehmungssteigerung" benutzen, von Sandberg wie folgt definiert: „die Verstärkung oder Erweiterung von den Kernkapazitäten des Verstandes durch Verbesserung oder Vermehrung von internen bzw. externen Prozessen zur Informationsbearbeitung."[16] Medikamente, die die Hirnchemie ändern, könnten negative Auswirkungen haben, indem sie die Wahrnehmung der Streitkräfte ihrer Maßnahmen und der Konsequenzen ihres Verhaltens ändern. Der Verlust emotionaler Anbindungen könnte die Soldaten daran hindern, die soziale Anbindung und das Vertrauen, dass zurzeit aufgrund ihrer Werte und ihres Ethos gelehrt wird, aufrecht zu erhalten.

Bekannte Mittel, die das Wahrnehmungsvermögen beeinflussen, sind u.a. Nikotin, das Wachsamkeit und kognitive Verarbeitung erhöht,[17] sowie Kaffein, das das Erregungsniveau verstärkt, vor allem bei Müdigkeit.[18] Allerdings benutzt

---

<https://www.gov.uk/drug-safety-update/off-label-or-unlicensed-use-of-medicines-prescribers-responsibilities,> (Zugriff: 4. Mai, 2020).

14 Nick Bostrom und Anders Sandberg, "Cognitive Enhancement: Methods, Ethics, Regulatory Challenges," (Kognitives Enhancement: Methoden, Ethik, Herausforderungen an die Regulierung) *Science and Engineering Ethics* 15, Nr. 3 (2009): 312.

15 *ebd.*, 314.

16 Sandberg und Bostrom, "Converging Cognitive Enhancements." (Konvergierende kognitive Enhancements), 201.

17 Carol S. Myers *et al.*, "Dose-Related Enhancement of Mood and Cognition in: Smokers Administered Nicotine Nasal Spray," (Dosisbezogenes Enhancdement von Laune und Kognition in Rauchern verabreichten nikotinhaltigen Nasensprays), *Neuropsychopharmacology* 33, Nr. 3 (2008): 594.

18 Tom M. McLellan, John A. Caldwell, und Harris R Lieberman, "A Review of Caffeine's Effects on Cognitive, Physical and Occupational Performance," (Eine Übersicht der Auswirkungen von Koffein auf kognitive, physische und berufliche Leistung), *Neuroscience & Biobehavioral Reviews* 71 (2016): 297.

diese Arbeit den Begriff von PCE nur für rezeptpflichtige Medikamente, und sowohl Nikotin als auch Kaffein sind rezeptfrei und leicht erhältlich, deshalb werden sie hier nicht weiter besprochen. Ein Beispiel eines kognitiven PCEs ist Modafinil, ein Arzneistoff, der für Narkolepsie lizensiert ist, Wachsamkeit erhöht und die kognitive Leistungsfähigkeit verbessert.[19] Da Modafinil Wachsamkeit mit nur geringen Nebenwirkungen erhöhen kann, kann es die Leistung der Soldaten für eine Off-Label-Indikation steigern.[20] Amphetamine sind eine weitere Gruppe Arzneistoffe, die als Anregungsmittel wirken können und wurden von der amerikanischen Luftwaffe für langfristige Einsätze benutzt.[21] Es sind Medikamente, die die Wahrnehmung beeinflussen und werden für die Behandlung psychischer Gesundheit benutzt, z.B. Propranolol, das einigen Erfolg auf dem Bereich der Behandlung von posttraumatischen Belastungsstörungen (PTSD) aufweisen kann. PTSD ist ein bekannter Zustand bei Soldaten, doch da Propranolol in diesem Fall eher als Behandlung als zum Enhancement benutzt wird, steht es für diese Arbeit nicht zur Diskussion.[22]

Mit Hinsicht auf die physischen Auswirkungen gibt es eine Reihe von PCEs, die benutzt werden können, um einen Soldaten aufzubauen, u.a. Anabolika, Erythropoietin (Blutdoping) und Wachstumshormone.[23] Zurzeit sind diese Mittel beim Militär nicht gestattet, es sei denn, sie werden von einem Arzt für ein bestimmtes Symptom verschrieben.[24] Man kann das Bestreben nachempfinden, "stärkere" Soldaten für Nahkämpfe zur Verfügung zu haben, und

19 Kelli J. Westcott, "Modafinil, Sleep Deprivation, and Cognitive Function in Military and Medical Settings," (Modafinil, Schlafentzug und die kognitive Funktion im militärischen und medizinischen Umfeld), *Military Medicine* 170, Nr. 4 (2005): 334.

20 *ebd.*

21 John A. Caldwell und J. Lynn Caldwell, "Fatigue in Military Aviation: An Overview of U.S. Military-Approved Pharmacological Countermeasures," (Müdigkeit in der Militärluftfahrt: Eine Übersicht der vom amerikanischen Militär zugelassenen pharmakologischen Gegenmaßnahmen), *Aviation, Space, and Environmental Medicine* 76, Nr. 7 (2005): C45.

22 Alain Brunet *et al.*, "Reduction of PTSD Symptoms With Pre-Reactivation Propranolol Therapy: A Randomized Controlled Trial," (Reduktion der PTS-Symptome mit Pre-Reaktivierungstherapie mit Propranolol), *American Journal of Psychiatry* 175, Nr. 5 (2018): 427–33.

23 Karl E. Friedl, "U.S. Army Research on Pharmacological Enhancement of Soldier Performance: Stimulants, Anabolic Hormones, and Blood Doping," (Forschungsprogramm der US-Streitkräfte zum pharmakologischen Enhancement der Streitkräfte: Stimulans, anabole Hormone und Blut-Doping) *The Journal of Strength & Conditioning Research* 29 (2015): S72.

24 British Army, "People, Drugs and Supplements," (Personen, Medikamente und Zusätze), <https://www.army.mod.uk/people/join-well/drugs-and-supplements/> (Zugriff: 6. Mai, 2020).

die britischen Streitkräfte haben kürzlich das erforderliche Fitnessniveau erhöht.[25] Andererseits wird die Wichtigkeit absoluter Stärke für Angehörige des Militärs im Kampf vielleicht als weniger kritisch angesehen, da seit 2018 Frauen als Infanteristinnen an der Front zugelassen wurden.[26] Zweifelsohne ist ein echter Vorteil der PCEs für physische Eigenschaften die Erhöhung von Durchhaltevermögen und Ausdauer, sowie eine Unterdrückung des Hungergefühls, aber dies ist weiterhin schwer erfassbar, da zusätzliche Nährstoffergänzung erforderlich ist, um diese vorteilhaften Auswirkungen zu erhalten.[27]

Der Erfolg von PCEs mit Auswirkung auf physische Eigenschaften wird nachstehend besprochen, doch trotz der Vielzahl von Personen, die PCEs benutzen, um ihr Erinnerungsvermögen oder ihre Wachsamkeit zu verbessern, zeigt Maslens Kritik der Fachliteratur, dass der Nachweis ihrer Wirksamkeit nicht eindeutig ist, mit begrenztem Enhancement in spezifischen Bereichen, zu bestimmten Dosierungen, für einen Teil der Benutzer.[28] Es ist interessant, dass die Forschung nicht festlegen konnte, ob die Vorteile von PCEs die Leistung von bemannten Waffensystemen und die Lebensqualität derer, die sie bemannen, steigern.[29] Außerdem stellen sich Fragen, ob PCEs routinemäßig zu

25 Joaquín Pérez-Guisado und Philip M Jakeman, "Citrulline Malate Enhances Athletic Anaerobic Performance and Relieves Muscle Soreness," (Citrullin-Malat steigert athletische anaerobe Leistung und lindert Muskelschmerzen), *The Journal of Strength & Conditioning Research* 24, Nr. 5 (2010), 1222.

26 British Army, "New Physical Employment Standards for the Army," (Neue physische Arbeitsnormen bei den Streitkräften), <https://www.army.mod.uk/physical-employment-standards/> (Zugriff: 6. Mai, 2020).

27 Lizzie Dearden, "Women Now Allowed to Apply for Royal Marines and All Other Frontline Military Roles, Defence Secretary Announces," (Frauen dürfen sich jetzt bei der Königlichen Marine und für militärischen Rollen an allen anderen Fronten anmelden), *The Independent*, 25. Oktober 25, 2018, <https://www.independent.co.uk/news/uk/home-news/women-soldiers-army-military-sas-defence-government-infantry-frontline-gavin-williamson-female-a8601371.html> (Zugriff: 2. April, 2020).

28 Hannah Maslen, Nadira Faulmüller, and Julian Savulescu, "Pharmacological Cognitive Enhancement – How Neuroscientific Research Could Advance Ethical Debate," (Pharmakologisches kognitives Enhancement – Wie die neurowissenschaftliche Forschung die ethische Debatte fördern könnte), *Frontiers in Systems Neuroscience* 8 (2014): 3.

29 Marten Meijer, "A Human Performance Perspective on the Ethical Use of Cogniceuticals: Commentary on 'Recommendations for the Ethical Use of Pharmacologic Fatigue Countermeasures in the U.S. Military,'" (Eine Perspektive der menschlichen Leistung zum ethischen Gebrauch von Arzneistoffen zur kognitiven Verstärkung – Kommentar zu den "empfohlenen Mitteln für den ethischen Gebrauch von pharmakologischen Müdigkeitsbekämpfern bei US-Streitkräften), *Aviation, Space, and Environmental Medicine* 78, Nr. 5 (2007): B133.

benutzen sind oder nur für bestimmte Einsätze, wenn Nichtgebrauch zu fatalen Konsequenzen führen könnten.

Warum sind PCEs jetzt relevant?

Die jetzige Relevanz der Debatte um PCEs im Militär ist nicht nur da, um ethische Diskussionen mit der sich rapide weiterentwickelnden Technologie in Einklang zu bringen, sondern auch, um sie mit denen im Sport zu vergleichen, wo die gleichen Probleme bezüglich Sicherheit und Strategie auftreten. Trotz der Versuche, Drogen vom Sport auszuschließen, bleibt ihr Einsatz weit verbreitet aufgrund des verlockenden Erfolgs und der hohen Einnahmen, zusammen mit dem geringen Risiko, erwischt zu werden und der geringen Strafmaße.[30] Die World Anti-Doping Agency (WDA) erklärte den Gebrauch von Arzneistoffen im Sport als illegal, aufgrund mangelnder Fairness und Gleichheit, wenn sie die Leistungen steigern, ein Gesundheitsrisiko darstellen oder gegen den „Sportgeist" verstoßen.[31] Die von der WDA verbotenen PCEs lassen sich im Großen und Ganzen in zwei Kategorien aufteilen, solche, die die Leistung steigern und solche die das Durchhaltevermögen erhöhen.[32] Viele Sportler haben aufgrund der Einnahme von PCEs außergewöhnlich positive Auswirkungen empfunden, um einen Wettbewerbsvorteil zu erhalten, die gleiche Auswirkung, die vom Militär erwünscht wird.[33]

Savulescu behauptet, dass Sport die „genetisch untauglichen" Personen benachteiligt und ein Gewinner jemand ist, der die Kombination von genetischem Potenzial hat und über die ideale Ausgewogenheit von Psychologie, Training und Urteilsvermögen verfügt. Aus diesem Grund befürwortet er, dass es Wettbewerbern möglich ist, PCEs zu nehmen, um faire

30 J. Savulescu, B. Foddy und M. Clayton, "Why We Should Allow Performance Enhancing Drugs in Sport," (Warum wir leistungssteigernde Arzneistoffe im Sport gestatten sollten), *British Journal of Sports Medicine* 38, Nr. 6 (2004): 666.

31 World Anti-Doping Agency, "World Anti-Doping Code" (Welt-Anti-Doping-Code), (Montreal: World Anti-Doping Agency, 2015), 14, 30, <https://www.wada-ama.org/sites/default/files/resources/files/wada_anti-doping_code_2019_english_final_revised_v1_linked.pdf> (Zugriff: 12. März, 2020).

32 Lincoln Allison, "Faster, Stronger, Higher," (Schneller, stärker, höher), *The Guardian*, 9. August, 2004, <https://www.theguardian.com/sport/2004/aug/09/athensolympics2004.olympicgames> (Zugriff: 1. Januar, 2020).

33 Kate Harvey, "Sports Science and Medicine," (Sportwissenschaft und Sportmedizin), *The Nuffield Council on Bioethics*, 2014, 5, <https://nuffieldbioethics.org/publications/sports-science-and-medicine> (Zugriff: 6. Januar, 2020).

Rahmenbedingungen zu schaffen, genetische Ungleichheiten auszugleichen und finanzielle Unterschiede zwischen reichen und armen Ländern zu beheben.[34] Die Argumente für oder gegen das Doping im Sport befassen sich mit Fairness und Gleichwertigkeit, im Gegensatz zum Militär, das darauf hinzielt, Fairness und Gleichwertigkeit zu vermeiden, da man einen Wettbewerbsvorteil vor dem Feind sucht, um den Kampf zu gewinnen. Ein weiteres Argument von Mehlman ist, dass die Gesellschaft von einem Sportler mit gesteigerter Leistung nicht profitiert, während die Leistungssteigerung von Militärpersonal zur Erhöhung der Erfolgswahrscheinlichkeit eines nationalen Einsatzes das Gesamtrisiko für die Gesellschaft insgesamt verringern könnte.[35] Beide Seiten der Dopingdebatte im Sport sind sich darin einig, dass die Gesundheit und Sicherheit des Einzelnen an erster Stelle steht. Im Gegensatz dazu sind es für das Militär die Gesundheit und Sicherheit der Einheit, oder sogar der Gesellschaft, die über das Wohl des Einzelnen gestellt werden.[36]

Warum wünschen Einzelne und das Militär die Benutzung von PCEs?

Das Militär könnte die Einnahme von PCEs aus drei Gründen befürworten: um einen Wettbewerbsvorteil zu erhalten, um sich der Fähigkeit des Gegners anzupassen, und wenn man als eine Koalition mit anderen Nationen zusammenarbeitet. Die Fähigkeit, die menschliche Leistungsfähigkeit zu steigern und dadurch einen Wettbewerbsvorteil dem Gegner gegenüber zu erhalten, ist nichts Neues. Der Krieg hat jahrhundertelang Kämpfe von Angesicht-zu-Angesicht ausgetragen, und selbst mit unserer modernen Technologie gilt es immer noch als menschliches Bemühen, wie man im Krieg gegen den Terrorismus und dem britischen Einsatz im Irak und in Afghanistan sehen konnte. Im 15. Jahrhundert kauten die Inkas Kola-Blätter, um Hunger- und Durstgefühle und Müdigkeit zu reduzieren; so verbesserte man das Durchhaltevermögen und die Leistungsfähigkeit.[37] Im 17. Jahrhundert teilte

34 Savulescu, Foddy und Clayton, “Why We Should Allow Performance Enhancing Drugs in Sport.” (Warum wir leistungssteigernde Arzneistoffe für Sport zulassen sollten), 667–8.

35 Mehlman, Lin, and Abney, “Enhanced Warfighters: A Policy Framework.” (Enhancement für Streitkräfte: Ein Strategierahmen), 114.

36 Julian Savulescu, Leon Creaney, and Anna Vondy, “Should Athletes Be Allowed to Use Performance Enhancing Drugs?”(Sollte es Athleten gestattet werden, leistungssteigernde Arzneistoffe zu benutzen?) *BMJ* (*Clinical Research Ed.*) 347 (2013): f6150.

37 L. Kamienski, *Shooting Up: A History of Drugs in Warfare,* (Spritzen: Eine Geschichte der Arzneistoffe in der Kriegsführung) (Oxford: Hurst, 2017), 46–47.

man Rum an die Soldaten und Seeleute aus, denn man glaubte, dass Alkohol sie zu besseren Kämpfern machte.[38] Der Gebrauch von Opium hatte unterschiedlichen Erfolg – die indischen Streitkräfte gewannen verstärkten Kampfgeist und eine gesteigerte Kampfleistung, während die Chinesen stark unter Missbrauch von Opium litten, die die Fähigkeit ihrer Truppen entschieden schwächte.[39]

In der Moderne wurden Amphetamine für ein verbessertes Durchhaltevermögen und um die Wachsamkeit aufrecht zu erhalten ausgegeben, indem man z.B. der Bemannung von deutschen Panzern die sogenannte Panzerschokolade verabreichte, und die RAF benutzte Benzedrin.[40] Im Krieg der USA mit Vietnam wurden unerhörte Mengen von sowohl ärztlich verschriebener als auch selbstverordneter psychoaktiver Arzneistoffe von den Truppen verzehrt, u.a. Amphetamine, Marihuana, LSD und Heroin.[41] Regelwidrig bewaffnete Gruppen, wie ISIS, Taliban und Al Qaeda haben Psychopharmaka benutzt, um ihre militärischen Defizite auszugleichen, und verteilten sie als Lohn und zur Rekrutierung, wie auch, um ihre menschlichen Leistungen zu steigern.[42] Die „Jihad Pille," die vor allem in Syrien hergestellt wurde, sorgte dafür, dass Daesh-Kämpfer furchtlos und euphorisch wurden.[43]

Alle Streitkräfte zielen auf einen Leistungsvorteil, um ihre Einsätze erfolgreich zu machen, ob es nun mittels Technologie, Training oder Doktrin ist, und ein kognitiver Vorteil unterscheidet sich nicht davon.[44] Dies ist umso wichtiger geworden, als das britische Militär in den letzten zehn Jahren die Zahl der Bediensteten reduziert hat, ohne die Leistung zu verringern. Obwohl moderne Kriegsschauplätze weniger Operateure und Wartungspersonal erfordern, bleibt das sich daraus ergebende Resultat ein überfordertes System unter Leistungsdruck. Die Auswirkung aufgrund von reduzierter Belastbarkeit des Personals ist noch stärker, wie die Medien besonders betonen, nach denen seit

38 ebd., 9.

39 ebd., 63.

40 ebd., 111, 117.

41 ebd., 188.

42 ebd., 233–235.

43 Mirren Gidda, "Drugs in War: What Is Captagon, the 'Jihad Pill' Used by Islamic State Militants?," (Arzneistoffe im Krieg: Was ist Fenetyllin, die 'Jihad-Pille', die von militanten Islamisten benutzt werden?), *Newsweek*, 12. Mai, 2017, <https://www.newsweek.com/drugs-captagon-islamic-state-jihad-war-amphetamines-saudi-arabia-608233> (Zugriff: 26. März, 2020).

44 Michael B. Russo, "Recommendations for the Ethical Use of Pharmacologic Fatigue Countermeasures in the U.S. Military," (Empfehlungen zum ethischen Gebrauch von pharmakologischen Müdigkeitsbekämpfern bei US-Streitkräften), *Aviation, Space, and Environmental Medicine* 78, Nr. 5 (2007): B125.

2018 einer von dreizehn Soldaten Antidepressiva gegen psychische Störungen verschrieben bekommt und die Selbstmordrate angestiegen ist.[45] Schlafentzug ist für die Truppen ein weiteres Problem, ob im Dienst oder nicht, und reduziert ihre kognitive Funktionsfähigkeit, was der übermäßige Genuss von Koffein und Alkohol noch schlimmer macht.[46] Wenn Schlafentzug das Risiko von menschlichem Versagen erhöht und Innovation reduziert, so könnte es eine ethische Notwendigkeit sein, Streitkämpfern PCEs zu geben, um Fehlentscheidungen aufgrund von unvermeidlicher Kampfmüdigkeit zu verhindern.[47]

Als zweites sehen sich alle modernen Streitkräfte immer mehr einer technologischen Gleichrangigkeit gegenübergestellt, und dies in einer äußerst fragilen Welt.[48] Die Erwartung, dass zukünftige Feinde ihre Streitkräfte mit PCEs versorgen, um Müdigkeit zu lindern, die Muskelkraft zu erhöhen oder andere Wettbewerbsvorteile zu erzeugen, ist nicht von der Hand zu weisen.[49] Das amerikanische Militär hat den Gebrauch von Dextroamphetaminen und die amerikanische Luftwaffe Modafinil für eine Auswahl von Truppen und Personal zugelassen.[50] Die USA verfügt über eine eigene Forschungsstelle in der militärmedizinischen Kognitionsforschung zur Schaffung und Bereitstellung von Spitzenkompetenzen.[51] Sie untersucht bereits PCEs, die Schmerztoleranz

45 Sean Rayment, "Thousands of Soldiers on Antidepressants as They Battle Mental Health Issues, New Figures Reveal," (Tausende von Soldaten nehmen Antidepressiva bei der Bekämpfung zur Bekämpfung von Problemen ihrer psychischen Gesundheit) *The Mirror*, 28. Juli, 2018, <https://www.mirror.co.uk/news/uk-news/thousands-soldiers-antidepressants-battle-mental-12996613>, Ministry of Defence., "FOI2017/13417," 2018, <https://assets.publishing.service.gov.uk/government/uploads/system/uploads/attachment_data/file/691866/2017-13417.pdf> (Zugriff: 31. März, 2020).

46 Paul Scharre und Lauren Fish, "Human Performance Enhancement," *Center for a New American Security*, 2018, 7, <https://www.cnas.org/publications/reports/human-performance-enhancement-1> (Zugriff: 6. Januar, 2020).

47 Olav Kjellevold Olsen, Ståle Pallesen, and Eid Jarle, "The Impact of Partial Sleep Deprivation on Moral Reasoning in Military Officers," (Die Auswirkung des teilweisen Schlafentzugs auf die moralische Argumentation bei Offizieren des Militärs?), *Sleep* 33, Nr. 8 (2010): 1086.

48 Kenneth Ford und Clark Glymour, "The Enhanced Warfighter.," (Der Streitkämpfer mit Enhancement), *Bulletin of the Atomic Scientists* 70, Nr. 1 (2014): 43.

49 ebd. 47.

50 Mary A. Kautz, Maria L. Thomas, und J. Lynn Caldwell, "Considerations of Pharmacology on Fitness for Duty in the Operational Environment," (Überlegungen zur Pharmakologie für Diensttauglichkeit im Einsatzumfeld), *Aviation, Space, and Environmental Medicine* 78, Nr. 5 (2007): B109.

51 Eric B. Schoomaker, "Military Medical Research on Cognitive Performance: The Warfighters Competitive Edge," (Militärische medizinische Forschung zur kognitiven Leistung: Der Wettbewerbsvorteil der Streitkräfte), *Aviation, Space, and Environmental Medicine* 78, Nr. 5 (2007): B4.

erhöht und verkapselten Sauerstoff, der im Körper abgelagert werden kann, um die Überlebenschance von verwundeten Kämpfern zu erhöhen.[52] Die Wahrscheinlichkeit, dass andere staatlichen und nicht-staatlichen Akteure das Gleiche tun, ist sehr hoch, und deshalb muss das Vereinigte Königreich diesem Beispiel folgen, um auf Augenhöhe mit den anderen zu bleiben.[53]

Drittens ist es möglich, dass das britische Militär PCEs benötigen könnte, um mit NATO, VN und anderen Koalitionsstreitkräften zusammenzuarbeiten, falls einige von ihnen oder alle anderen Nationen PCEs benutzen. In Situationen, in denen eine Nation etwas ethisch akzeptieren kann, eine andere jedoch nicht, gibt es unvermeidliche Risiken einer Diskrepanz. Man nehme das Beispiel der Fidschianer, denen der Genuss von Alkohol von einem westlichen Kommandanten der Koalition verboten wurde, er ihnen aber gestattete, Kava zu produzieren und zu trinken, eine Substanz, die psychoaktive Mittel enthält und die Nachtsicht beeinflusst.[54] Was passiert, wenn ein Koalitionssoldat, der seine Wachsamkeit mithilfe von PCEs fördert, sich in einer Notlage befindet und die Hilfe eines britischen Soldaten benötigt, der solche Mittel nicht genommen hat und der schläfrig und nicht in der Lage zu reagieren ist?

Es gibt eine Reihe von Gründen, warum ein Soldat PCEs nimmt oder nicht. Schelle ist der Ansicht, dass Gruppendruck ein wichtiger Faktor für diese Entscheidung ist.[55] Normalerweise ist dies positiv zu bewerten, weil eine Person eher bereit ist, ein PCE einzunehmen, wenn Freunde und Kollegen das auch tun, aber es kann auch umgekehrt der Fall sein, dass bei starker Missbilligung der anderen die Bereitschaft, PCEs zu benutzen, verringert wird. Dieser Effekt kann durch sozialen Druck außerhalb der direkten Freundschaftsgruppe multipliziert werden. Eine deutsche Umfrage unter Universitätsstudenten ergab, dass die Bereitschaft PCEs zu benutzen von persönlicher Einstellung

---

52 James Patrey *et al.*, "Human Performance Enhancement for NATO Military Operations (Science, Technology, and Ethics)," (Human Performance Enhancement für NATO-Militäreinsätze (Wissenschaft, Technologie und Ethik), in: *NATO Research and Technology Organisation* (Virginia, USA: Office of Naval Research Warfighter Performance Department, 2009), 1, <https://apps.dtic.mil/dtic/tr/fulltext/u2/a562561.pdf> (Zugriff: 6. Januar, 2020).

53 President's Council on Bioethics, *Beyond Therapy: Biotechnology and the Pursuit of Happiness* (New York: Regan Books, 2003), 136.

54 Russo, "Recommendations for the Ethical Use of Pharmacologic Fatigue Countermeasures in the U.S. Military." (Empfehlungen für den ethischen Gebrauch von Arzneistoffen zur Müdigkeitsbekämpfung bei US-Streitkräften), B121.

55 Kimberly J. Schelle *et al.*, "Attitudes toward Pharmacological Cognitive Enhancement – a Review," (Einstellungen zum pharmakologischen kognitiven Enhancement – eine Übersicht), *Frontiers in Systems Neuroscience* 8 (2014): 8.

zu Risiken, Bereitschaft unter Gleichrangigen, Kosten und Nebenwirkungen abhängt.[56]

Die Medien haben auch Einfluss darauf, ob eine Person PCEs einnimmt oder nicht, indem sie ihr Profil und die allgemeine öffentliche Meinung ansprechen. Ein Magazin der Universität Cambridge, Varsity, behauptete, dass 10% der Studenten Substanzen wie Modafinil und Ritalin einnahmen, um ihre akademische Leistung zu verbessern. Dies betonte die Vorteile und Normalität der Einnahme von Arzneistoffen.[57] Trotz der Kenntnisnahme von Nebenwirkungen berichtete sogar die BBC in ihren Nachrichten über die ungefähren Kosten, die ein Student für sogenannte „Smart Pills" zu bezahlen hat, obschon sie auch auf die Illegalität ihres Verkaufs hinwies.[58] Die Gesellschaft kann ihre Sichtweise und Einstellung schnell ändern; einfach durch Berührung mit PCEs und mit genügend Medienberichterstattung könnte der Gebrauch von PCE sehr schnell akzeptiert werden.[59]

Ein weiterer Grund, PCEs als Selbstmedikation einzunehmen ist eine Lifestyle-Entscheidung, um sich schneller vom Training oder physischen Aktivitäten zu erholen, oder um die physische Leistung zu verbessern. Ein Großteil des militärischen Personals benutzt bereits Zusätze, von Nahrungsergänzungsmitteln bis hin zu verbotenen Substanzen; laut einer Untersuchung nehmen bis zu 38% der britischen, im Training befindlichen Rekruten PCEs.[60] Es ist erstaunlich, dass Soldaten trotz einer Nulltoleranzpolitik weiterhin verbotene Substanzen zu sich nehmen.[61] Es gibt besondere Gründe, weshalb Soldaten bereit sind, PCEs zu nehmen, die mit militärischen Werten und einem Ethos zu tun haben,

---

56 Sebastian Sattler *et al.*, "Evaluating the Drivers of and Obstacles to the Willingness to Use Cognitive Enhancement Drugs: The Influence of Drug Characteristics, Social Environment, and Personal Characteristics," (Bewertung der Anreger für den Gebrauch von PCEs und Gründe, die die Bereitschaft behindern: Der Einfluss von Arzneistoffmerkmalen, sozialem Umfeld und persönlichen Charakteristiken), *Substance Abuse Treatment, Prevention, and Policy* 9, Nr. 1 (2014): 5.

57 Natasha Lennard, "One in Ten Takes Drugs to Study," (Einer in zehn nimmt Arzneistoffe für das Studium ein), *Varsity*, 6. März 6, 2009, <https://www.varsity.co.uk/news/1307> (Zugriff: 31. März, 2020).

58 BBC News, "Sussex University Students Illegally Buying 'Smart Pills,'" (Studenten an der Sussex University kaufen illegal "Smart Pills"), *BBC News*, 13. März, 2018, <https://www.bbc.co.uk/news/uk-england-43383717> (Zugriff: 31. März, 2020).

59 Adam Bear and Joshua Knobe, "Normality: Part Descriptive, Part Prescriptive," (Normalität: zum Teil beschreibt es, zum Teil wird es verschrieben),*Cognition* 167 (2017): 25.

60 Anna Casey *et al.*, "Supplement Use by UK-Based British Army Soldiers in Training," (Der Gebrauch von Zusätzen bei britischen Streitkräften beim Training in Großbritiannien), *The British Journal of Nutrition* 112, Nr. 7 (2014): 1178–1180.

61 British Army, "People. Drugs and Supplements." (Personen, Arzneistoffe und Zusätze).

die ihnen beim Beitritt fest eingeimpft wurden. Dazu gehört, dass sie es als Teil eines moralischen Kodex betrachten, im Glauben, dass dies ehrenhaft ist, oder sogar Schuldgefühle empfinden Kameraden gegenüber, die bereits im Einsatz sind. Ein Soldat könnte ein PCE einnehmen, das bei nachfolgenden Einsätzen die Aggression erhöht, um den Tod eines gefallenen Kameraden zu rächen.

Zuletzt gibt es einige Berufe, in denen Personen verpflichtet sind, gewisse Maßnahmen zu treffen, zum Beispiel wenn Chirurgen sich vor einer OP die Hände waschen, und obligatorische Ruhepausen für Fernfahrer.[62] Diese beruflichen Verpflichtungen setzen die Einwilligung des Einzelnen zu bestimmten Maßnahmen voraus und beziehen sich vor allem auf die Erhaltung ihrer Gesundheit und Sicherheit. Das Militär könnte deshalb einen beruflichen Grund dafür finden, dass sein Personal diese Medikamente auf ähnliche Weise nimmt wie die Piloten in den USA, die aufgefordert werden, bei langen Einsätzen stimulierende Mittel zu sich zu nehmen. Dies ist jedoch bei der Mehrzahl der PCEs kaum der Fall, bei denen das Verhältnis zwischen Risiko und Nutzen nicht so eindeutig ist.

Welche militärischen Bedenken begleiten den Gebrauch von PCEs?

Es gibt eine Reihe von Fragen zum Einsatz leistungssteigender Arzneistoffe beim Militär, darunter rechtliche, politische und operative Aspekte, das Verhältnis der Zivilbevölkerung zum Militär und IC. Britische Streitkräfte müssen sowohl das Dienst- als auch das Zivilrecht einhalten. *„Damit die Streitkräfte effektiv arbeiten können, ist die Aufrechterhaltung sowohl der persönlichen als auch der auferlegten Disziplin erforderlich.*[63] Wenn PCEs im nichtmilitärischen Bereich als illegal gelten oder vom Militär verboten werden, können sie nicht selbstverschrieben werden, und wenn sie gesetzlich erlaubt sind, muss es eine Politik geben, die ihre Verwendung unterstützt.

Das Verbot der PCEs oder die Begrenzung des Zugriffs auf sie könnte zu einem rapide wachsenden Schwarzmarkt zur Beschaffung führen, der die Sicherheit beeinträchtigt. Wir führen hier Viagra an, das die MHRA dazu zwang, das Mittel von rezeptpflichtig als rezeptfrei einzustufen.[64] Weitere

---

62 Maslen, Faulmüller, and Savulescu, "Pharmacological Cognitive Enhancement – How Neuroscientific Research Could Advance Ethical Debate," (PCE – inwiefern die neurowissenschaftliche Forschung die ethische Debatte fördern könnte), 6.

63 United Kingdom. Ministry of Defence, *JSP 830: The Manual of Service Law* (London: HMSO, 2016), 1-1-3.

64 Sabrina Barr, "Viagra Now Available over the Counter without Prescription in UK," (Viagra ist jetzt im Vereinigten Königreich nicht länger rezeptpflichtig), *The Independent*, 27.

Untersuchungen, um Sicherheit und Wirksamkeit zu bestimmen, geben den Verbrauchern das Vertrauen, PCEs zu benutzen, und indem sie legalisiert werden, wird ihre Entwicklung gefördert, sodass sie letztendlich billiger und sicherer sind.[65] Das Militär sollte Scharres Empfehlung für eine Überprüfung auf höchster Ebene befolgen, bei der jedes PCE von Fall zu Fall auf seine Wirksamkeit, Sicherheit und seinen Nutzen hin untersucht wird.[66] Zudem sollte der Einsatz von PCEs in der Forschung oder in Einsätzen freiwillig sein.

Laut Tabelle 17 der britischen Arzneimittelvorschriften ist das Militär berechtigt, Medikamente für Soldaten zu liefern und zu verabreichen und so die Verschreibung von einem zugelassenen Arzt zu umgehen.[67] Diese Ausnahme soll Truppen in Umgebungen decken, in denen ein unmittelbarer Zugang zu Ärzten nicht möglich ist. Im Idealfall sollten alle verschriebenen Behandlungen von geschulten Sanitätern verschrieben werden,[68] deren Kompetenz von einem Arzt beglaubigt wird, oder aber, sollte kein Personal mit medizinischer Ausbildung vorhanden sein, sollte die Erlaubnis möglichst über die Kommunikation mit einem Arzt eingeholt werden. Was hindert die Befehlshaber von Einsatzkräften daran, ihren Sanitätern zu befehlen, PCEs zu verschreiben und den Soldaten zu befehlen, sie einzunehmen, oder sogar die Soldaten dazu zu bringen, sie sich selbst zu verabreichen, auf ähnliche Weise wie Fentanyl-Lutschtabletten?[69] Obwohl dies legal ist, müssen in diesem Fall Autorität und Verantwortlichkeit bestehen bleiben, um die Sicherheit und den Schutz des Soldaten zu gewährleisten.

März, 2018, <https://www.independent.co.uk/life-style/health-and-families/viagra-buy-without-prescription-over-counter-uk-pharmacies-male-impotence-erectile-dysfunction-a8275461.html> (Zugriff: 3. April, 2020).

65 Bostrom und Sandberg, "Cognitive Enhancement: Methods, Ethics, Regulatory Challenges." (Kognitives Enhancement: Methoden, Ethik, Herausforderungen aufgrund der Regulierungen), 333.

66 Scharre und Fish, "Human Performance Enhancement.," 3.

67 United Kingdom, "The Human Medicines Regulations 2012," Pub. L. Nr. 1916, Schedule 17 (2012), Pt 2, 10, Pt 5, 17, <http://www.legislation.gov.uk/uksi/2012/1916/schedule/17/made> (Zugriff: 6. April, 2020).

68 Medic is a term used to cover a combat medical technician of the British Army and its sister service equivalents. They are trained to diagnose, prescribe and manage medical emergencies but do not come under a National regulatory body. (Sanitäter ist ein Begriff im britischen Militär und anverwandten Organisationen. Sie sind in der Lage, medizinische Notfälle zu diagnostizieren, Medikamente zu verschreiben und medizinische Notfälle zu bearbeiten, aber sind ärztlichen Vorschriften nicht unterstellt).

69 CBRN Delivery Team, *2017DIN04–165. Fentanyl Lozenge 800 Micrograms (OTFC) Single – Introduction into Service as Self Administered Operational Analgesia.* (Bristol: Ministry of Defence, 2017).

Von der Sicht des Einsatzes und Befehlsgewalt aus werden Elemente der Nötigung oder des Ungehorsams in dem Abschnitt über IC erörtert, aber der Gebrauch von PCEs hat andere potenzielle Auswirkungen auf die Beschäftigung. Würde die Karriere eines Soldaten durch die Einnahme von PCEs beschleunigt, da dies ihn befähigte, an kritischeren Missionen teilzunehmen? Ebenso könnte dieser Faktor sich auf die Bezahlung, Beförderung und den Verleih von Orden auswirken. Der Zusammenhalt und die Moral in einer Einheit sind von höchster Wichtigkeit für das Gelingen einer Mission; dies geht über Kommunikation, Teamarbeit und gemeinsamer Ethik vor sich. Wäre es das Gleiche mit oder ohne leistungssteigernde Mittel? Könnte es die Soldaten, die sie nicht verabreicht bekamen, dazu bewegen eine „wir und sie"-Haltung anzunehmen und das Gefühl erzeugen, zweitrangig zu sein oder etwas verpasst zu haben? Noch wichtiger ist, dass ein Einsatz abgeblasen werden könnte, wenn die Beteiligten daran diese Enhancements nicht erhalten hätten.

Soldaten vertreten die Gesellschaft und ihre Werte, und man verlässt sich auf sie, diese zu beschützen und dabei zugleich die Menschenrechte und das internationale humanitäre Völkerrecht achten.[70] Das Vereinigte Königreich verfügt über einen moralischen Vertrag, den Armed Forces Covenant (AFC), der anerkennt, dass Soldaten die Bedürfnisse des Dienstes über die eigenen stellen, potenziell also bereit sind, ihr Leben zu opfern, und dass die Gesellschaft die Pflicht hat, dafür zu sorgen, dass sie gerecht behandelt werden. Folglich entsteht ein gegenseitiger Nutzen sowohl für das Militär als auch für die Gesellschaft.[71] Dieser AFC formuliert eine Sorgfaltspflicht für Angehörige des Militärs, die die auferlegte Disziplin und somit eingeschränkte Autonomie akzeptiert haben, und das bedeutet, dass die Öffentlichkeit die Anwendung von PCEs nicht unterstützen würde, wenn sie als nicht sicher oder ungerecht erachtet würden. Diese Sorgfaltspflicht galt als dermaßen wichtig, dass die Regierung alle einzelnen Dienste angewiesen hat, ihre rechtlichen und moralischen Verpflichtungen zu aktualisieren und darüber hinaus ihre Werte, Normen und ihr Ethos zu bekräftigen.[72]

---

70 British Army, *Values and Standards of the British Army*, *AC 64649* (Andover: Army Headquarters, 2018), 25.

71 Helen McCartney, "The Military Covenant and the Civil–Military Contract in Britain,"(Der Militärpakt und der zivil-militärische Pakt in Großbritannien) (*International Affairs* 86, Nr. 2 (2010): 413 .

72 House of Commons Defence Committee, *Duty of Care. Third Report of Session 2004–05. Band I. HC63-I* (London: The Stationery Office Limited, 2005), 5.

KAPITEL 2

die Einwilligungserklärung

Die Theorie der Einwilligungserklärung

Bevor wir die Probleme im Umfeld der Einwilligungserklärung im Militär beschreiben, müssen wir seine Entwicklung verstehen. Das 20. Jahrhundert zählt eine Reihe von grundlegenden Ereignissen, die die Entwicklung der Einwilligungserklärung geprägt haben; das erste fand während des 2. Weltkriegs statt, als die Nazis die Gefangenen in den Konzentrationslagern für Forschungszwecke und grausame Experimente gegen ihren Willen benutzten. Aus den nachfolgenden Prozessen, in denen Ärzte für ihre Handlungen zur Rechenschaft gezogen wurden, entstand 1947 der Nürnberger Kodex, der zehn ausdrückliche Grundsätze für Ärzte, die an Menschen experimentieren, aufstellt und Versuche an Gefangenen verbietet.[1] Das erste Prinzip war der Erhalt einer freiwilligen Einwilligungserklärung der Versuchsperson.[2] Im folgenden Jahr verabschiedeten die Vereinten Nationen eine Allgemeine Erklärung der Menschenrechte mit Hinsicht auf die weitreichenden Nazi-Gräuel, die Artikel 5 beinhaltete, wonach niemand grausamen oder unmenschlichen Behandlungen ausgesetzt werden darf.[3]

Die Deklaration von Helsinki (1964), vom Weltärztebund (World Medical Association, WMA) verabschiedet, erließ die ethischen Prinzipien zur Durchführung von Forschungsarbeiten am Menschen oder identifizierbarem menschlichen Material und Daten, mit der Unterscheidung zwischen therapeutischen und nicht-therapeutischen Verfahren.[4] Sie verpflichten den Arzt vor allem anderen, als oberstes Gebot die Gesundheit der Patienten zu

1 British Medical Journal, "The Nuremberg Code (1947)," (Der Nürnberger Kodex (1947)) (*British Medical Journal* 313, Nr. 7070 (1996): 1448.

2 Michael Gross, *Military Medical Research Ethics: Investigational Drugs, Clinical Trials and Enhancement* (Militärische medizinische Forschungsethik: Prüfpräparate, klinische Versuche und Enhancement), (Oxford: Oxford University Press, 2019), 2.

3 United Nations, "Universal Declaration of Human Rights," (Allgemeine Erklärung der Menschenrechte), 1948, <https://www.un.org/en/universal-declaration-human-rights/> (Zugriff: 9. Januar, 2020).

4 World Medical Association, "Ethical Principles for Medical Research Involving Human Subjects," (Ethische Prinzipien für medizinische Forschung am Menschen), *WMA Declaration of Helsinki*, 2018, <https://www.wma.net/policies-post/wma-declaration-of-helsinki-ethical-principles-for-medical-research-involving-human-subjects/>, (Zugriff: 7. April, 2020).

 | DOI:10.1163/9789004677746_009

fördern und ihre Rechte bei Forschungen am Menschen zu schützen, und er wird für beides verantwortlich gemacht. Die Richtlinie sagt aus, dass jegliche Risiken einer Studie die Vorteile nicht überwiegen dürfen, sie muss von einer Ethik-Kommission (REC) zugelassen werden und die freiwillige informierte Einwilligung ist unerlässlich, wobei ein Abhängigkeitsverhältnis zwischen Arzt und Versuchsperson zu beachten ist. Die Erklärung wies darauf hin, dass, wenn eine Behandlung sich als nicht effektiv erweisen sollte, sie dennoch fortgesetzt werden dürfte, vorausgesetzt, dass ein angemessener IC vorliegt und sie nach Urteil des Arztes Leben retten, die Gesundheit wiederherstellen oder Leiden mildern würde.

Der Belmont-Bericht aus dem Jahr 1979 war ein Versuch, die bisherigen ethischen Erkenntnisse zusammenzufassen.[5] Der Bericht nannte drei forschungsethische Grundprinzipien: Achtung der Menschenwürde, Benefizienz und Gerechtigkeit.[6] Achtung der Menschenwürde bedeutet, den Einzelnen als autonom und selbstbestimmungsfähig zu behandeln und dabei solche Menschen zu schützen, die als verletzlich gelten. Mit Benefizienz ist im Wesentlichen gemeint, anderen Menschen nicht zu schaden, Risiken zu minimieren und den Nutzen bei der Behandlung eines Einzelnen zu maximieren. Abschließend ist Gerechtigkeit mit Fairness verbunden, sodass die Gesellschaft an den Vorteilen der Forschung teilhat, sowie auch an ihren Lasten.

Nürnberg, Helsinki und Belmont waren sämtlich auf die Forschungsethik ausgerichtet, sowie auf die Notwendigkeit des freiwilligen Konsenses. Das Konzept des IC entstand in den 1950er Jahren; es entfernte sich von der einfachen Offenlegung durch die Ärzte und betonte das Verständnis der Versuchsperson. Vor den 1950er Jahren enthielt jeder Konsens eine minimale Offenlegung von Informationen, die den Patienten beunruhigen könnten.[7] Der Begriff von IC entstand aus dem Gerichtsverfahren der Universität Salgo in 1957, mit der Auflage, dass es eine Pflicht ist, Behandlungsrisiken und Optionen offenzulegen, nachdem ein Mann nach einer routinemäßigen Behandlung

---

5 The National Commission for the Protection of Human Subjects of Biomedical and Behavioural Research, "The Belmont Report: Ethical Principles and Guidelines for the Protection of Human Subjects of Research," (Der Belmont-Report: Ethische Prinzipien und Richtlinien für den Schutz von Menschen als Probanden), 1979, <https://www.hhs.gov/ohrp/sites/default/files/the-belmont-report-508c_FINAL.pdf,> (Zugriff: 8. Januar, 2020).

6 ebd. 4.

7 Tom L. Beauchamp, "Informed Consent: Its History, Meaning, and Present Challenges," (Einwilligungserklärung: Ihre Geschichte, Bedeutung und derzeitige Herausforderungen), *Cambridge Quarterly of Healthcare Ethics* 20, Nr. 4 (2011): 515.

Lähmungen erlitt und der Fall als Körperverletzung eingestuft wurde.[8] Einige Jahre später entschied das Gericht im Falle Natanson, dass das Versäumnis des Arztes, die Aufklärung vorzunehmen, von einer Körperverletzung zu einer Fahrlässigkeit umgedeutet wird, ein Stand, der immer noch gültig ist.[9] 1972 fällten drei verschiedene amerikanische Gerichtshöfe Entscheidungen, die eine patientenorientiertere Offenlegung zum Standard erhoben. Das besagte, dass der Patient genügend Informationen erhalten musste, um eine intelligente Wahl zu treffen.[10] Die Ärzteschaft war nicht besonders begeistert davon, sie waren der Meinung, dass diese an sie gestellten Anforderungen zu aufwändig seien und sogar der guten Patientenversorgung im Wege stünden.

Wenn man die Geschichte zusammenfasst, ist IC auf Respekt vor der Autonomie und Selbstbestimmung des Patienten basiert. Das Wort Autonomie stammt aus dem Griechischen: *auto* bedeutet Selbst und *nomos* Regel, Bestimmung.[11] IC ist eine autonome Zulassung der Person, um einer medizinischen Fachkraft zu gestatten, sie nur dann medizinisch zu behandeln, wenn die zu behandelnde Person mündig ist und nicht unter der Kontrolle anderer steht. Berg definierte IC als etwas, dass „sich auf gesetzliche Regeln bezieht, die Ärzten und anderen Fachleuten im Gesundheitswesen Verhaltensweisen im Umgang mit Patienten vorschreiben."[12] Beide Parteien müssen beteiligt sein, für den Patienten ist der informierte Konsens ein Recht, für einen Arzt ist sie eine Pflicht bzw. Verbindlichkeit.[13] Man kann IC auch im Licht von institutionellen und strategischen Regelungen sehen, wenn im Gesundheitswesen die NHS-Regeln der Einwilligung befolgt werden, so sind sie gültig und informiert.[14] (NHS: National Health Service, Britischer Nationaler Gesundheitsdienst).

Während der letzten 50 Jahre war die informierte Einwilligung eine ethisch vertretbare medizinische Praxis, begründet auf Autonomie und individuellem Wohlbefinden, jetzt mit Verlagerung des Schwerpunktes auf gemeinsame

---

8 R. R. Faden, T. L. Beauchamp und N. M. P. King, *A History and Theory of Informed Consent* (Eine Geschichte und Theorie der Einwilligungserklärung), New York: Oxford University Press, 1986), 125.

9 ebd., 129.

10 ebd., 132.

11 J. W. Berg *et al.*, *Informed Consent: Legal Theory and Clinical Practice*, (Informierter Konsens: Rechtswissenschaftliche Theorie und klinischer Versuch), Second (New York: Oxford University Press, 2001), 15.

12 ebd., 3.

13 ebd., 14.

14 Beauchamp, "Informed Consent: Its History, Meaning, and Present Challenges," (Einwilligungserklärung: Ihre Geschichte, Bedeutung und gegenwärtige Herausforderungen), 518.

Entscheidungsfindung von Patient und Arzt. Wie Berg es beschreibt, impliziert IC offizielle Maßnahmen mit rechtlichen Beiklängen, die oftmals auch dokumentiert werden müssen, wie zum Beispiel bei OPs. Bei diesen offiziellen Maßnahmen wird erwartet, dass beide Parteien über die Vorteile der Behandlung und potenzielle negative Ausgänge vollständig in Kenntnis gesetzt sind, wobei der Patient sein Vertrauen in die Gesundheitsexperten setzt. Viele Aspekte außerhalb der Medizin gewinnen an Formalität und sind oft im Verbraucherschutz und dem detaillierten Kleingedruckten, das ein Produkt oder eine Dienstleistung begleitet, zu finden. Letztlich scheint das Betreiben von Formalität und schriftlichen Einwilligungserklärungen ein Schutz der Behandelnden vor Anklage, Rechtsstreitigkeiten und Wiedergutmachung zu sein.[15]

Zusammenfassend muss eine Person vier Kriterien erfüllen, damit die informierte Einwilligung für das Gesundheitswesen gültig ist:

1. Sie muss geistig zurechnungsfähig sein – dies schließt potenziell betreuungsbedürftige Personen aus, d.h. solche die sehr alt und solche, die bewusstlos sind.
2. Sie muss die Risiken, den Nutzen und alternative Optionen verstehen, einschließlich der Option nichts zu tun, und die Möglichkeit haben, Fragen zu stellen.
3. Sie muss in der Lage sein, die Einwilligung jederzeit zu widerrufen.
4. Sie darf nicht unter Zwang stehen.

Dies erscheint schlicht und unkompliziert, aber Corrigan bespricht ein Modell der „leeren Ethik,"gemäß dem jede autonome Person, wenn sie genügend Informationen erhält, sowie die Zeit, diese zu verarbeiten, die Entscheidung treffen wird, ob sie eine Behandlung akzeptiert oder nicht. Das setzt einen universalen Standard voraus und ignoriert kulturelle Differenzen.[16] Die Fähigkeit einer jeden Person, voll in Kenntnis gesetzt zu sein, erfordert eine unterschiedliche Menge an Informationen und Zeit, was bedeutet, dass das Verfahren des IC auf den Einzelnen zugeschnitten sein sollte.

15 O. O'Neill, "Some Limits of Informed Consent," (Einige Einschränkungen von Einwilligungserklärungen), *Journal of Medical Ethics* 29, Nr. 1 (2003): 4.

16 Oonagh Corrigan, "Empty Ethics: The Problem with Informed Consent," (Leere Ethik: Das Problem mit IC), *Sociology of Health & Illness* 25, Nr. 3 (2003): 770.

Militärische Aspekte der Einwilligungserklärung

Früher richtete das Militär sein Verfahren zur Einwilligungserklärung nach dem für die Zivilbevölkerung aus, doch umging es sie unter gewissen Umständen und fügte seinen Soldaten Schaden zu; gleichzeitig vernachlässigte es die Sorgfaltspflicht für sie. Das erste Prinzip der Nürnberger Deklaration besagt, dass eine freiwillig gegebene informierte Einwilligung des Probanden unerlässlich ist.[17] Trotz dieses Prinzips experimentierten sowohl das Vereinigte Königreich als auch die USA während des kalten Krieges an ihren Soldaten, indem sie sie Strahlungen, chemischen Wirkstoffen und LSD aussetzten.[18] In jüngerer Zeit erhielt das amerikanische Verteidigungsministerium (DOD) eine IC-Ausnahmegenehmigung von der bundesstaatlichen Behörde zur Überwachung von Nahrungs- und Arzneimitteln (FDA) für die Verabreichung von Pyridostigmin und Botulinumtoxin-Impfstoff an Truppen für die Operation Desert Storm (Wüstensturm).[19] Der Grund für diese Ausnahme war angeblich, dass es unmöglich gewesen sei, Einwilligungserklärungen von mehr als 500.000 Soldaten zu erhalten, und einige hätten sie nicht gegeben und wären somit in Gefahr gebracht.[20] Die Impfung, allerdings nicht Pyridostigmin, wurde schließlich auf freiwilliger Basis ausgegeben, mit der Begründung von „Experimentieren" im Vergleich zu „Schutz" der Truppen. Pyridostigmin galt nach jahrzehntelanger Erfahrung mit der Behandlung von Myasthenia Gravis (schwere Myasthenie, Muskelschwund) als sicher, während der Impfstoff auf seine Effektivität untersucht wurde.[21]

17 Gross, *Military Medical Research Ethics: Investigational Drugs, Clinical Trials and Enhancement*, (Militärische medizinische Forschungsethik: Prüfpräparate, klinische Versuche und Enhancement), 2.

18 George J. Annas, "Changing the Consent Rules for Desert Storm," (Änderung der Einwilligungsregeln für Desert Storm), *New England Journal of Medicine* 326, Nr. 11 (12. März, 1992): 771, Adam Lusher, "The Bizarre True Story of When the UK Military Tested LSD on Royal Marines," (Die bizarre wahre Geschichte von den Versuchen des britischen Militärs an Mitgliedern der Königlichen Marine), *The Independent*, 24. Mai, 2018, <https://www.independent.co.uk/news/uk/home-news/lsd-video-porton-down-chemical-weapons-experiments-trials-uk-military-army-marines-sixties-acid-a8366906.html> (Zugriff: 29. April, 2020).

19 Joel Martin Schofer, "Violations of Informed Consent During War," (Verstöße gegen Einwilligungserklärungen im Krieg), *JAMA* 281, Nr. 17 (1999): 1657.

20 Annas, "Changing the Consent Rules for Desert Storm." (Änderung der Einwilligungsregeln für Desert Storm), 770.

21 ebd., 772.

Wenn auf IC für Verteidigungszwecke verzichtet werden kann, so ist dies ein gefährlicher Präzedenzfall. Damit ein DOD-Verzicht jedoch gültig ist, müssen sehr strenge Bedingungen erfüllt werden:

> um die Ausführung des militärischen Einsatzes zu erleichtern, erfordern die Erhaltung der Gesundheit des Einzelnen und die Sicherheit das Personals, dass eine bestimmte Behandlung einer vorgegebenen Gruppe von Angehörigen des Militärs verabreicht wird, ungeachtet dessen, ob die einzelne Person es vorzieht, nicht behandelt zu werden oder eine alternative Behandlung zu erhalten.[22]

Die Leute, die diese Medikamente ablehnen, müssten entweder das Einsatzgebiet verlassen und so ihre militärischen Pflichten nicht erfüllen, oder ungeschützt bleiben, also sich Risiken aussetzen, ihre Kameraden in Gefahr bringen und die Erfolgschancen des Einsatzes reduzieren.[23] Der amerikanische Fall der Verabreichung von nicht zugelassenen Medikamenten kam vor das Gericht; der Prozess wurde verloren, einschließlich der Berufungen, doch keiner der Prozesse erwähnte den Nürnberger Kodex, und in allen Fällen wurde der Einsatz von Pyridostigmin unterstützt, da dies als eine Behandlung galt.[24]

2002 kehrten zwei Piloten von einer langfristigen Übung in Afghanistan nach Kuweit zurück, verwechselten scharfe Schüsse mit einem Angriff von feindlichen Aufständischen und töteten vier kanadische Piloten bei einer Tragödie durch eigenen Beschuss. In der darauf folgenden Gerichtsverhandlung argumentierten die Verteidiger, dass die Piloten gezwungen worden waren, Dextroamphetamin zu sich zu nehmen, ein Wirkstoff, der ihre Aufmerksamkeit beeinträchtigte und zu dem versehentlichen Bombardement führte. Die Anklagen wurden fallengelassen, und obwohl der Wirkstoff nie verantwortlich gemacht wurde, wurde das Problem des Mangels an IC für ein

---

22 Richard A. Rettig, *Military Use of Drugs Not Yet Approved by the FDA for CW/BW Defense: Lessons from the Gulf War* (Militärische Benutzung von Arzneistoffen, die noch nicht von der FDA für CW/BW Verteidigung zugelassen wurden: Was vom Golfkrieg gelernt wurde) (Santa Monica: RAND Corporation, 1999), xii.

23 Richard A. Rettig, *Waiving Informed Consent: Military Use of Non-FDA-Approved Drugs in Combat* (*Verzicht auf Einwilligungserklärung: Militärischer Gebrauch von seitens der FDA nicht zugelassenen Arzneistoffen im Kampf*) (Santa Monica: RAND Corporation, 2000), <https://www.rand.org/pubs/research_briefs/RB7534.html> (Zugriff: 20. April, 2020).

24 George J. Annas, "Protecting Soldiers from Friendly Fire: The Consent Requirement for Using Investigational Drugs and Vaccines in Combat," (Schutz für Soldaten vor Eigenbeschuss: Die Einwilligungserklärung für den Gebrauch von Prüfpräparaten und Impfstoffen im Kampf) *American Journal of Law & Medicine* 24, Nr. 2/3 (1998): 249.

verschriebenes Medikament deutlich.[25] Wirkte sich das Dextroamphetamin auf ihre geistige Leistungsfähigkeit aus, oder beeinflusste es ihre Fähigkeit, ihr Verhalten unter Kontrolle zu halten, oder war es doch nur ein Pilotenfehler, der Schluss, zu dem der Untersuchungsausschuss gekommen war?[26] Wurde also das Dextroamphetamin zur „Behandlung" eingesetzt und war erforderlich, damit sie für Kampfeinsätze geeignet waren?[27] Die amerikanische Heeresdienstvorschrift sagt folgendes aus: „Ein Soldat des Heeres im aktiven Dienst, oder im aktiven Dienst während einer Übung, ist normalerweise verpflichtet, sich ärztlicher Betreuung zu unterziehen, die erforderlich ist, um sein Leben zu sichern, unnötige Leiden zu lindern oder das Wohl der anderen zu schützen oder zu erhalten."[28]

Die wichtigste Frage ist, ob das Einnehmen von PCEs standardmäßig zur „medizinischen Betreuung" gehört, um „das Wohl der anderen zu schützen oder zu erhalten"?

Im Zuge der Verstöße in der Vergangenheit gegen die Rechte und die Ethik des Militärpersonals und angesichts der daraus entstehenden Gefahren, dass der Verteidigungssektor rechtliche Ausnahmeregelungen zum IC erhält, passte Mehlman die Belmont-Prinzipien dem Gebrauch für das Militär an. Benefizienz, Achtung vor der Person und Gerechtigkeit wurden nun zu Verhältnismäßigkeit, staatlicher Bevormundung und Fairness.[29] Zum ersten deckt Verhältnismäßigkeit die Auflage eines biomedizinischen Risikos für Truppen nur, wenn es für einen legitimen Einsatz erforderlich ist, in dem das

25 Lauren R. Robbins, "Refusing to Be All That You Can Be: Regulating against Forced Cognitive Enhancement in the Military," (Verweigerung alles das zu sein, was du sein kannst: Schutzregulierung des aufgezwungen kognitiven Enhancements im Militär), in *Military Medical Ethics for the 21st Century*, Hsg. M. L. Gross and D. Carrick, Military and Defence Ethics (Farnham: Ashgate Publishing Limited, 2013), 127.

26 Oliver Burkeman und Richard Norton-Taylor, "US Pilots Blame Drug for Friendly Fire Deaths," (Amerikanische Piloten machen Arzneistoff für Eigenbeschuss verantwortlich), *The Guardian*, 4. Januar, 2003, <https://www.theguardian.com/world/2003/jan/04/afghanistan.richardnortontaylor>.

27 Annas, "Protecting Soldiers from Friendly Fire: The Consent Requirement for Using Investigational Drugs and Vaccines in Combat.," (Schutz für Soldaten vor Eigenbeschuss: Die Einwilligungserklärung für den Gebrauch von Prüfpräparaten und Impfstoffen im Kampf) 250.

28 Stephen E. Deardorff, "Informed Consent, Termination of Medical Treatment, and the Federal Tort Claims Act – A New Proposal for the Military Health Care System," (Einwilligungserklärung, Einstellung von medizinischer Behandlung und das Gesetz für bundesstaatliche Ansprüche von unerlaubten Handlungen – Ein neuer Plan für das militärische Gesundheitssystem), *Military Law Review* 115, Nr. Winter (1987): 68.

29 Maxwell J. Mehlman und Stephanie Corley, "A Framework for Military Bioethics," (Ein Rahmen für militärische Bioethik) *Journal of Military Ethics* 13, Nr. 4 (2014): 337.

Risiko im Verhältnis zu dem gewonnenen militärischen Vorteil steht. Zweitens ist eine staatliche Bevormundung erforderlich, aufgrund der reduzierten Autonomie und der Pflicht zum Gehorsam, die die Fähigkeit eines Soldaten, seine Einwilligung zu verweigern, eingrenzt. Deshalb muss ein Kommandant sicherstellen, dass die Gefährdungen angemessen sind und die Privatsphäre, Würde und Vertraulichkeit der Person bewahrt wird.[30] Zum Schluss ist Fairness ein schwieriger Bereich für Kommandanten, die vielleicht eine Gruppe ihrer Untergebenen einem biomedizinischen Risiko aussetzen, jedoch gleichzeitig sicherstellen müssen, dass dies in einer diskriminierungsfreien Weise geschieht und nicht als eine Strafe benutzt wird.[31]

Obwohl die Belmont-Prinzipien als Leitlinie für die Forschung gedacht waren, enthalten Mehlmans angepasste militärische Prinzipien zusammen im Wesentlichen das, was Sorgfaltspflicht bedeutet, ein Begriff, der alle moralischen und gesetzlichen Verantwortlichkeiten deckt, von Verwundung bis hin zur Sicherheit am Arbeitsplatz. Sorgfaltspflicht ist ein wichtiges Konzept für das gesamte Militärpersonal oberhalb der Rangniedrigsten, das die ihnen Untergebenen betreut und für sie verantwortlich ist.[32] Wenn neue Rekruten dem Militär beitreten, geben sie einen Teil ihrer Autonomie auf und nehmen zur Kenntnis, dass man ihnen befehlen kann, sich in lebensgefährliche Situationen zu bringen.[33] Der neue Rekrut erklärt sich zu einer Reihe von Tätigkeiten bereit, um legitime militärische Zwecke zu erfüllen, im Wissen und gutem Vertrauen darauf, dass das Militär im Rahmen seiner Sorgfaltspflicht die Risiken so gering wie möglich hält. Ein Soldat akzeptiert neue Waffen und die Ausbildung dafür, die laufend entwickelt werden; kann dies also mit neuen Arzneimitteln verglichen werden, für die eine stillschweigende Einwilligung abzugeben ist? Es wird allgemein akzeptiert, dass Militärangehörige eventuell in den Krieg ziehen und möglicherweise ihr Leben aufs Spiel setzen müssen, aber gleichzeitig ist nicht allgemein bekannt, das PCEs zur Verfügung stehen. Allerdings ändert sich so etwas mit der Zeit, und wenn der Einsatz von PCE alltäglich wird, könnte die stillschweigende Einwilligung gültig sein.

---

30 Michael L. Gross, *Bioethics and Armed Conflict. Moral Dilemmas of Medicine and War* (Bioethik und bewaffnete Konflikte. Die moralischen Dilemmas in der Medizin und im Krieg) (Cambridge: MIT Press, 2006), 45.

31 Mehlman und Corley, "A Framework for Military Bioethics," (Ein Rahmen für militärische Bioethik) 339–340.

32 House of Commons Defence Committee, *Duty of Care. Third Report of Session 2004–05. Band I. HC 63-I*, 29.

33 William J. FitzPatrick und Lee L. Zwanziger, "Defending Against Biochemical Warfare," (Verteidigung gegen biochemische Kriegsführung) *The Journal of Philosophy, Science & Law* 3, Nr. 2 (2003): 9.

Die militärische Kommandokette trägt die Verantwortung dafür, dass jedes Risiko so gering wie möglich gehalten wird, sowie auch für die Einhaltung der Sorgfaltspflicht; Teil dieser Kette ist im Vereinigten Königreich die Competent Medical Authority (Zuständige militärische Behörde, CMA. Die CMA ist ein ranghoher Militärarzt, der die medizinischen Aspekte eines Einsatzplans genehmigt hat und dafür rechenschaftspflichtig ist. Wer ist jedoch letztendlich rechenschaftspflichtig, und ist diese Dienststelle in der Lage, zu verhindern, dass das Militär sich selbst gefährdet, um seine Ziele zu erfüllen?[34] Da PCES als Medikamente eingestuft sind, würde der militärärztliche Dienst (Defence Medical Services (DMS)) die militärische Autorität darstellen und sein Drei-Sterne-General (Generalleutnant) die volle Verantwortung tragen.[35] Zum Glück gibt es externe, unabhängige Prüfungsstellen, ergänzt durch die Care Quality Commission (Ausschuss für Pflegequalitä), die die DMS strafrechtlich verfolgen können, falls medizinische Standards verletzt werden, auch wenn Menschen geschädigt oder in Gefahr gebracht werden.[36]

Ist es hinnehmbar, dass das Militär gegen den Einwilligungsprozess verstößt und den Stand der staatlichen Bevormundung einnimmt, wenn es der Meinung ist, es wahre die Sorgfaltspflicht? Paternalismus oder Bevormundung wurde als „die Einmischung eines Staates oder einer Person in die Belange einer anderen Person, gegen ihren Willen, und von einem Anspruch berechtigt oder mit der Motivierung, dass die Person, in deren Belange man sich einmischt, davon profitiert oder vor Schädigung beschützt wird“ definiert.[37] Paternalistische Strategien grenzen die Wahl des Einzelnen ein, sind aber gestattet, wenn die relevante Behörde dies als vorrangig von Vorteil für diese Person erachtet.[38] Obschon die Medizin sich von Bevormundung abgewendet

---

34 Jessica Wolfendale und Steve Clarke, "Paternalism, Consent, and the Use of Experimental Drugs in the Military," (Staatliche Bevormundung, Einwilligung und der Gebrauch von experimentellen Medikamenten im Militär), *The Journal of Medicine and Philosophy: A Forum for Bioethics and Philosophy of Medicine* 33, Nr. 4 (2008): 347.

35 United Kingdom. HM Government, "Defence Medical Services," (Dachorganisation des britischen Verteidigungsministeriums), <https://www.gov.uk/government/groups/defence-medical-services> (Zugriff: 18. Mai, 2020).

36 Care Quality Commission, "Defence Medical Services," 2019, <https://www.cqc.org.uk/what-we-do/services-we-regulate/defence-medical-services>, (Zugriff: 9. April, 2020).

37 Gerald Dworkin, "Paternalism," (Staatliche Bevormundung), Hsg. Edward N. Zalta, *The Stanford Encyclopedia of Philosophy* (Stanford: Metaphysics Research Lab, Stanford University, 2019), <https://plato.stanford.edu/entries/paternalism/>, (Zugriff: 8. Januar, 2020).

38 Wolfendale und Clarke, "Paternalism, Consent, and the Use of Experimental Drugs in the Military." (Staatliche Bevormundung, Einwilligung und der Gebrauch von experimentellen Medikamenten im Militär), 339.

hat, herrscht diese noch immer im Militär vor; das IC-Verfahren könnte außer Kraft gesetzt werden, wenn eine Person, die ihre eigenen Vorzüge in den Vordergrund stellt, ihr eigenes Leben und das von anderen riskiert,[39] da die persönliche Gesundheit eines Soldaten Auswirkungen auf sein Umfeld haben kann.[40] Wird auf die Einwilligung für PCEs verzichtet, wird dann der Einzelne zum Versuchskaninchen, und wird der Arzneistoff in eine experimentale oder Forschungsmittel-Kategorie eingestuft, mit der sich daraus ergebenden Notwendigkeit für ein höheres Niveau von IC? Das Vertrauen in die Verantwortungstragenden muss erhalten bleiben, wobei die Sorgfaltspflicht bei der Entscheidungsfindung als höchste Priorität gilt, wenn man auf die Einwilligungserklärung verzichtet, wie man dem Fall von Pyridostigmin und dem Gebrauch experimentaler Arzneistoffe im Kampf entnehmen kann.[41]

Von einer „antizipativen Einwilligung" spricht man, wenn die Person ihre Einwilligung nicht geben kann, aufgrund eines kurzfristigen Kapazitätsdefizits, z.B. bei der Injektion eines Combo-Pen, ein notwendiges Gegenmittel, wenn ein Soldat aufgrund eines Nervenkampfstoffs außer Gefecht gesetzt wird.[42] Dies könnte mit PCEs übereinstimmen, zum Beispiel, die Bereitstellung von Medikamenten, wenn in kritischen Momenten Müdigkeit bekämpft werden muss und keine Zeit für eine ausführliche Diskussion bleibt. Allerdings handelt es sich hier eher um eine Behandlung als um eine Leistungsverstärkung. In gewissen Bereichen des Militärdienstes, für die in Zukunft eine antizipative Einwilligung erforderlich werden könnte, könnte ein weitgehenderer Konsens angenommen werden, der allgemeinerer Art ist und weniger spezifisch ist. Dies umreißt Themen, denen die Soldaten möglicherweise zustimmen müssen, und ermöglicht Flexibilität und einen Grundstock an Informationen.[43] Eine solche Einwilligungserklärung könnte mit der Rekrutierung beginnen, jährlich erneuert werden, sowie wenn neue Entwicklungen oder erweiterte wissenschaftliche Erkenntnisse auftreten.[44] Der Vorteil eines weitgehenderen

---

39 ebd. 341.

40 Edmund G. Howe und Edward D. Martin, "Treating the Troops," (Ärztliche Behandlung von Streitkräften), *Hastings Center Report* 21, Nr. 2 (1991): 23.

41 Wolfendale und Clarke, "Paternalism, Consent, and the Use of Experimental Drugs in the Military." (Staatliche Bevormundung, Einwilligung und der Gebrauch von experimentellen Medikamenten im Militär), 345.

42 iMedi.co.uk, "Autoject (Combopen) Nerve Agent Antidote L4a1," (Autoject (Combopen) als Gegenmittel gegen Nervenkampfstoff), 2009, <https://imedi.co.uk/autoject-combopen-nerve-agent-antidote-l4a1> (Zugriff: 30. April, 2020).

43 Gert Helgesson, "In Defense of Broad Consent," (Verteidigung des weitgehenden Konsenses) *Cambridge Quarterly of Healthcare Ethics* 21, Nr. 1 (2012): 40.

44 Rettig, "Military Use of Drugs Not Yet Approved by the FDA for CW/BW Defense: Lessons from the Gulf War.," 4. Kapitel.

jährlichen Konsenses ist, dass Wiederholung und Aufbau von Informationen ein besseres Verständnis mit sich bringen, die Gefahr jedoch besteht, etwas zu unterzeichnen, dessen Bedeutung man nur begrenzt verstehen kann.[45]

Von den hervorgehobenen Fragen aus gesehen wäre es für den Einsatz der PCES logisch, dass Verzichtserklärungen zu vermeiden sind und dass, wo immer möglich, sowohl weitgehender Konsens als auch informierter Konsens benutzt werden. Doch O'Neill widerspricht dem Einsatz von IC, weil er glaubt, dass seine Befürworter schlechte Argumente und übertriebene Ansprüche anführen, wobei er auf die viel zu vielen Ausnahmen für IC in der medizinischen Praxis hinweist, z.B. für geistig Behinderte, Bewusstlose und solche, die unter Zwang stehen, z.B. Gefängnisinsassen.[46] Weiter beschreibt er eine *„Opazität der Einwilligung,"* wenn ein Einzelner einer bestimmten Handlung zustimmt, ohne sich darüber im Klaren zu sein, dass dies eine weitere notwendige Maßnahme mit sich bringen könnte.[47] Diese Opazität wurde von dem Alder Hey-Kinderkrankenhaus ans Licht gebracht, das die Organe von Kindern nach ihrem Tod zurückbehielt. Zwar hatten die Eltern zugestimmt, dass Gewebeteile für die Forschung benutzt werden, aber nicht, dass ganze Organe entfernt werden dürften, obgleich die Organe aus Gewebe bestehen.[48] Dies führt dazu, dass Entscheidungsträger IC-Verfahren einführen oder verschärfen, um das Wohl der Patienten besser zu schützen und ihnen die Möglichkeit zu geben, eine informierte Wahl zu treffen.[49]

Die Bedeutung von Einwilligungserklärung für die militärische Forschung

Um IC für biomedizinische Forschung zu erhalten, braucht man ein höheres Niveau von IC, um Patienten und gesunde Freiwillige vor Ausnutzung und Schäden zu schützen, wie in der Helsinki-Deklaration und den Belmont-Prinzipien beschrieben. Die einzigen zivilrechtlichen Ausnahmen, wenn IC nicht für die Forschung erforderlich ist, sind retrospektive und

45 FitzPatrick und Zwanziger, "Defending Against Biochemical Warfare," (Verteidigung gegen biochemische Kriegsführung), 15.

46 O'Neill, "Some Limits of Informed Consent," (Einige Einschränkungen des IC), 4.

47 ebd., 6.

48 Clare Dyer, "Consent Needed For Organ Retention, BMA Says," (Der Konsens, der für Organaufbewahrung erforderlich ist), *British Medical Journal* 321, Nr. 7269 (2000): 1098.

49 Corrigan, "Empty Ethics: The Problem with Informed Consent." (Leere Ethik: Das Problem mit IC), 769.

Notfallstudien.[50] In den USA kann nach dem Defence Appropriations Act (Genehmigungsgesetz zur nationalen Verteidigung) auf die Einwilligungserklärung verzichtet werden, wenn die Forschung den Probanden direkt zugutekommt, die Entwicklung von für das Militär notwendigen medizinischen Produkten notwendig ist und alle normalen Gesetze und Vorschriften einhält.[51] Seit 2002 wurden keine Verzichtserklärungen mehr ausgegeben, aber Gross ist der Meinung, dass, um die medizinische Militärforschung zu verbessern, die derzeitigen Vorschriften mithilfe von Verzichtserklärungen zu nutzen sind und der Geltungsbereich der medizinischen Zivilforschung für militärische Zwecke zu erweitern ist.[52]

Um die britischen Truppen vor Instrumentalisierung zu schützen, verfügt das britische Verteidigungsministerium über seinen eigenen ethischen Forschungsausschuss (ethics research committee (MODREC)), bestehend aus Experten und Unabhängigen.[53] Die Rolle der Unabhängigen ist von großer Wichtigkeit als Fürsprecher außerhalb des militärischen Einflusses, um die Sicherheit der Teilnehmer an dem Forschungsprogramm zu schützen und eine „Befehlskultur“ zu vermeiden.[54] MODREC hat seine Prinzipien veröffentlicht, die „die Interessen von Teilnehmern schützen und fördern, indem sie ein solides wissenschaftliches und ethisches Verhalten und angemessene, auf Vertrauen basierende Führung der Forschung mit menschlichen Versuchspersonen beschreiben.“[55] Sie sind mit nationalen und internationalen ethischen Prinzipien ausgerichtet, laut denen die Rechte der Versuchspersonen

---

50 Gross, *Military Medical Research Ethics: Investigational Drugs, Clinical Trials and Enhancement,* (Ethik in der medizinischen Forschung: Prüfpräparate, klinische Versuche und Enhancement) 6.

51 John McManus *et al.*, “Informed Consent and Ethical Issues in Military Medical Research,” (Einwilligungserklärung und ethische Probleme in der militärischen medizinischen Forschung), *Academic Emergency Medicine* 12, Nr. 11 (2005): 1123.

52 Gross, *Military Medical Research Ethics: Investigational Drugs, Clinical Trials and Enhancement,* (Ethik in der militärischen medizinischen Forschung: Prüfpräparate, klinische Versuche und Enhancement) 7.

53 United Kingdom, Ministry of Defence, “Ministry of Defence Research Ethics Committee,” (Ethik-Ausschuss des britischen Verteidigungsministeriums), <https://www.gov.uk/government/groups/ministry-of-defence-research-ethics-committees#guidance-documents> (Zugriff: 9. Januar, 2020).

54 United Kingdom, Ministry of Defence, *JSP 536. Governance of Research Involving Human Participants.* (*Regelung der Forschung mithilfe von menschlichen Probanden, Teil 1: Richtlinie,* 3. Ausgabe. (London: HMSO, 2020), 5–5, Mehlman, Lin, und Abney, “Enhanced Warfighters: A Policy Framework,” (Enhancement für Streitkräfte: Risiken, Ethik und Strategie)115.

55 United Kingdom. Ministry of Defence, *JSP 536. Governance of Research Involving Human Participants. Part 1: Directive, 1–1* (siehe oben).

„Vorrang vor den Interessen der Wissenschaft und der Gesellschaft haben."[56] Mit Hinsicht auf IC erklärt MODREC ausdrücklich, dass ein Soldat sich weigern kann, an irgendeinem Forschungsprojekt teilzunehmen, und dass die für die Studie erstellten Informationen in einem geeigneten Format und in einem angemessenen Verhältnis zu der zu erwartenden Nutzen-Risiko-Analyse stehen müssen.[57] Verhältnismäßigkeit bedeutet hier, dass bei hohen Risiken, oder wenn die Untersuchung von den üblichen Verfahren abweicht, weit mehr Informationen verfügbar gemacht werden, und unterstützt die Verhältnismäßigkeit, wie sie von Mehlmans angepassten Belmont-Prinzipien dargestellt wird.

Dem Einzelnen ist eine „angemessene Zeit" zu geben, in der er entscheiden kann, ob er teilnehmen möchte, und das kann nicht am gleichen Tag des Erhalts der Informationen geschehen.[58] Corrigan erkannte im Laufe ihrer eigenen Forschung, dass Probanden nicht immer alle Informationen verstanden, was getestet wurde oder ob es sich um eine aktive Behandlung handelte.[59] Als Gründe dafür wurden das Vertrauen in medizinische Experten und die Erwartung genannt, dass Ärzte in erster Linie zu ihrem Wohl handeln würden.[60] Die Vorstellungen von Einzelpersonen in der medizinischen Forschung sind je nach Herkunft und kulturellen Normen unterschiedlich.[61] Selbst der Titel des Forschungsprojekts wirkte sich auf die Wahrnehmung aus, denn wenn er das Wort „Experiment" enthielt, hatte das eine negative Bedeutung, während „Untersuchung" am beliebtesten war.[62] Am meisten Sorgen bereitet es, warum Personen sich für Forschungszwecke anbieten, und gemäß Corrigans kleiner Untersuchung gaben mehr als 96% ihre Einwilligung aus finanziellen Gründen, einige auch, um ihrem Arzt gefällig zu sein.[63] Sie kam

56 United Kingdom, "The Medicines for Human Use (Clinical Trials) Regulations," (Die Vorschriften für Medikament für den menschlichen Verzehr (klinische Versuche), Pub. L. Nr. 1031, Schedule 1, pt. 2, para. 3, (2004), <http://www.legislation.gov.uk/uksi/2004/1031/schedule/1/part/2/paragraph/3/made#text%3Dinformed consent> (Zugriff: 1. Januar, 2020).

57 United Kingdom. Ministry of Defence, *JSP 536. Governance of Research Involving Human Participants. Part 1: Directive*, 3–4 (*Regelung der Forschung mithilfe von menschlichen Probanden, Teil 1: Richtlinie*).

58 ebd.

59 Corrigan, "Empty Ethics: The Problem with Informed Consent," (Leere Ethik: Das Problem mit IC), 774–775.

60 ebd. 778–780.

61 ebd. 777.

62 Ruth R. Faden, *Advisory Committee on Human Radiation Experiments. Final Report.* (Beratungsausschuss zu Strahlungsexperimenten an Menschen), (Washington DC: U.S. Government Printing Office, 1995), 734.

63 Corrigan, "Empty Ethics: The Problem with Informed Consent.," (Leere Ethik: Das Problem mit IC), 782–784.

zu dem Schluss, dass das IC-Verfahren selbst zu einer *„leeren Ethik"* führte, bei der die Grundsätze von IC den sozialen Kontext nicht berücksichtigten.[64]

Faden vertrat die Ansicht, dass ein IC nicht für alle Forschungsarbeiten erforderlich ist, insbesondere für die vergleichende Wirkungsforschung, die seiner Meinung nach einen übertriebenen Patientenschutz betreibt, wo doch die Forschung sich nur minimal auf das, was wichtig für die Patienten ist, auswirkt und ihnen nur dann nicht genügend Schutz vor Fehlern und Management bietet, wenn die erforderlichen Untersuchungen, um diese Probleme zu reduzieren, zu lästig werden.[65] Wenn eine Einrichtung eine Vision kontinuierlicher Weiterbildung, um die Patientenversorgung mit absoluter Transparenz zu verbessern, dann wäre es ethisch vertretbar, die Patienten einfach über eine Studie zu informieren und ihnen die Möglichkeit zu geben, sie abzulehnen. Dies funktioniert nur, wenn es vergleichende Behandlungsoptionen gibt und nicht, wenn ein höheres Risiko oder Ungewissheit besteht, oder wenn genauere Informationen erforderlich sind.[66] Wie man nun festlegt, was ein geringes Risiko in randomisierten kontrollierten Versuchen darstellt, wird als klinisch gleichwertig beschrieben und untersteht dem derzeitigen Pflegestandard.[67]

Ebenfalls wichtig für die Untersuchungen ist das Problem der vorrangigen militärischen Bedürfnisse, und die Erhaltung der Autonomie des Patienten ist hier sehr relevant. Der Erfolg eines militärischen Einsatzes kann die Rechte des einzelnen Soldaten außer Kraft setzen, und wie Groß sagt: „die Militärmedizin konzentriert sich nicht ausschließlich auf den Patienten. Ihre Aufgabe ist es eher, die Bereitschaft der Streitkräfte aufrecht zu erhalten."[68] Da pharmakologisches Enhancement bei gesunden militärischen Versuchspersonen in Off-Label-Anwendungen benutzt wird, ist es nach Meinung eines holländischen Autors unwahrscheinlich, dass so ein Versuch vor einem Ethik-Komitee bestehen würde.[69] PCEs sind noch nicht standardmäßig Teil der

64 ebd. 787.

65 Ruth R. Faden, Tom L. Beauchamp, and Nancy E. Kass, "Informed Consent, Comparative Effectiveness, and Learning Health Care," (IC, vergleichende Nutzenbewertung und Weiterbildung im Gesundheitswesen), *New England Journal of Medicine* 370, Nr. 8 (2014): 766.

66 ebd. 767.

67 Marilyn C. Morris und Robert M. Nelson, "Randomized, Controlled Trials as Minimal Risk: An Ethical Analysis*," (Randomisierte geregelte Versuche als minimales Risiko) *Critical Care Medicine* 35, Nr. 3 (2007): 943.

68 Gross, *Military Medical Research Ethics: Investigational Drugs, Clinical Trials and Enhancement*, (Ethik in der militärischen medizinischen Forschung: Prüfpräparate, klinische Versuche und Enhancement) 4.

69 D. O. E. Gebhardt, "Off-Label Administration of Drugs to Healthy Military Personnel. Dubious Ethics of Preventive Measures," (Off-Label Vergabe von Arzneistoffen an

Sorgfaltspflicht und stellen potenziell ein hohes Risiko da, sodass eine komplette Einwilligungserklärung (IC) für die Untersuchung erforderlich wird. Das Vereinigte Königreich sollte es den USA nicht gleichtun und Ausnahmen vom IC zulassen, sondern sich an die etablierte Forschungsethik halten. um Kenntnisse zu erhalten, die die Streitkräfte im Rahmen der Sorgfaltspflicht bei Einsätzen besser schützt. Auf diese Weise sollte das Militär Mehlmans Rat befolgen, nämlich dass eine langfristige Periode rigoroser Tests, die nur schrittweise eingeführt werden können, für alle PCEs erforderlich ist.[70]

gesundes Militärpersonal. Zweifelhafte Ethik bei vorbeugenden Maßnahmen) *Journal of Medical Ethics* 31, Nr. 5 (2005): 268.

70 Mehlman, Lin, und Abney, "Enhanced Warfighters: Risk, Ethics, and Policy." (Enhancement von Streitkräften: Risiko, Ethik und Strategie), 65.

KAPITEL 3

Die Zukunft der Einwilligungs-erklärung

Wie informiert und wie konsensuell ist eine Einwilligungserklärung?

Um zu sichern, dass Soldaten wirklich gut informiert sind, müssen ihnen die erwünschten Vorteile, unerwünschten Auswirkungen und Risiken klar gemacht werden und zwar so, dass sie verständlich sind. Das Hauptrisiko der PCEs sind ihre Nebenwirklungen, die von Medikament zu Medikament unterschiedlich sind. PCEs, die sich auf den Körper auswirken, wie anabole Steroide können dauerhafte Leberschäden erzeugen, und Wachstumshormone können zu Verlust des Sehvermögens und Diabetes führen.[1] Aufputschmittel wie Amphetamine verursachen Unruhe, Nervosität, Schlaflosigkeit, Gereiztheit und Übelkeit.[2] Modafinil kann Kopfschmerzen, Magen-Darm-Beschwerden, Schlafstörungen, Depressionen und Selbstmordgedanken erzeugen, die als so wichtig erachtet wurden, dass die Europäische Arzneimittelagentur beschloss, es für viele Erkrankungen nicht mehr verschreiben zu lassen, einschließlich bei Schlafstörungen für Schichtarbeiter.[3]

Die Risiken und der Nutzen müssen wenn immer möglich quantitativ angegeben sein, um die Entscheidungsfindung zu erleichtern, zum Beispiel kann Droge A 20% der Benutzer ein kognitives Enhancement vermitteln, doch 1% von ihnen begehen Selbstmord. Dies führt zu dem Zwiespalt, wer die Entscheidung treffen soll, wann das Risiko-Nutzen-Verhältnis zu hoch ist: das CMA, der Einsatzkommandant oder der Kämpfer? Zieht man zusätzlich das ungekannte Risiko von Tod oder Verwundung während eines Einsatzes hinzu und vergleicht dann, ob ein Soldat ein steigerndes Mittel erhalten hat oder nicht, so wird die Analyse schwierig. Bekannt ist, dass eine erhöhte Wahrscheinlichkeit von Nebenwirkungen die Bereitschaft PCEs einzunehmen,

1 U.S. Anti-Doping Agency, "Effects of Performance-Enhancing Drugs," (Auswirkungen von leistungssteigernden Arzneistoffen) <https://www.usada.org/athletes/substances/effects-of-performance-enhancing-drugs/> (Zugriff: 8. Mai, 2020).

2 Scharre und Fish, "Human Performance Enhancement," (Leistungssteigerung des Menschen) 8.

3 European Medicines Agency, "Modafinil," 2010, <https://www.ema.europa.eu/en/medicines/human/referrals/modafinil>.

 | DOI:10.1163/9789004677746_010

vermindert[4] und obwohl die Verträglichkeit von Nebenwirkungen individuell ist, kann sich dies kollektiv auf den Erfolg des Einsatzes auswirken. Nach Bostrom besteht Einigkeit darüber, dass individuelle Autonomie Vorrang vor geringfügigen medizinischen Risiken haben kann, und dass die geeigneten Personen, die entscheiden, ob die Vorteile die Risiken wert sind, nicht unbedingt medizinische Experten sein müssen.[5]

Ein unerlässlicher Bestandteil des IC ist das Verständnis der Informationen, da jede Person über eine andere Ansicht oder Aufnahmefähigkeit verfügt, vor allem, wenn es um statistische Risiken geht. Der Grad der Aufnahmefähigkeit von Soldaten kann auf Grund ihrer Lese- und Schreibfertigkeiten begrenzt sein; das Militär hat jüngst Rekruten mit einer Lesefertigkeit von nur fünf Jahren aufgenommen, und fast 40% haben die Lese- und Schreibfertigkeit von Elfjährigen.[6] Deshalb kann man junge Soldaten nicht als informiert betrachten, wenn die begrenzte Auffassungsgabe bedeutet, dass sie grundsätzlich nicht verstehen, wofür sie ihre Einwilligung geben.

PCEs sollten reversibel sein, sodass die leistungssteigernden Auswirkungen und die damit verbundenen Risiken beseitigt werden können, wenn die Notwendigkeit nicht mehr besteht, z.B. bei der Rückkehr von einem Einsatz oder der Entlassung aus dem Wehrdienst. Allerdings würden PCEs, die sich auf kognitive Verarbeitung auswirken, wahrscheinlich nicht reversible Effekte mit sich bringen, aufgrund der komplizierten neuronalen Verarbeitung und der Anpassung der Hirnzellen an eine veränderte Neurochemie. Dies wirft Bedenken auf, wenn Angehörige des Militärs dazu gebracht werden, Medikamente ohne Wahlmöglichkeit einzunehmen. Ist das PCE nicht reversibel, wird es sich auf die Gesellschaft auswirken, wenn eine Person mit Enhancement unter ihnen ist.[7] Mehr als die Hälfte der Bevölkerung glaubt, dass PCEs ihren Benutzern einen unfairen Vorteil gewähren, ungeachtet dessen, ob

---

4 Sattler *et al.*, “Evaluating the Drivers of and Obstacles to the Willingness to Use Cognitive Enhancement Drugs: The Influence of Drug Characteristics, Social Environment, and Personal Characteristics.,” (Auswertung der Befürworter und die Hindernisse zur Bereitschaft, PCEs zu benutzen), 9.

5 Bostrom und Sandberg, “Cognitive Enhancement: Methods, Ethics, Regulatory Challenges.,” (Kognitives Enhancement: Methoden, Ethik, regulatorische Herausforderungen), 323.

6 Neil Sears, “Army Signs up Recruits with a Reading Age as Young as FIVE in: Desperate Bid to Boost Troop Numbers,” *The Daily Mail*, 5. April, 2020, <https://www.dailymail.co.uk/news/article-8190009/Army-signs-recruits-reading-age-young-FIVE-desperate-bid-boost-troop-numbers.html>; Katherine Sellgren, “Almost 40% of Army Recruits Have Reading Age of 11, MPs Warn,” *BBC News*, 18. Juli 18, 2013, <https://www.bbc.co.uk/news/education-23346693> (Zugriff: 1. Mai, 2020).

7 Allhoff *et al.*, “Ethics of Human Enhancement: 25 Questions & Answers,” (Ethik des Human Enhancements: 25 Fragen und Antworten), 15.

dies als Betrug gilt oder nicht.[8] Trotzdem kann eine umfassendere Benutzung von PCEs der Gesellschaft dienlich sein, wenn eine erhöhte Produktivität Armut reduziert.[9] Buchanan geht noch einen Schritt weiter und erkennt einen dramatischen positiven Vorteil für die Gesellschaft und die Gesamtwirtschaft aufgrund von Enhancement.[10]

Andere Überlegungen drehen sich um das Risiko der Abhängigkeit und des Missbrauchs; hierzu veröffentlichte eine amerikanische Umfrage 2006, dass 13% der Personen, die Stimulans wie Amphetamine benutzen, die Kriterien für Abhängigkeit oder Missbrauch erfüllen, die Auswirkungen auf die Gesellschaft haben könnten.[11] Unvorhergesehene Konsequenzen der PCEs könnten sich auf den Einzelnen auswirken und die Leistungen solcher, die bereits in gewissen Bereichen Spitzenleistungen hervorbringen, beeinträchtigen, wie man es im Falle von Amphetaminen und Kreativität gesehen hat.[12] Was wäre, wenn Designer-PCEs zu einer selbstzerstörerischen, sogenannten „Black Ball"-Technologie würden, die das Ende der Zivilisation herbeiführten?[13] Man denke an ein kognitives PCE, das das menschliche Verhalten grundsätzlich verändern würde, sodass seine Benutzer nach mehreren Jahren stärker mit Gewalt und Zerstörung reagierten. Wenn der genaue Mechanismus einer Maßnahme und ihre Nebenwirkungen nicht verstanden werden, kann man noch von informierter Einwilligung reden? Doch trotz aller Fortschritte in der Wissenschaft wird ein komplettes Verständnis der Arbeitsweise von PCEs und ihre langfristigen Nebenwirkungen wahrscheinlich nie möglich sein und deshalb können die erstellten Informationen immer nur das weitergeben, was zurzeit bekannt ist und sich zu Lücken und Einschränkungen bekennen.

Katz ist der Meinung, dass Ärzte Langlebigkeit höher bewerten als Lebensqualität, und dass die Medizin, nicht das Gesetz, die Doktrin zum IC festlegen sollten, und dies mit größerer Betonung auf Information als auf

8 Schelle *et al.*, "Attitudes toward Pharmacological Cognitive Enhancement – a Review," (Einstellungen zu PCEs – eine Übersicht).

9 Mohamed, "Neuroethical issues in Pharmacological Cognitive Enhancement," (Neuroethische Fragen zu PCEs), 537.

10 A. E. Buchanan, *"Beyond Humanity: The Ethics of Biochemical Enhancement,"* (Über die Menschheit hinaus?: Die Ethik des biochemischen Enhancement), 537.

11 Larry A. Kroutil *et al.*, "Nonmedical Use of Prescription Stimulants in the United States," (Nichtmedizinische Benutzung von verschreibungspflichtigen Stimulans in den Vereinigten Staaten), *Drug and Alcohol Dependence* 84, Nr. 2 (2006): 140.

12 Martha J. Farah *et al.*, "When We Enhance Cognition with Adderall, Do We Sacrifice Creativity? A Preliminary Study," (Wenn wir Kognition mit Adderall steigern, ist das auf Kosten von Kreativität? Eine Vorstudie.), *Psychopharmacology* 202, Nr. 1 (2009): 541.

13 Nick Bostrom, "The Vulnerable World Hypothesis," (Die Hypothese von der verletzbaren Welt), *Global Policy* 10, Nr. 4 (2019): 455.

Konsens.[14] Tatsächlich aber wollen die Ärzte mit ihrer Offenlegung die rechtliche Haftung für eine angebliche Nichtoffenlegung vermeiden.[15] Wie können Soldaten über PCEs informiert werden, wenn die Ärzte nur sehr ungern ihr Unwissen über Vorteile und Risiken und alternative Behandlungen zugeben und ihre Informationen dann in einer leicht-verdaulichen Version den Patienten vorstellen?[16] Nach Katzs Ermessen ist der höchste Wert auf Autonomie als ultimativen Schutz zu legen, während Wohltätigkeit die Person als krank abstempeln könnte, man weniger Sorgfalt anwenden und die Wahrscheinlichkeit erhöhen könnte, dass dem Arzt die Entscheidung im Namen des Patienten überlassen wird.[17] Er kam zu dem Schluss, dass Ärzte das Ausmaß ihrer wissenschaftlichen Kenntnisse oder ihren Mangel daran zugeben, eine gemeinsame Entscheidungsfindung anstreben und den Patienten gestatten sollten, die endgültige Wahl zu treffen.[18]

Da ein gewisses Maß an Autonomie beim Eintritt in das Militär verloren geht, besteht die Gefahr, dass die Soldaten über die PCE-Anforderungen „informiert" werden, während der Teil der „Einwilligung" umgangen wird.[19] Um sicherzugehen, dass die Anwendung von PCEs für Soldaten konsensuell ist, ist das Belmont-Prinzip der Achtung der Person die Hauptsache, wenn militärische Rekruten als angreifbare Gruppe angesehen werden könnten und gefährdet sind, in Zwangslagen Anweisungen seitens der Befehlskette zu befolgen. Wie bereits beschrieben, erleichtert die Kameradschaft einer Einheit den Gruppendruck auf den Einzelnen, sich einer Reihe gemeinsamer Werte anzupassen und ihn eventuell zu verleiten, PCEs gegen „besseres Wissen" einzunehmen. Wenn es Soldaten direkt befohlen wird, ein PCE zu nehmen, müssten sie, wenn es ein rechtmäßiger Befehl wäre, gehorchen. Es ist jedoch nicht immer der Fall, dass dies für alle rechtmäßigen Befehle möglich ist, da sie durch die Notwendigkeit, andere Vorschriften zu erfüllen, ersetzt werden können, wie zum Beispiel die Genfer Konvention oder das Recht der bewaffneten Konflikte.[20]

---

14 Jay Katz, "Informed Consent – Must It Remain a Fairy Tale," (IC – muss es ein Märchen bleiben?), *Journal of Contemporary Health Law and Policy* 10 (1994): 71.

15 ebd. 77.

16 ebd. 80–83.

17 ebd. 85.

18 ebd. 90–91.

19 Robbins, "Refusing to Be All That You Can Be: Regulating against Forced Cognitive Enhancement in the Military." (Verweigerung alles das zu sein, was du sein kannst: Schutzregulierung des aufgezwungen kognitiven Enhancements im Militär),148.

20 United Kingdom. Development Concepts and Doctrine Centre, (Entwicklungskonzepte und Lehrzentrum), *JSP 383. The Joint Service Manual of the Law of Armed Conflict* (Shrivenham: DCDC, 2004), 13–14, 21–26.

Intelligente Menschen sind fähig, ihre eigenen autonomen Wahlen zu treffen, aber wie liegt der Fall, wenn bestimmte Maßnahmen der gesamten militärischen Einheit zugutekommt? Gibt es Umstände, in denen die persönliche Autonomie auf angemessene Weise geopfert werden muss, um die Sicherheit und somit die Gesundheit der größeren Gruppe zu fördern? Nach Pellegrino fördert dies die Vorbeugung, mittels der der Sozialvertrag den einzelnen Personen auferlegt, ihre „Autonomie für gewisse Vorteile aufzugeben" und dass absolutes „Selbstinteresse mit dem Leben in einer zivilisierten Gemeinschaft unvereinbar ist."[21] Beispiele sind das obligatorische Tragen von Motorradhelmen, um Kopfverletzungen bei Motorradunfällen zu reduzieren, und von Sicherheitsgurten in Fahrzeugen, um ein Polytrauma bei einem Unfall zu vermeiden. Bemerkenswert ist, dass die wirksamsten vorbeugenden Maßnahmen gesetzlich vorgeschrieben sind, statt durch eine einschränkende Wahl.[22] Ähnlich ist es, wenn in gewissem Grade die Autonomie beim Eintritt ins Militär und das vorgeschriebene Tragen von vorbeugender Schutzkleidung, wie Schutzwesten oder feuerfeste Uniformen, aufgegeben wird.

Wenn denn die Einnahme von PCEs die Gesundheit und Überlebensmöglichkeit des Einzelnen und der Gruppe steigern, so sollte sie im Sinne der Gesundheitsvorsorge Pflicht sein und keinen Konsens erfordern. Annas stimmt hier nicht zu; sie glaubt, dass verschreibungspflichtige Medikamente den Soldaten nicht aufgezwungen werden und Militärärzte nicht gezwungen werden sollten, sie zu verschreiben.[23] Wenn Soldaten ein PCE ablehnen, heißt das, dass sie für Einsätze nicht zu gebrauchen sind und somit ihre zukünftigen Karriereoptionen einschränken? Verweigert ein Soldat die medizinische Versorgung, die seine Gesundheit oder die anderer im aktiven Dienst erhält, kann dies als Disziplinarvergehen gewertet werden. Verweigert ein Soldat die medizinische Versorgung, die seine Gesundheit oder die anderer im aktiven Dienst erhält, kann dies als Disziplinarvergehen gewertet werden.[24] Ablehnung anderer Arten von medizinischer Versorgung wird an den ärztlichen Beirat geleitet, um festzustellen, ob diese Ablehnung angemessen

21 Edmund D. Pellegrino, "Autonomy and Coercion in Disease Prevention and Health Promotion," (Autonomie und Zwangsmittel bei der vorbeugenden Medizin und der Gesundheitsförderung), *Theoretical Medicine* 5, Nr. 1 (1984): 88.

22 ebd. 90.

23 Catherine L. Annas und George J. Annas, "Enhancing the Fighting Force: Medical Research on American Soldiers," (Enhancement der Streitkraft: Medizinische Forschung an amerikanischen Soldaten), *Journal of Contemporary Health Law and Policy* 25, Nr. 2 (2009): 308.

24 Annas, "Changing the Consent Rules for Desert Storm," (Änderung der IC-Regeln für Desert Storm), 772.

ist oder nicht.[25] Der Ausschuss entscheidet, ob die medizinische Versorgung erforderlich ist, um die Gesundheit des Soldaten oder die Gesundheit anderer zu schützen oder ihm die ordnungsgemäße Erfüllung seiner Pflicht zu ermöglichen. Kommt man zu dem Schluss, dass diese Behandlung erforderlich ist, wird der Soldat einem Disziplinarverfahren unterzogen oder aus dem Dienst entlassen.[26] Robbins denkt, dass die Verantwortung bei den Soldaten liegt, die das Recht haben sollten, abzulehnen, ohne dass dies seine Freiheit beeinträchtigt.[27] Wenn ein Soldat sich vor dem Einsatz weigert, kann eine andere Person seinen Platz einnehmen, aber eine Ablehnung auf dem Schlachtfeld würde andere in Gefahr bringen. Es ist deutlich, dass es eine Politik geben muss, die die Vorschriften und Richtlinien von PCEs festlegt, die, wo immer möglich, einen einvernehmlichen Ansatz beinhalten und eine akute Situation der Ablehnung während des Konflikts vermeiden sollte.

Da PCEs Medikamente sind, die von einem zugelassenen Arzt verschrieben werden müssen, könnte ein Militärarzt entscheiden, dass der Nutzen der Anwendung von PCEs für den Einzelnen oder das im Einsatz befindliche Team die Einholung einer Zustimmung überflüssig macht, ungeachtet der informierten Komponente? Dies lenkt die Aufmerksamkeit auf die Frage, ob Militärärzte nur Ärzte sind, oder auch Offiziere, oder beides, und welche von beiden Kompetenzen den Vorrang hat. Für Annas ist die Antwort klar: der Militärarzt sollte „zuerst, zuletzt und immer Arzt sein."[28] Medizinische Ethik sollte sich für einen Arzt, ob im militärischen oder zivilen Bereich, ob im Frieden oder im Krieg, nie ändern, aber es gab historische Umstände, unter denen Variationen von normalen medizinischen ethischen Verpflichtungen scheinbar gerechtfertigt waren. Während des 2. Weltkrieges wurden Kämpfer mit Geschlechtskrankheiten vorrangig vor den Verwundeten mit Penicillin versorgt, da erstere schneller an die Front zurückkehren konnten, und in jüngerer Zeit wurde geraten, stimmungsstabilisierende Mittel zu verschreiben,

25 Robbins, "Refusing to Be All That You Can Be: Regulating against Forced Cognitive Enhancement in the Military," (Verweigerung alles das zu sein, was du sein kannst: Schutzregulierung des aufgezwungen kognitiven Enhancements im Militär), 129.

26 ebd. 130.

27 Robbins, "Refusing to Be All That You Can Be: Regulating against Forced Cognitive Enhancement in the Military," (Verweigerung alles das zu sein, was du sein kannst: Schutzregulierung des aufgezwungen kognitiven Enhancements im Militär), 134.

28 George J. Annas, "Military Medical Ethics – Physician First, Last, Always," (Militärische medizinische Ethik – Arzt zuerst, zuletzt, immer), *New England Journal of Medicine* 359, Nr. 11 (2008): 1090.

um sicherzustellen, dass Soldaten auf die Schlachtfelder vom Irak oder von Afghanistan zurückkehren.[29]

Der Rollenkonflikt, beides, sowohl Soldat als auch Arzt zu sein, verursacht ein Dilemma der zweifachen Loyalität gegenüber beiden Berufen. Dies ist leicht zu lösen, wenn internationale Richtlinien befolgt werden, wie die des Weltärztebundes (World Medical Association), die besagen, dass während eines bewaffneten Konflikts es die erste Pflicht des Arztes ist, dem Patienten zu helfen, und die der Genfer Konvention, die besagt, dass die medizinische Behandlung aus medizinischen Gründen und im Einklang mit der medizinischen Ethik erfolgen soll.[30] Beide Richtlinien weisen potenzielle Schwachstellen auf. PCEs sind keine Behandlungen aus medizinischen Gründen, und die wichtigste Pflicht dem Patienten gegenüber könnte es sein, den Einsatz von PCEs zu seinem eigenen Schutz zu erzwingen. Es bestehen jedoch Bedenken, dass, wenn die militärische Notwendigkeit den Gebrauch von PCEs erzwingt, die Prinzipien und Ethik des Arztes außer Kraft gesetzt werden und dass potenziell ein Missbrauch möglich ist.[31]

Die professionelle Verantwortung eines Arztes besteht der Gesellschaft gegenüber, der er dient, und dieser Verantwortungsbereich wird sowohl vom Berufsstand als auch von unabhängigen Aufsichtsbehörden bestimmt.[32] Für einen Militärarzt schließt dies Vorschriften von der Ärztekammer (General Medical Council), der Fakultät für Fachmedizin (medical specialty professional college) und dem entsprechenden Dienst ein.[33]

---

29 ebd. 1088.

30 Daniel Messelken and Hans Ulrich Baer, "Hovering Between Roles: Military Medical Ethics," (Schweben zwischen den rollen: Militärische medizinische Ethik), in *Military Medical Ethics for the 21st Century*, Hsg. M. L. Gross und D. Carrick, Military and Defence Ethics (Farnham: Ashgate Publishing Limited, 2013), 268.

31 ebd. 270.

32 Dan W. Brock, "Conscientious Refusal by Physicians and Pharmacists: Who Is Obligated to Do What, and Why?," (Weigerungen aus Gewissensgründen von Ärzten und Apothekern: Wer ist verpflichtet was zu tun und warum?) *Theoretical Medicine and Bioethics* 29, Nr. 3 (2008): 193.

33 Examples of these regulations are General Medical Council, "Good Medical Practice," (Beispiele dieser Regeln sind General Medical Council, "Gute medizinische Praxis") 2019, <https://www.gmc-uk.org/ethical-guidance/ethical-guidance-for-doctors/good-medical-practice>, The Royal College of Anaesthetists, "Guidelines for the Provision of Anaesthetic Services,"(Richtlinien für die Erstellung von Anästhetikum-Dienste), 2020, <https://www.rcoa.ac.uk/safety-standards-quality/guidance-resources/guidelines-provision-anaesthetic-services>, United Kingdom. Ministry of Defence, *The Queen's Regulations for the Army 1975. AC13206,* (London: Ministry of Defence, 2019), <https://assets.publishing.service.gov.uk/government/uploads/system/uploads/attachment_data/file/826092/The_Queen_s_Regulations_for_the_Army_1975.pdf> (Zugriff: 6. April, 2020).

Es gibt kein definitives Verfahren, um irgendwelche Konflikte zwischen diesen unterschiedlichen Aufsichtsbehörden zu lösen.[34] Ist der Militärarzt vor allem zuerst ein Offizier, der gesetzmäßige Befehle geben und ihnen gehorchen muss, oder ein Arzt, dessen Hauptanliegen das Wohl des Patienten ist? Cantor schlägt vor, dass Ärzte ihre Pflicht zu tun haben, ungeachtet ihrer Einstellungen, aber dies galt für Kriegsdienstverweigerung aus Gewissensgründen, und bedeutete, die Pflicht eines Arztes setzt alles andere außer Kraft.[35] Die Nürnberger Prozesse wiesen nach, dass es keine Rechtfertigung ist, einem eines Befehls zu gehorchen, der gegen den eigenen Moralkodex verstößt.[36] Im Gegensatz dazu ist Mehlman, nicht der Meinung, dass Militärärzte, die medizinische Ethik und moralische Pflichten befolgen, dies über ihre militärischen Pflichten setzen können, und er ist der Ansicht, dass sie das biomedizinische Risiko den Entscheidungsträgern darlegen und die Absichten ihrer Kommandeure energisch in Frage stellen sollten.[37]

Ärzte können nur medizinische Handlungen unterstützen, die die Gesundheit fördern und wiederherstellen, das wird von ihnen erwartet, und sie sind nicht verpflichtet, nichtmedizinische Dienstleistungen zu erstellen. Letzteres wird von Gamble unterstützt, der betont: „Soldaten, die freiwillig dem Militär beitreten, können nicht einfach verpflichtet werden, für alle Aufgaben, die in ihr erworbenes Wissen fallen, zuständig zu sein, und dies sollte auch für Ärzte gelten."[38] Wenn die Verschreibung eines PCEs einen gesundheitlichen Vorteil mit sich bringt, so wäre das eine medizinische Handlung, aber wenn es verschrieben wird, ohne dass Symptome oder eine Krankheit vorliegen,

---

34 Nathan K. Gamble und Michal Pruski, "Medical Acts and Conscientious Objection: What Can a Physician Be Compelled to Do?," (Medizinische Handlungen und Kriegsverweigerung: Wozu kann man einen Arzt zwingen?) *The New Bioethics* 25, Nr. 3 (2019): 263.

35 Julie D. Cantor, "Conscientious Objection Gone Awry – Restoring Selfless Professionalism in Medicine," (Wenn die Kriegsverweigerung schief läuft – Wiederherstellung des selbstlosen Professionalismus in der Medizin), *New England Journal of Medicine* 360, Nr. 15 (2009): 1485.

36 Harvard Law School Library, "Nuremberg – Transcript Viewer – Transcript for NMT 1: *Medical Case*," (Nürnberg – Protokollansicht – Protokoll für NMT 1: Medizinischer Fall) *Nuremberg Trials Project*, 2016, <http://nuremberg.law.harvard.edu/transcripts/1-transcript-for-nmt-1-medical-case?seq=2586> (Zugriff: 11. März, 2020).

37 Mehlman und Corley, "A Framework for Military Bioethics," (Ein Rahmen für militärische Bioethik) 345.

38 Gamble und Pruski, "Medical Acts and Conscientious Objection: What Can a Physician Be Compelled to Do?" (Medizinische Handlungen und Kriegsverweigerung: Wozu kann man einen Arzt zwingen?) 268.

sondern aus rein militärischen Gründen, so stellt dies eine sozialklinische Handlung dar, beschrieben von Gamble als Verfahren für soziale Anliegen, wie z.B. Schönheitschirurgie.[39] Diese Arbeit hat PCEs als ein Enhancement und nicht als eine Behandlung geschildert, folglich ist ihre Verschreibung ein sozialklinischer Akt, und Gamble ist der Meinung, dass Militärärzte nicht verpflichtet sein sollten, ihn zu unterstützen.

Gegenwärtig steht keine schriftliche Richtlinie zur Verfügung, die sich zu dem Thema äußert, ob es einem Militärarzt befohlen werden kann, ein Medikament, das er als unethisch erachtet, zu verschreiben. Eine Ausnahme könnte gemacht werden, wenn es für Notfälle auf dem Schlachtfeld therapeutisch sein könnte. Diese ethische Abweichung kann dem Patienten Schaden zufügen, wie man sah, als ein Blutgerinnungshemmer gegeben wurde, um Leben bei einem Polytrauma zu retten. Es wurde von hochrangigen Sanitätsoffizieren befohlen, obwohl die Untersuchungen bezüglich seiner Auswirkungen noch nicht beendet waren. Weitere Untersuchungen wiesen nach, dass sein Einsatz zu unnötigen Todesfällen geführt hatte und selbst damals im Jahre 2006 Ärzten im Lazarett in Bagdad Sorgen bereiteten: „Ich befürchte, dass einige Soldaten aufgrund von übereifriger Anwendung unerprobter Therapien zu Schaden kamen."[40] Die Auswirkungen werden noch verstärkt, wenn ein Soldat zwar die medizinische Standardbehandlung akzeptieren muss oder mit Disziplinarmaßnahmen rechnen muss, aber nicht verpflichtet ist, Eingriffe zu akzeptieren, die von der Ärzteschaft nicht als Standardverfahren anerkannt sind.[41] Ähnlich wie in der Sache mit den PCEs war die Anwendung von Blutgerinnungsmitteln kein Standardverfahren und hätte nur mit einer Einwilligungserklärung verabreicht werden dürfen oder, in Notfällen und ohne Zustimmung, hätte es einer bekannten allgemein akzeptierten Risiko-Vorteil-Analyse unterzogen werden müssen.

39 ebd. 275.

40 Robert Little, "Army Medicine: Untested in Battle," (Militärmedizin: Nicht im Kampf erprobt) *The Baltimore Sun*, 29. März, 2009, <https://www.baltimoresun.com/news/nation-world/bal-te.militarymed29mar29-story.html> (Zugriff: 30. März, 2020).

41 Annas, "Protecting Soldiers from Friendly Fire: The Consent Requirement for Using Investigational Drugs and Vaccines in Combat.," (Schutz für Soldaten vor Eigenbeschuss: Die Einwilligungserklärung für den Gebrauch von Prüfpräparaten und Impfstoffen im Kampf) 257.

Die Übermittlung einer wirksamen militärischen Einwilligungserklärung

Dieser letzte Abschnitt dieser Arbeit untersucht die praktischen Aspekte einer militärischen Einwilligungserklärung (IC), bespricht wie und wann sie gegeben werden soll, um die informierten und einwilligenden Bestandteile zu optimieren, sowie den Strategierahmen zur Förderung der Anwendung von PCEs. IC muss von effektiver Kommunikation zwischen der informierenden und der einwilligenden Person unterstützt werden. Im 1. Golfkrieg von 1991 war die Anthrax-Impfung (Milzbrandimpfung) keine Pflicht, aber wurde dennoch mit stillschweigender Einwilligung verabreicht.[42] Später meldeten Kriegsveteranen häufigere Gesundheitsschäden, für die viele die Anthrax-Impfung verantwortlich machten, was zu Furcht und Misstrauen der militärischen Einrichtung gegenüber führte. Um diesem im Irak-Krieg von 2003 entgegenzuwirken, wurde die ausdrückliche Einwilligung verwendet, zusammen mit einem Informationsprogramm, bestehend aus schriftlichen Dokumenten, verbaler Aufklärung und Videoaufnahmen. Es wurde eine Bedenkzeit eingeräumt, bevor man eine Einwilligungserklärung unterschrieb, um den IC-Prozess zu erhärten.[43] Trotzdem verweigerte mehr als die Hälfte des britischen Militärs das Anthrax-Impfprogramm.[44] Eine Umfrage unter den im Irak-Krieg 2003 eingesetzten Soldaten ergab, dass die Bedenken hinsichtlich der Sicherheit, der Wirksamkeit und des IC im Vordergrund standen.[45] Trotz aller Information und Kommunikation verfehlte das Programm eine ausgeglichene Ansicht und konnte die Besorgnis, dass die Impfung vielleicht nicht wirkungsvoll sei und zukünftige Krankheiten verursachen könnte, nicht wegräumen.[46] Man konnte nicht verstehen, warum das Impfprogramm jetzt freiwillig war und IC erforderte, wenn es doch zuvor Pflicht war. Dies führte zu

---

42 Dominic Murphy *et al.*, "UK Armed Forces Responses to an Informed Consent Policy for Anthrax Vaccination: A Paradoxical Effect?," (Die Reaktion der britischen Streitkräfte zu einer IC-Strategie für ein Anthrax-Impfprogramm: eine paradoxe Auswirkung?), *Vaccine* 24, Nr. 16 (2006): 3109.

43 ebd. 3110.

44 Cathel Kerr, "Anthrax Vaccine Gets Cold Shoulder from Troops," (Soldaten zeigen dem Anthrax-Impfprogramm sie kalte Schulter), *Canadian Medical Association Journal* 168, Nr. 10 (2003): 1308.

45 Murphy *et al.*, "UK Armed Forces Responses to an Informed Consent Policy for Anthrax Vaccination: A Paradoxical Effect?," (Die Reaktion der britischen Streitkräfte zu einer IC-Strategie für ein Anthrax-Impfprogramm: eine paradoxe Auswirkung?), 3111.

46 Dominic Murphy, Neil Greenberg, und Duncan Bland, "Health Concerns in UK Armed Forces Personnel," (Gesundheitsbedenken beim Personal des britischen Militärs), *Journal of the Royal Society of Medicine* 102, Nr. 4 (2009): 144.

einem Vertrauensverlust in das Verteidigungsministerium, dem man zutraute, schädliche Nebenwirkungen unter den Teppich zu kehren. Das Resultat war, dass IC vielleicht aus ethischen oder legalen Gründen wünschenswert ist, aber nicht unbedingt zu dem erwarteten positiven Effekt führt.[47] Deshalb wird eine IC-Strategie für PCEs, die Besorgnis erhöht und die Akzeptanz reduziert, ihr Ziel nicht erreichen.

Die Kommunikationsmethode für IC ist von äußerster Wichtigkeit, um zu bestätigen, dass das Individuum voll informiert ist, vor allen Dingen auch die Risiken zur Kenntnis genommen hat und freiwillig seine Einwilligung gab. Man kann von der Art und Weise lernen, wie öffentliche Gesundheitsbehörden Risikoinformationen verbreiten, wobei die Kommunikation das allgemeine Ziel verfolgt, die Informationen so zu präsentieren, dass sie verständlich und verwertbar sind, sodass der Einzelne das Risiko beurteilen kann und aktiv vom Informanten unterstützt wird.[48] Nicholson betonte, dass Risiken mündlich zu besprechen sind, und das in einer verständlichen Sprache und auf einfühlweise Weise, offen und ehrlich und kompetent.[49] Außerdem bemerkte er, dass legere Kleidung eine effektive Kommunikation besonders fördert. Dies könnte ein wichtiger Punkt für das Militär sein, wo das Tragen der Uniform die Differenzen in der Rangstufen besonders deutlich macht und potenziell als Zwangsmittel angesehen wird.

Die Weltgesundheitsorganisation nahm zur Kenntnis, dass die öffentliche Wahrnehmung von Informationen sich verlagert hat. Das Vertrauen in Aussagen von Experten und Behörden ist gesunken, und die Menschen nutzen zunehmend Online-Quellen und soziale Medien, um sich Rat zu holen, unter Bevorzugung von auf Meinungen basierten Informationen anstelle solcher, die nachweisbar sind.[50] Der Schlüssel zu dem Dilemma ist, Vertrauen aufzubauen, und glücklicherweise sind Ärzte diejenigen, denen die Öffentlichkeit am meisten Vertrauen schenkt,[51] folglich sollten sie statt der nichtmedizinischen Beamten des Verteidigungsministeriums diese Informationen verbreiten. Eine Überfrachtung mit Informationen kann das Verständnis behindern,

47 Murphy *et al.*, "UK Armed Forces Responses to an Informed Consent Policy for Anthrax Vaccination: A Paradoxical Effect?," (Die Reaktion der britischen Streitkräfte zu einer IC-Strategie für ein Anthrax-Impfprogramm: eine paradoxe Auswirkung?).

48 P. J. Nicholson, "Communicating Health Risk," (Kommunikation von Gesundheitsrisiken), *Occupational Medicine* 49, Nr. 4 (1999): 253.

49 ebd. 254.

50 World Health Organisation, "An Introduction to Risk Communication," (Eine Einführung in die Risikokommunikation), 1, <https://www.who.int/risk-communication/introduction-to-risk-communication.pdf?ua=1>, (Zugriff: 12. März, 2020).

51 Nicholson, "Communicating Health Risk," (Kommunikation von Gesundheitsrisiken) 254.

deshalb sollten sie zu mehreren Anlässen geliefert werden, wobei jedes Mal einige zentrale Botschaften und Fakten vermittelt werden, die auf dem zuvor Gesagten aufbauen. Im Laufe der Zeit werden neue Informationen ins Spiel gebracht und sollten so schnell wie möglich weitergegeben werden, um den IC zu erhalten.[52]

Für Soldaten, die eine militärische Laufbahn einschlagen, sollte sowohl eine weitgehende Einwilligung als auch IC für zukünftige Benutzung von PCEs vorhanden sein. Der weitgehende Konsens an sich läuft Gefahr, ausgenutzt zu werden, wie es bei dem Indianerstamm der Havasupai gesehen werden konnte. Diese unterzeichneten einen weitgehenden Konsens für die Diabetesforschung, die dann für breitere Zwecke benutzt wurde, zu der sie, hätten sie es denn gewusst, ihre Einwilligung nicht gegeben hätten.[53] Der Stamm galt als eine besonders gefährdete Bevölkerung, vielleicht nicht ungleich neuer Rekruten zum Militär. Ein weitgehender Konsens könnte verbessert werden, wenn es ungefähre Grenzen gäbe, für das, was damit abgedeckt werden könnte, aber dies verlagert die Verantwortung für die Sorgfaltspflicht auf die Befehlskette. Die breite Zustimmung würde verbessert, wenn es ungefähre Grenzen dafür gäbe, was damit abgedeckt werden könnte, aber dies verlagert die Verantwortung für die Sorgfaltspflicht auf die Befehlskette. Grundsätzlich sollte jedoch für jeden Rekruten beim Beitritt ins Militär eine umfassende Zustimmung zur potenziellen künftigen Verwendung von PCE unternommen werden, dieser sollte dann die Möglichkeit haben, sich dagegen zu entscheiden und den Dienst zu diesem Zeitpunkt zu verlassen. Diese breite Zustimmung sollte bei jeder Beförderung und bei jeder Änderung oder Verlängerung der Dienstzeit wiederholt werden. Diese Wiederholung gleicht die Häufigkeit aus und vermeidet, Verfahren mechanisch abzuhaken. Vor allem aber trägt sie der Tatsache Rechnung, dass der Einzelne im Laufe seiner Entwicklung vom neuen Rekruten zum ausgebildeten Soldaten heranreift und im Laufe seiner Karriere Lebens- und Militärerfahrung sammelt, die sein Verständnis und seine Einstellung zum Risiko verändert.[54]

Ein kompletter IC mit allen spezifischen Details sollte sofort vorgenommen werden, wenn ein Soldat einer Einheit, die PCEs für den Erfolg von Einsätzen

52 Mahmood Adil, "Risk Communication in Healthcare: An Overview," (Risikokommunikation im Gesundheitswesen: Eine Übersicht), *Journal of Communication in Healthcare* 1, Nr. 4 (2008): 365.

53 Beauchamp, "Informed Consent: Its History, Meaning, and Present Challenges.," (IC: Seine Geschichte, Bedeutung und derzeitigen Herausforderungen), 521.

54 Thomas Dohmen *et al.*, "Risk Attitudes across the Life Course," (Einstellungen zu Risiken im Laufe eines Lebens), *The Economic Journal* 127, Nr. 605 (2017): F114.

erfordert, beitritt und dann als Teil der einsatzvorbereitenden Ausbildung (PDT) wiederholt werden. Beide Konsensformen räumen rechtzeitige Zeitpunkte ein, zu denen man seine Zustimmung für den Gebrauch eines PCE verweigern kann; die PDT ist der letzte Moment, an dem eine Verweigerung noch möglich ist. Ist man einmal in einer Einsatzumgebung eingesetzt, in der PCEs als kritisch für den Erfolg des Einsatzes identifiziert wurde, kann ein Teammitglied, das kein leistungssteigerndes Mittel eingenommen hat, das Risiko für sich selbst und die Einheit erhöhen und eine Gefährdung darstellen. In diesem Fall sollte der Konsens umgangen und der Soldat verpflichtet werden, das PCE zu nehmen. Werden Soldaten aus Forschungsgründen rekrutiert, so ist, um einer Ausbeutung vorzubeugen, ein IC in ausführlicherer Form und im Einklang mit dem Belmont-Report und der MODREC-Zulassung vorgeschrieben.

Um jeglichen Aspekt des Zwangs zu vermeiden und ein Vertrauensverhältnis zu erhalten, sollten die IC-Informationen in einer geeigneten Umgebung von einem Arzt, der in Risikokommunikation geschult ist, mitgeteilt werden, jemand, der sich mit dem aktuellen Stand der PCEs auskennt, am besten nicht uniformiert und ohne Anwesenheit von Vorgesetzten.[55] Man sollte zu Fragen aufmuntern und Hintergrundinformationen in allen Formen der Medien zur Verfügung stellen, mit einer Liste von häufig gestellten Fragen und ihren Antworten, auf die der Zugriff im Internet und im Intranet des Verteidigungsministeriums unkompliziert ist. Durch die Einbeziehung der Befehlskette können Soldaten sogar zum Teil ihre Autonomie zurückgewinnen, da sie die Kontrolle über die Zeitplanung und die Art der Durchführung der PCE erhalten.

Sollte es ein unterzeichnetes Formular für PCEs geben, auch wenn für andere Medikament-Verschreibungen eine stillschweigende Einwilligung benutzt wird?[56] Eine unterschriebene Einwilligung bedeutet nicht unbedingt, dass ein IC vorhanden ist und dass jedes Risiko vollständig offengelegt wurde, oder nur die bekannten Vorteile oder ein minimal mitgeteiltes Wissen. Welche Informationen auch immer vom Arzt mitgeteilt werden, sie müssen im Einklang mit seinen professionellen Richtlinien wahrheitsgemäß sein. Wie jedoch bereits besprochen, beschönigen Ärzte oftmals Bereiche, in denen ihr Wissen sich in Grenzen hält oder über die die Fakten noch unbekannt sind, und dies muss überwunden werden. Trotzdem ist ein unterzeichnetes Formular ein Nachweis eines dokumentierten Treffens, es könnte die Informationsbereiche, die besprochen wurden, hervorheben und bietet dem Militärarzt Schutz als

55 McManus *et al.*, "Informed Consent and Ethical Issues in Military Medical Research." (IC und ethische Fragen in militärischer medizinischer Forschung), 1122.

56 Beauchamp, "Informed Consent: Its History, Meaning, and Present Challenges," (IC: Seine Geschichte, Bedeutung und derzeitigen Herausforderungen) 517.

Grundlage für eine rechtliche Verteidigung, falls eine Beschwerde erhoben wird.[57] Alles in allem sollte ein unterschriebenes IC-Formular für Soldaten, die PCEs akzeptieren, aus Gründen der Transparenz und Rechenschaftspflicht verwendet werden und als Teil ihrer medizinischen Unterlagen sicher gespeichert werden.

Selbstverständlich müssen Richtlinien mit Hinsicht auf die Verwendung von PCEs eingeführt werden, einschließlich aller rechtlichen Aspekte, z.B. wer ist verantwortlich, wenn eine falsche Dosis verabreicht wird. Ist es der Arzt, die Person, der Befehlshaber oder der Hersteller? Maslen weist darauf hin, dass eine wirklich informierte und ethische Politik nur dann möglich ist, wenn der persönliche Nutzen und die vollen Risiken von Enhancement bekannt sind.[58] Da eine solch komplette Information vielleicht nie vorhanden ist, so sollte die Ausgangsbasis einer jeden Politik die vier Komponenten für ethische Entscheidungsfindung bei der Verwendung von PCEs beinhalten. Diese werden vom amerikanischen flugmedzinischen Forschungslabor (US Army Aeromedical Research Laboratory) wie folgend beschrieben:[59]

i. Der Gebrauch ist freiwillig.
ii. Das Medikament ist für die vorgesehene Anwendung sicher.
iii. Dosierung und Anwendung entsprechen seiner Funktion.
iv. Zuvor wurden alternative nicht-pharmakologische Mittel untersucht.

Dies steht im Einklang mit Mehlmans angepassten Belmont-Prinzipien der Verhältnismäßigkeit, der staatlichen Bevormundung und der Fairness sowie seinem zuvor veröffentlichten hybriden Rahmenwerk, das sich mit den umfassenderen Fragen der Transparenz gegenüber der Öffentlichkeit und der Rechenschaftspflicht derjenigen befasst, die die Entscheidungen der Notwendigkeit treffen.[60]

57 ebd. 519.
58 Maslen, Faulmüller, and Savulescu, "Pharmacological Cognitive Enhancement – How Neuroscientific Research Could Advance Ethical Debate," (PCE – wie neurowissenschaftliche Forschung die ethische Debatte fördern könnte), 8.
59 Scharre and Fish, "Human Performance Enhancement," 10.
60 Mehlman, Lin, und Abney, "Enhanced Warfighters: Risk, Ethics, and Policy." (Enhancement für Streitkämpfer: Risiko, Ethik und Strategie), 75–76.

Schlussfolgerung

Das Potenzial für Human Enhancement ist bereits vorhanden, und das Vereinigte Königreich muss die Anwendung von PCEs in Betracht ziehen, entweder mit einem positiven Entschluss, in diese Technologie zu investieren, oder zwangsmäßig, um den Gegnern in einem Konflikt gleich stark begegnen zu können. Dieses Thema verdient kritische Aufmerksamkeit, da wir uns in relativen Friedenszeiten befinden, denn während Kriegszeiten oder eines Konflikts ist es sehr viel schwieriger, eine rationale und rigorose Debatte darüber zu führen. In welche Richtung das Vereinigte Königreich auch geht, es scheint sinnvoll, Annas Rat für Militärärzte zu befolgen und eine eindeutige Politik zu verfolgen, die auf traditioneller Ethik beruht, gemäß der die medizinische Versorgung des Einzelnen vorrangig ist.[1] PCEs sollten nicht als medizinische Behandlung angesehen werden, sondern als eine Gruppe von Medikamenten, die nur von einem zugelassenen Arzt verschrieben werden können und die die Fähigkeit der Streitkräfte über das Normalmaß hinaus steigern.

Diese Arbeit stimmt mit Gross's Aussage überein, dass „militärische Ethik nur die informierte Einwilligung *gestattet.*"[2] Deshalb erfordert die Nutzung von PCEs im Militär ein IC-Verfahren, um den Einzelnen zu schützen, der im Gegensatz zu seinem zivilen Pendant einen Teil seiner Autonomie beim Beitritt in das Militär aufgegeben hat und der einem Gruppendruck, unbeabsichtigten und vorsätzlichen Zwangsmaßnahmen seitens seiner Befehlshaber ausgesetzt ist. In der Vergangenheit hat das Militär mit Bezug auf IC versagt und Soldaten ausgenutzt, und damit tatsächliche und potenzielle Schäden verursacht. Deshalb ist ein überarbeitetes IC-Verfahren, das sich an den derzeitigen zivilen Verfahren orientiert, unbedingt erforderlich.

Eine Einwilligung kann nur als informiert gelten, wenn die Risiken, die Vorteile und die Dauer von Nebenwirkungen genügend verstanden und diese dem Empfänger dieser Informationen so vermittelt werden, wie es seinen geistigen Fähigkeiten entspricht, um sicherzugehen, dass er voll im Bilde ist. Viel von diesem Fachwissen wird aus neuen Untersuchungen stammen, und da die Forschungspopulation wahrscheinlich dem Militär angehört, sollte der IC für Enhancement wie im Belmont-Bericht beschrieben befolgt werden, zusammen

1 Annas, "Protecting Soldiers from Friendly Fire: The Consent Requirement for Using Investigational Drugs and Vaccines in Combat," (Schutz für Soldaten vor Eigenbeschuss: Die Einwilligungserklärung für den Gebrauch von Prüfpräparaten und Impfstoffen im Kampf), 275.

2 Gross, *Bioethics and Armed Conflict. Moral Dilemmas of Medicine and War.*, (Bioethik und bewaffneter Konflikt. Moralische Dilemmas in der Medizin und der Kriegsführung), 107.

 | DOI:10.1163/9789004677746_011

mit der etablierten MODREC-Zulassung, die die Rechte der Militärangehörigen schützt. Wenn nicht genügend Fachwissen vorhanden ist, müssen Ärzte das Vertrauen aufrechterhalten, indem sie ehrlich sind und etwaige Lücken oder Einschränkungen zugeben.

Um zu gewährleisten, dass PCEs weiterhin einem Konsens unterstehen, muss es gestattet sein, auszusteigen, ohne dass mit einem Disziplinarverfahren gedroht wird, und jegliche Auswirkungen auf einen Karriereanstieg müssen mit einer frühzeitigen Offenlegung so gering wie möglich gehalten werden. Selbst wenn zuvor eine Einwilligung gegeben wurde, sollte die Verweigerung, PCEs zu irgendeinem Zeitpunkt vor einem Einsatz zu nehmen, unbeschadet akzeptiert werden. Wenn jedoch ein Einsatz begonnen hat, könnte die Benutzung von PCEs befohlen werden. Die Rechtfertigung für diese nicht einvernehmliche Verwendung ist, dass es im Interesse der Einheit, des Einsatzes oder des Staates ist, die die Rechte des Einzelnen außer Kraft zu setzen.[3] Der Bereich der unvorhergesehenen Folgen von PCEs bleibt problematisch, da sie eventuell jahrelang nicht bekannt werden, und wer entscheidet, dass die Risiken von PCEs für den Erfolg des Einsatzes wesentlich sind und die Vorteile überwiegen?

Das IC-Verfahren für die Anwendung von PCE im Militär sollte durch eine Politik und die akzeptierte Denkweise untermauert sein, dass IC ein laufender Prozess ist und keine einmalige Angelegenheit. Dieser Prozess kann mit einer breiten Zustimmung beim Beitritt in die Streitkräfte beginnen, die bei jeder Beförderung und Laufbahnverlängerung oder wenn neue wichtige Kenntnisse ans Licht kommen, wiederholt wird. Wie diese Arbeit es definierte, sollte dieser Konsens beim Beitritt in eine militärische Einheit, deren Einsätze wahrscheinlich PCEs erfordern, mit einem vollständigen IC verstärkt werden, und dann noch einmal während der Vorbereitung auf den Einsatz. Für das IC, nicht aber für den weitgehenden Konsens, sollte eine Unterschrift erforderlich sein, und die Informationen sollten von einem Militärarzt mitgeteilt werden, der in Risiko-Kommunikation geschult ist, in einer Umgebung, die Rangunterschiede so gering wie möglich hält und somit ein einvernehmliches Herangehen erleichtert und jeglichen Zwang vermeidet. Der Online-Zugriff auf Hintergrundinformationen und über alle anderen Medien muss frei zugänglich sein. Wenn das Militär diese Methode des IC anwendet, so gewährt es den Personen, denen PCEs verabreicht werden, den besten Schutz, indem es ein Gleichgewicht zwischen Verhältnismäßigkeit, Bevormundung

3 Mehlman, Lin, and Abney, "Enhanced Warfighters: Risk, Ethics, and Policy," (Enhancement für Streitkämpfer: Risiko, Ethik und Strategie), 58.

und Fairness gewährleistet. Hinzu schützt es die verordnenden Militärärzte vor Fahrlässigkeit und schützt die Befehlshaber durch Transparenz und Rechenschaftspflicht.

Bibliographie

Adil, Mahmood. "Risk Communication in Healthcare: An Overview." *Journal of Communication in Healthcare* 1, Nr. 4 (2008): 363–72. DOI: 10.1179/cih.2008.1.4.363.

Advisory Committee on Human Radiation Experiments. "Executive Summary and Guide to Final Report," 1995. <https://www.osti.gov/opennet/servlets/purl/120931/120931.pdf> (Zugriff: 9. Januar, 2020).

Allhoff, Fritz, Lin Patrick, Moor James, and Weckert John. "Ethics of Human Enhancement: 25 Questions & Answers." *Studies in Ethics, Law, and Technology* 4, Nr. 1 (2010) 1–39. DOI: 10.2202/1941-6008.1110.

Allison, Lincoln. "Faster, Stronger, Higher." *The Guardian*, August 9, 2004, <https://www.theguardian.com/sport/2004/aug/09/athensolympics2004.olympicgames> (Zugriff: 1. April, 2020).

Annas, Catherine L., and George J. Annas. "Enhancing the Fighting Force: Medical Research on American Soldiers." *Journal of Contemporary Health Law and Policy* 25, Nr. 2 (2009): 283–308.

Annas, George J. "Changing the Consent Rules for Desert Storm." *New England Journal of Medicine* 326, Nr. 11 (1992): 770–73. DOI: 10.1056/NEJM199203123261117.

Annas, George J. "Military Medical Ethics – Physician First, Last, Always," *New England Journal of Medicine* 359, Nr. 11 (2008): 1087–90. DOI: 10.1056/NEJMp0805975.

Annas, George J. "Protecting Soldiers from Friendly Fire: The Consent Requirement for Using Investigational Drugs and Vaccines in Combat," *American Journal of Law & Medicine* 24, Nr. 2/3 (1998): 245–60.

Barr, Sabrina. "Viagra Now Available over the Counter without Prescription in UK," *The Independent*, 27. März, 2018, <https://www.independent.co.uk/life-style/health-and-families/viagra-buy-without-prescription-over-counter-uk-pharmacies-male-impotence-erectile-dysfunction-a8275461.html> (Zugriff: 3. April, 2020).

BBC News. "Sussex University Students Illegally Buying 'Smart Pills,'" *BBC News*, 13. März, 2018, <https://www.bbc.co.uk/news/uk-england-43383717> (Zugriff: 31. März, 2020).

Bear, Adam, und Joshua Knobe. "Normality: Part Descriptive, Part Prescriptive," *Cognition* 167 (2017): 25–37. DOI: <https://doi.org/10.1016/j.cognition.2016.10.024>.

Beauchamp, Tom L. "Informed Consent: Its History, Meaning, and Present Challenges," *Cambridge Quarterly of Healthcare Ethics* 20, Nr. 4 (2011): 515–523. DOI: 10.1017/S0963180111000259.

Berg, J. W., P. S. Appelbaum, C. W. Lidz, und L. S. Parker. *Informed Consent: Legal Theory and Clinical Practice*. Second. New York: Oxford University Press, 2001.

Beutler, Ernest, und Jill Waalen. "The Definition of Anemia: What Is the Lower Limit of Normal of the Blood Hemoglobin Concentration?" *Blood* 107, Nr. 5 (März 2006): 1747–50. DOI: 10.1182/blood-2005-07-3046.

Bostrom, Nick. "The Vulnerable World Hypothesis." *Global Policy* 10, Nr. 4 (2019): 455–76. DOI: 10.1111/1758-5899.12718.

Bostrom, Nick, and Anders Sandberg. "Cognitive Enhancement: Methods, Ethics, Regulatory Challenges." *Science and Engineering Ethics* 15, Nr. 3 (2009): 311–41. DOI: 10.1007/s11948-009-9142-5.

British Army. "New Physical Employment Standards for the Army." <https://www.army.mod.uk/physical-employment-standards/> (Zugriff: 6. Mai, 2020).

British Army. "People. Drugs and Supplements." <https://www.army.mod.uk/people/join-well/drugs-and-supplements/> (Zugriff: 30. März, 2020).

British Army. *Values and Standards of the British Army. AC 64649*. Andover: Army Headquarters, 2018, <https://www.army.mod.uk/media/5219/20180910-values_standards_2018_final.pdf> (Zugriff: 26. März, 2020).

British Medical Journal. "The Nuremberg Code (1947)." *British Medical Journal* 313, Nr. 7070 (1996): 1448. DOI: 10.1136/bmj.313.7070.1448.

Brock, Dan W. "Conscientious Refusal by Physicians and Pharmacists: Who Is Obligated to Do What, and Why?" *Theoretical Medicine and Bioethics* 29, Nr. 3 (2008): 187–200. DOI: 10.1007/s11017-008-9076-y.

Brunet, Alain, Daniel Saumier, Aihua Liu, David L Streiner, Jacques Tremblay, und Roger K Pitman. "Reduction of PTSD Symptoms With Pre-Reactivation Propranolol Therapy: A Randomized Controlled Trial." *American Journal of Psychiatry* 175, Nr. 5 (12. Januar, 2018): 427–33. DOI: 10.1176/appi.ajp.2017.17050481.

Buchanan, A. E. *Beyond Humanity?: The Ethics of Biomedical Enhancement*. Oxford: OUP Oxford, 2011.

Burkeman, Oliver, und Richard Norton-Taylor. "US Pilots Blame Drug for Friendly Fire Deaths," *The Guardian*, 4, Januar, 2003, <https://www.theguardian.com/world/2003/jan/04/afghanistan.richardnortontaylor> (Zugriff: 27. März, 2020).

Caldwell, John A., und J. Lynn Caldwell. "Fatigue in Military Aviation: An Overview of U.S. Military-Approved Pharmacological Countermeasures." *Aviation, Space, and Environmental Medicine* 76, Nr. 7 (2005): C39–51.

Cantor, Julie D. "Conscientious Objection Gone Awry – Restoring Selfless Professionalism in Medicine," *New England Journal of Medicine* 360, Nr. 15 (2009): 1484–85. DOI: 10.1056/NEJMp0902019.

Care Quality Commission. "Defence Medical Services," 2019. <https://www.cqc.org.uk/what-we-do/services-we-regulate/defence-medical-services> (Zugriff: 9. April, 2020).

Carrick, D., P. M. L. Gross, P. J. Connelly, P. G. Lucas, und P. P. Robinson. *Military Medical Ethics for the 21st Century*. Military and Defence Ethics. Ashgate Publishing Limited, 2013.

Casey, Anna, Jason Hughes, Rachel M Izard, und Julie P Greeves. "Supplement Use by UK-Based British Army Soldiers in Training," *The British Journal of Nutrition* 112, Nr. 7 (2014): 1175–84. DOI: 10.1017/S0007114514001597.

CBRN Delivery Team. *2017DIN04-165. Fentanyl Lozenge 800 Micrograms (OTFC) Single – Introduction into Service as Self Administered Operational Analgesia*. Bristol: Ministry of Defence, 2017.

Corrigan, Oonagh. "Empty Ethics: The Problem with Informed Consent," *Sociology of Health & Illness* 25, Nr. 3 (2003): 768–92.

Dearden, Lizzie. "Women Now Allowed to Apply for Royal Marines and All Other Frontline Military Roles, Defence Secretary Announces," *The Independent*, 25. Oktober, 2018. <https://www.independent.co.uk/news/uk/home-news/women-soldiers-army-military-sas-defence-government-infantry-frontline-gavin-williamson-female-a8601371.html> (Zugriff: 2. April, 2020).

Deardorff, Stephen E. "Informed Consent, Termination of Medical Treatment, and the Federal Tort Claims Act – A New Proposal for the Military Health Care System," *Military Law Review* 115, Nr. Winter (1987): 1–120.

Dohmen, Thomas, Armin Falk, Bart H H Golsteyn, David Huffman, und Uwe Sunde. "Risk Attitudes across the Life Course," *The Economic Journal* 127, Nr. 605 (2017): F95–116. DOI: 10.1111/ecoj.12322.

Drabiak-Syed, Katherine. "Reining In the Pharmacological Enhancement Train: We Should Remain Vigilant about Regulatory Standards for Prescribing Controlled Substances," *The Journal of Law, Medicine & Ethics* 39, Nr. 2 (2011): 272–79. DOI: 10.1111/j.1748-720X.2011.00596.x.

Dunne, T. "Liberalism," in: *The Globalisation of World Politics. An Introduction to World Politics*, edited by John Baylis, Steve Smith, und Patricia Owens, 102–13. Oxford: Oxford University Press, 2011.

Dworkin, Gerald. "Paternalism." Hsg. Edward N. Zalta. *The Stanford Encyclopedia of Philosophy*. Stanford: Metaphysics Research Lab, Stanford University, 2019. <https://plato.stanford.edu/entries/paternalism/> (Zugriff: 8. Januar, 2020).

Dyer, Clare. "Consent Needed For Organ Retention, BMA Says," *British Medical Journal* 321, Nr. 7269 (2000): 1098.

European Medicines Agency. "Modafinil," 2010. <https://www.ema.europa.eu/en/medicines/human/referrals/modafinil> (Zugriff: 31. März, 2020).

Faden, R. R., T. L. Beauchamp, und N. M. P. King. *A History and Theory of Informed Consent*. New York: Oxford University Press, 1986.

Faden, Ruth R. *Advisory Committee on Human Radiation Experiments. Final Report.* Washington DC: U.S. Government Printing Office, 1995.

Faden, Ruth R., Tom L. Beauchamp, und Nancy E. Kass. "Informed Consent, Comparative Effectiveness, and Learning Health Care," *New England Journal of Medicine* 370, Nr. 8 (2014): 766–68. DOI: 10.1056/NEJMhle1313674.

Farah, Martha J., Caroline Haimm, Geena Sankoorikal, und Anjan Chatterjee. "When We Enhance Cognition with Adderall, Do We Sacrifice Creativity? A Preliminary Study." *Psychopharmacology* 202, Nr. 1 (2009): 541–47. DOI: 10.1007/s00213-008-1369-3.

FitzPatrick, William J., und Lee L. Zwanziger. "Defending Against Biochemical Warfare." *The Journal of Philosophy, Science & Law* 3, Nr. 2 (2003): 1–19. DOI: 10.5840/jpsl2003323.

Ford, Kenneth, und Clark Glymour. "The Enhanced Warfighter." *Bulletin of the Atomic Scientists* 70, Nr. 1 (2014): 43–53.

Friedl, Karl E. "U.S. Army Research on Pharmacological Enhancement of Soldier Performance: Stimulants, Anabolic Hormones, and Blood Doping." *The Journal of Strength & Conditioning Research* 29 (2015): S71–76.

Galliott, J., und M Lotz. *Super Soldiers: The Ethical, Legal and Social Implications.* Emerging Technologies, Ethics and International Affairs. Farnham: Taylor & Francis, 2016.

Gamble, Nathan K., and Michal Pruski. "Medical Acts and Conscientious Objection: What Can a Physician Be Compelled to Do?" *The New Bioethics* 25, Nr. 3 (2019): 262–82. DOI: 10.1080/20502877.2019.1649871.

Gebhardt, D. O. E. "Off-Label Administration of Drugs to Healthy Military Personnel. Dubious Ethics of Preventive Measures," *Journal of Medical Ethics* 31, Nr. 5 (2005): 268. DOI: 10.1136/jme.2004.008821.

General Medical Council. "Good Medical Practice," 2019. <https://www.gmc-uk.org/ethical-guidance/ethical-guidance-for-doctors/good-medical-practice> (Zugriff: 6. April, 2020).

Gidda, Mirren. "Drugs in War: What Is Captagon, the 'Jihad Pill' Used by Islamic State Militants?" *Newsweek*, 12. Mai, 2017. <https://www.newsweek.com/drugs-captagon-islamic-state-jihad-war-amphetamines-saudi-arabia-608233> (Zugriff: 26. März, 26, 2020).

Gross, Michael. *Military Medical Research Ethics: Investigational Drugs, Clinical Trials and Enhancement.* Oxford: Oxford University Press, 2019.

Gross, Michael L. *Bioethics and Armed Conflict. Moral Dilemmas of Medicine and War.* Cambridge: MIT Press, 2006.

Harvard Law School Library. "Nuremberg – Transcript Viewer – Transcript for NMT 1: *Medical Case.*" Nuremberg Trials Project, 2016. <http://nuremberg.law.harvard.edu/transcripts/1-transcript-for-nmt-1-medical-case?seq=2586> (Zugriff: 11. März, 2020).

Harvey, Kate. "Sports Science and Medicine." *The Nuffield Council on Bioethics*, 2014, <https://nuffieldbioethics.org/publications/sports-science-and-medicine> (Zugriff: 6. Januar, 2020).

Helgesson, Gert. "In Defense of Broad Consent." *Cambridge Quarterly of Healthcare Ethics* 21, Nr. 1 (2012): 40–50. DOI: 10.1017/S096318011100048X.

House of Commons Defence Committee. *Duty of Care. Third Report of Session 2004–05. Volume I. HC 63-I*. London: The Stationery Office Limited, 2005.

Howe, Edmund G., and Edward D. Martin. "Treating the Troops." *Hastings Center Report* 21, Nr. 2 (1991): 21–24. DOI: 10.2307/3562332.

iMedi.co.uk. "Autoject (Combopen) Nerve Agent Antidote L4a1," 2009. <https://imedi.co.uk/autoject-combopen-nerve-agent-antidote-l4a1> (Zugriff: 30. April, 2020).

JASON. JSR-07-625. "Human Performance." Virginia, USA, 2008, <https://fas.org/irp/agency/dod/jason/human.pdf> (Zugriff: 9. April, 2020).

Juengst, Eric T. "What Does Enhancement Mean?" In *Enhancing Human Traits: Ethical and Social Implications*, edited by Eric Parens, 29–47; Hastings Center Studies in Ethics Series. Washington DC: Georgetown University Press, 2000.

Kamienski, L. *Shooting Up: A History of Drugs in Warfare*. Oxford: Hurst, 2017.

Kamm, Frances M. "Is There a Problem With Enhancement?" *The American Journal of Bioethics* 5, Nr. 3 (2005): 5–14. DOI: 10.1080/15265160590945101.

Katz, Jay. "Informed Consent – Must It Remain a Fairy Tale." *Journal of Contemporary Health Law and Policy* 10 (1994): 69–92.

Katz, J., und A. M. Capron. *The Silent World of Doctor and Patient*. Baltimore: Johns Hopkins University Press, 2002.

Kautz, Mary A., Maria L. Thomas, and J. Lynn Caldwell. "Considerations of Pharmacology on Fitness for Duty in the Operational Environment." *Aviation, Space, and Environmental Medicine* 78, Nr. 5 (2007): B107–12.

Kerr, Cathel. "Anthrax Vaccine Gets Cold Shoulder from Troops." *Canadian Medical Association Journal* 168, Nr. 10 (2003): 1308.

Kroutil, Larry A., David L. Van Brunt, Mindy A. Herman-Stahl, David C. Heller, Robert M. Bray, and Michael A. Penne. "Nonmedical Use of Prescription Stimulants in the United States." *Drug and Alcohol Dependence* 84, Nr. 2 (2006): 135–43.

Lennard, Natasha. "One in Ten Takes Drugs to Study." *Varsity*. 6. März, 2009. <https://www.varsity.co.uk/news/1307> (Zugriff: 31. März, 2020).

Little, Robert. "Army Medicine: Untested in Battle." *The Baltimore Sun*, 29. März, 2009. <https://www.baltimoresun.com/news/nation-world/bal-te.militarymed29mar29-story.html> (Zugriff: 30. März, 2020).

Lusher, Adam. "The Bizarre True Story of When the UK Military Tested LSD on Royal Marines." *The Independent*. 24. Mai, 2018. <https://www.independent.co.uk/news/uk/home-news/lsd-video-porton-down-chemical-weapons-experiments-trials-uk-military-army-marines-sixties-acid-a8366906.html> (Zugriff: 29. April, 2020).

Maheshwari, Nidhi, und Vineeth V Kumar. *Military Psychology : Concepts, Trends and Interventions*. New Delhi, India: Sage Publications Pvt. Ltd, 2016.

Maslen, Hannah, Nadira Faulmüller, und Julian Savulescu. "Pharmacological Cognitive Enhancement – How Neuroscientific Research Could Advance Ethical Debate." *Frontiers in Systems Neuroscience* 8 (2014): 1–12. DOI: 10.3389/fnsys.2014.00107.

McCartney, Helen. "The Military Covenant and the Civil–Military Contract in Britain." *International Affairs* 86, Nr. 2 (2010): 411–28. DOI: 10.1111/j.1468-2346.2010.00889.x.

McLellan, Tom M., John A. Caldwell, and Harris R. Lieberman. "A Review of Caffeine's Effects on Cognitive, Physical and Occupational Performance." *Neuroscience & Biobehavioral Reviews* 71 (2016): 294–312. DOI: <https://doi.org/10.1016/j.neubio rev.2016.09.001>.

McManus, John, Sumeru G. Mehta, Annette R. McClinton, Robert A. De Lorenzo, und Toney W. Baskin. "Informed Consent and Ethical Issues in Military Medical Research." *Academic Emergency Medicine* 12, Nr. 11 (2005): 1120–26. DOI: 10.1197/j.aem.2005.05.037.

Mehlman, Maxwell. "Bioethics of Military Performance Enhancement." *Journal of the Royal Army Medical Corps* 165, Nr. 4 (2019): 226–231. DOI: 10.1136/jramc-2018-001130.

Mehlman, Maxwell J., und Stephanie Corley. "A Framework for Military Bioethics." *Journal of Military Ethics* 13, Nr. 4 (2014): 331–49. DOI: 10.1080/15027570.2014.992214.

Mehlman, Maxwell J., Patrick Lin, und Keith Abney. "Enhanced Warfighters: A Policy Framework," in: *Military Medical Ethics for the 21st Century*, Hsgs. M. L. Gross und D. Carrick, 113–26. Military and Defence Ethics. Farnham: Ashgate Publishing Limited, 2013.

Mehlman, Maxwell, Patrick Lin, und Keith Abney. "Enhanced Warfighters: Risk, Ethics, and Policy." *Case Legal Studies Research Paper Nr. 2013–2*. Elsevier BV, 18. Januar, 2013. DOI: 10.2139/ssrn.2202982.

Meijer, Marten. "A Human Performance Perspective on the Ethical Use of Cogniceuticals: Commentary on 'Recommendations for the Ethical Use of Pharmacologic Fatigue Countermeasures in the U.S. Military.'" *Aviation, Space, and Environmental Medicine* 78, Nr. 5 (2007): B131–33.

Messelken, Daniel, und Hans Ulrich Baer. "Hovering Between Roles: Military Medical Ethics." In *Military Medical Ethics for the 21st Century*, edited by M. L. Gross and D. Carrick, 261–77. Military and Defence Ethics. Farnham: Ashgate Publishing Limited, 2013.

Mohamed, Ahmed Dahir. "Neuroethical Issues in: Pharmacological Cognitive Enhancement." *WIREs Cognitive Science* 5, Nr. 5 (2014): 533–49. DOI: 10.1002/wcs.1306.

Morris, Marilyn C., and Robert M. Nelson. "Randomized, Controlled Trials as Minimal Risk: An Ethical Analysis*." *Critical Care Medicine* 35, Nr. 3 (2007): 940–44.

Murphy, Dominic, Christopher Dandeker, Oded Horn, Matthew Hotopf, Lisa Hull, Margaret Jones, Theresa Marteau, Roberto Rona, and Simon Wessely. "UK Armed Forces Responses to an Informed Consent Policy for Anthrax

Vaccination: A Paradoxical Effect?" *Vaccine* 24, Nr. 16 (2006): 3109–14. DOI: 10.1016/j.vaccine.2006.01.043.

Murphy, Dominic, Neil Greenberg, and Duncan Bland. "Health Concerns in UK Armed Forces Personnel." *Journal of the Royal Society of Medicine* 102, Nr. 4 (2009): 143–47. DOI: 10.1258/jrsm.2009.080387.

Myers, Carol S., Richard C. Taylor, Eric T. Moolchan, and Stephen J. Heishman. "Dose-Related Enhancement of Mood and Cognition in Smokers Administered Nicotine Nasal Spray." *Neuropsychopharmacology* 33, Nr. 3 (2008): 588–98. DOI: 10.1038/sj.npp.1301425.

Newlands, Emma. "'They Even Gave Us Oranges on One Occasion': Human Experimentation in the British Army During the Second World War." *War & Society* 32, Nr. 1 (2013): 19–63. DOI: 10.1179/0729247312Z.00000000016.

Nicholson, P. J. "Communicating Health Risk." *Occupational Medicine* 49, Nr. 4 (1999): 253–56. DOI: 10.1093/occmed/49.4.253.

O'Neill, O. "Some Limits of Informed Consent." *Journal of Medical Ethics* 29, Nr. 1 (2003): 4–7. DOI: 10.1136/jme.29.1.4.

Olsen, Olav Kjellevold, Ståle Pallesen, and Eid Jarle. "The Impact of Partial Sleep Deprivation on Moral Reasoning in Military Officers." *Sleep* 33, Nr. 8 (2010): 1086–90. DOI: 10.1093/sleep/33.8.1086.

Parens, E. *Enhancing Human Traits: Ethical and Social Implications*. Hastings Center Studies in Ethics Series. Washington DC: Georgetown University Press, 2000.

Patrey, James, Judith Lytle, William Sobotka, GeorgiAnna Sheppard, and Susan R. Kayar. "Human Performance Enhancement for NATO Military Operations (Science, Technology, and Ethics)." In *NATO Research and Technology Organisation*, 1–7. Virginia, USA: Office of Naval Research Warfighter Performance Department, 2009, <https://apps.dtic.mil/dtic/tr/fulltext/u2/a562561.pdf> (Zugriff: 6. Januar, 2020).

Pellegrino, Edmund D. "Autonomy and Coercion in Disease Prevention and Health Promotion." *Theoretical Medicine* 5, Nr. 1 (1984): 83–91. DOI: 10.1007/BF00489248.

Pérez-Guisado, Joaquín, and Philip M Jakeman. "Citrulline Malate Enhances Athletic Anaerobic Performance and Relieves Muscle Soreness." *The Journal of Strength & Conditioning Research* 24, Nr. 5 (2010): 1215–22.

President's Council on Bioethics. *Beyond Therapy: Biotechnology and the Pursuit of Happiness*. New York: Regan Books, 2003.

Rayment, Sean. "Thousands of Soldiers on Antidepressants as They Battle Mental Health Issues, New Figures Reveal." *The Mirror*, 28. Juli, 2018. <https://www.mirror.co.uk/news/uk-news/thousands-soldiers-antidepressants-battle-mental-12996613> (Zugriff: 31. März, 2020).

Rettig, Richard. *Waiving Informed Consent: Military Use of Non-FDA-Approved Drugs in Combat*. Santa Monica: RAND Corporation, 2000. DOI: 10.7249/rb7534 (Zugriff: 30. April, 2020).

Rettig, Richard A. "Military Use of Drugs Not Yet Approved by the FDA for CW/BW Defense: Lessons from the Gulf War," Santa Monica: RAND Corporation, 1999. <https://www.rand.org/pubs/monograph_reports/MR1018z9.html> (Zugriff: 11. März, 2020).

Robbins, Lauren R. "Refusing to Be All That You Can Be: Regulating against Forced Cognitive Enhancement in the Military," in: *Military Medical Ethics for the 21st Century*, edited by M. L. Gross and D. Carrick, 127–38. Military and Defence Ethics. Farnham: Ashgate Publishing Limited, 2013.

Rosenbaum, S. "100 Years of Heights and Weights." *Journal of the Royal Statistical Society. Series A (Statistics in Society)* 151, Nr. 2 (1988): 276–309. DOI: 10.2307/2982758.

Russo, Michael B. "Recommendations for the Ethical Use of Pharmacologic Fatigue Countermeasures in the U.S. Military." *Aviation, Space, and Environmental Medicine* 78, Nr. 5 (2007): B119–27.

Sandberg, Anders, and Nick Bostrom. "Converging Cognitive Enhancements." *Annals New York Academy of Sciences* 1093 (2006): 201–27. DOI: 10.1196/annals.1382.015.

Sattler, Sebastian, Guido Mehlkop, Peter Graeff, and Carsten Sauer. "Evaluating the Drivers of and Obstacles to the Willingness to Use Cognitive Enhancement Drugs: The Influence of Drug Characteristics, Social Environment, and Personal Characteristics." *Substance Abuse Treatment, Prevention, and Policy* 9, Nr. 1 (2014): 1–14. DOI: 10.1186/1747-597X-9-8.

Savulescu, Julian. "Conscientious Objection in Medicine." *BMJ* 332, Nr. 7536 (2006): 294–97. DOI: 10.1136/bmj.332.7536.294.

Savulescu, J., and N Bostrom. *Human Enhancement*. Oxford: OUP Oxford, 2009.

Savulescu, J., B. Foddy, and M. Clayton. "Why We Should Allow Performance Enhancing Drugs in Sport." *British Journal of Sports Medicine* 38, Nr. 6 (2004): 666–670. DOI: 10.1136/bjsm.2003.005249.

Savulescu, Julian, Leon Creaney, and Anna Vondy. "Should Athletes Be Allowed to Use Performance Enhancing Drugs?" *BMJ (Clinical Research Ed.)* 347 (2013): f6150. DOI: 10.1136/bmj.f6150.

Scharre, Paul, and Lauren Fish. "Human Performance Enhancement." *Center for a New American Security*, 2018. <https://www.cnas.org/publications/reports/human-performance-enhancement-1> (Zugriff: 6. Januar, 2020).

Schelle, Kimberly J., Nadira Faulmüller, Lucius Caviola, and Miles Hewstone. "Attitudes toward Pharmacological Cognitive Enhancement – a Review." *Frontiers in Systems Neuroscience* 8 (2014): 1–14. DOI: 10.3389/fnsys.2014.00053.

Schofer, Joel Martin. "Violations of Informed Consent During War." *JAMA* 281, Nr. 17 (5. Mai, 1999): 1657.

Schoomaker, Eric B. "Military Medical Research on Cognitive Performance: The Warfighters Competitive Edge." *Aviation, Space, and Environmental Medicine* 78, Nr. 5 (2007): B4–6.

Sears, Neil. “Army Signs up Recruits with a Reading Age as Young as FIVE in Desperate Bid to Boost Troop Numbers,” *The Daily Mail.* April 5, 2020. <https://www.dailymail.co.uk/news/article-8190009/Army-signs-recruits-reading-age-young-FIVE-desperate-bid-boost-troop-numbers.html> (Zugriff: 1. Mai, 2020).

Sellgren, Katherine. “Almost 40% of Army Recruits Have Reading Age of 11, MPs Warn.” *BBC News*, 18. Juli, 2013. <https://www.bbc.co.uk/news/education-23346693> (Zugriff: 1. Mai, 2020).

Support, Macmillan Cancer. “Familial Adenomatous Polyposis (FAP).” <https://www.macmillan.org.uk/cancer-information-and-support/worried-about-cancer/causes-and-risk-factors/familial-adenomatous-polyposis-fap> (Zugriff: 6. April, 2020).

The National Commission for the Protection of Human Subjects of Biomedical and Behavioural Research. “The Belmont Report: Ethical Principles and Guidelines for the Protection of Human Subjects of Research,” 1979. <https://www.hhs.gov/ohrp/sites/default/files/the-belmont-report-508c_FINAL.pdf> (Zugriff: 8. Januar, 2020).

The Royal College of Anaesthetists. “Guidelines for the Provision of Anaesthetic Services,” 2020. <https://www.rcoa.ac.uk/safety-standards-quality/guidance-resources/guidelines-provision-anaesthetic-services> (Zugriff: 6. April, 2020).

U.S. Anti-Doping Agency. “Effects of Performance-Enhancing Drugs.” <https://www.usada.org/athletes/substances/effects-of-performance-enhancing-drugs/> (Zugriff: 8. Mai, 2020).

United Kingdom. Department of Health. “About Us – Medicines and Healthcare Products Regulatory Agency.” <https://www.gov.uk/government/organisations/medicines-and-healthcare-products-regulatory-agency/about#our-responsibilities> (Zugriff: 26. März, 2020).

United Kingdom. Department of Health. “The Controlled Drugs (Supervision of Management and Use) Regulations 2013. Information about the Regulations,” 2013. <https://assets.publishing.service.gov.uk/government/uploads/system/uploads/attachment_data/file/214915/15-02-2013-controlled-drugs-regulation-information.pdf> (Zugriff: 26. März, 2020).

United Kingdom. Development Concepts and Doctrine Centre. *JSP 383. The Joint Service Manual of the Law of Armed Conflict.* Shrivenham: DCDC, 2004.

United Kingdom. HM Government. “Defence Medical Services.” <https://www.gov.uk/government/groups/defence-medical-services> (Zugriff: 18. Mai, 2020).

United Kingdom. HM Government. “Off-Label or Unlicensed Use of Medicines: Prescribers’ Responsibilities,” 2014. <https://www.gov.uk/drug-safety-update/off-label-or-unlicensed-use-of-medicines-prescribers-responsibilities> (Zugriff: 4. Mai, 2020).

United Kingdom. HM Government. “Misuse of Drugs Act 1971,” 1971, <http://www.legislation.gov.uk/ukpga/1971/38/contents> (Zugriff: 26. März, 2020).

United Kingdom. Ministry of Defence. "FOI2017/13417," 2018. <https://assets.publishing.service.gov.uk/government/uploads/system/uploads/attachment_data/file/691866/2017-13417.pdf> (Zugriff: 31. März, 2020).

United Kingdom. Ministry of Defence. *JSP 536. Governance of Research Involving Human Participants. Part 1: Directive*. 3. Ausgabe London: HMSO, 2020.

United Kingdom. Ministry of Defence. *JSP 830: The Manual of Service Law*. London: HMSO, 2016.

United Kingdom. Ministry of Defence. *The Queen's Regulations for the Army 1975. AC13206*. London: Ministry of Defence, 2019.

United Kingdom. Ministry of Defence. "Ministry of Defence Research Ethics Committee." <https://www.gov.uk/government/groups/ministry-of-defence-research-ethics-committees#guidance-documents> (Zugriff: 9. Januar, 2020).

United Kingdom. The Human Medicines Regulations 2012, Pub. L. Nr. 1916, Schedule 17 (2012). <http://www.legislation.gov.uk/uksi/2012/1916/schedule/17/made> (Zugriff: 6. April, 2020).

United Kingdom. The Medicines for Human Use (Clinical Trials) Regulations, Pub. L. Nr. 1031, Schedule 1 (2004). <http://www.legislation.gov.uk/uksi/2004/1031/schedule/1/part/2/paragraph/3/made#text%3Dinformed%consent> (Zugriff: 1. Januar, 2020).

United Nations. "Universal Declaration of Human Rights," 1948. <https://www.un.org/en/universal-declaration-human-rights/> (Zugriff: 9. Januar, 2020).

Wamberg, Jacob, Mads Rosendahl Thomsen, and Kasper Lippert-Rasmussen. *The Posthuman Condition : Ethics, Aesthetics and Politics of Biotechnological Challenges*. Aarhus, Denmark: Aarhus University Press, 2012.

Westcott, Kelli J. "Modafinil, Sleep Deprivation, and Cognitive Function in Military and Medical Settings." *Military Medicine* 170, Nr. 4 (2005): 333–35. DOI: 10.7205/MILMED.170.4.333.

Wilson, Jacque. "Lance Armstrong's Doping Drugs – CNN." *CNN*, 18. Januar, 2013. <https://edition.cnn.com/2013/01/15/health/armstrong-ped-explainer/index.html> (Zugriff: April 12, 2020).

Wolfendale, Jessica. "Performance-Enhancing Technologies and Moral Responsibility in the Military." *The American Journal of Bioethics* 8, Nr. 2 (2008): 28–38. DOI: 10.1080/15265160802014969.

Wolfendale, Jessica, and Steve Clarke. "Paternalism, Consent, and the Use of Experimental Drugs in the Military." *The Journal of Medicine and Philosophy: A Forum for Bioethics and Philosophy of Medicine* 33, Nr. 4 (2008): 337–55. DOI: 10.1093/jmp/jhn014.

World Anti-Doping Agency. "World Anti-Doping Code." Montreal: World Anti-Doping Agency, 2015. <https://www.wada-ama.org/sites/default/files/resources/files/wada_anti-doping_code_2019_english_final_revised_v1_linked.pdf> (Zugriff: 12. März, 2020).

World Health Organisation. "An Introduction to Risk Communication." Zugriff: 12. März, 2020. <https://www.who.int/risk-communication/introduction-to-risk-communication.pdf?ua=1> (Zugriff: 12. März, 2020).

World Medical Association. "Ethical Principles for Medical Research Involving Human Subjects." *WMA Declaration of Helsinki*, 2018. <https://www.wma.net/policies-post/wma-declaration-of-helsinki-ethical-principles-for-medical-research-involving-human-subjects/> (Zugriff: 9. Januar, 2020).

Quel consentement éclairé dans les Armées pour l'augmentation des capacités par voie pharmacologique ?

Introduction

Les êtres humains constituent une espèce fragile qui a survécu et dominé la planète grâce à son intelligence, son ingéniosité et sa capacité d'adaptation. Cette capacité à survivre et à s'adapter s'applique aussi dans les conflits armés, dans lesquels un soldat[1] doit surmonter ses émotions – comme la peur – et réagir aux exigences physiques comme la faim, la soif et la fatigue. L'entraînement peut contribuer à lutter contre ces faiblesses potentielles, mais la possibilité d'utiliser les derniers progrès de la science et de la technologie pour améliorer l'action d'un soldat pourrait procurer l'avantage souhaité pour vaincre l'adversaire. Ceci devient encore plus important lorsque les acteurs d'autres États ou indépendants de tout État peuvent aussi avoir accès à cette technologie.

L'augmentation des capacités humaines est un domaine en évolution rapide ; Allhoff est convaincu que « nous approchons du début de la Révolution de l'augmentation des capacités humaines »[2]. La technologie progresse à un rythme tel que les questions éthiques qui la concernent accusent un retard entre le moment où elle devient disponible et celui où elle est effectivement utilisée. Ceci est vrai aussi bien pour ce qui est de l'augmentation pharmacologique (PCE) que pour les exosquelettes et l'interface homme-machine. Plusieurs organismes militaires et civils ont massivement investi dans l'augmentation des capacités humaines, tirant parti des avancées scientifiques dans les neurosciences, la biotechnologie, la robotique et les possibilités de miniaturisation technologique[3]. Des « médicaments » d'augmentation sont déjà disponibles, procurant jusqu'à 20 % d'amélioration des capacités chez ceux qui les prennent lors de tests spécifiques[4]. Il est par conséquent souhaitable de mettre en place une politique d'emploi de l'augmentation pharmacologique (PCE) permettant des délais de réflexion plutôt que de se trouver au pied du mur.

1 Le terme « soldat » est employé pour désigner tous les membres de toutes les Armées des Forces Armées du Royaume-Uni.

2 Fritz Allhoff *et al*, "Ethics of Human Enhancement: 25 Questions & Answers." (« Ethique de l'augmentation des capacités humaines : 25 questions et réponses ») *Studies in Ethics, Law, and Technology* 4, n° 1 (2010), 1.

3 Maxwell J. Mehlman, Patrick Lin et Keith Abney, "Enhanced Warfighters: A Policy Framework" (« Le soldat augmenté : un cadre politique, » dans Military Medical Ethics for the 21st century, édition M.L. Gross et D. Carrick, *Military and defence ethics* (Farnham: Ashgate Publishing Limited, 2013), 113.

4 Anders Sandberg et Nick Bostrom, "Converging Cognitive Enhancements," (« Augmentations cognitives convergentes »), *Annals New York Academy of Sciences* 1093 (2006), 205.

 DOI:10.1163/9789004677746_012

Parmi les problèmes éthiques posés par l'augmentation des capacités humaines figurent l'autonomie, la sécurité et la dignité[5]. Les deux premiers constituent les pierres angulaires de l'éthique appliquée au consentement éclairé, émanant de la nécessité de protéger les êtres humains contre les risques présentés par la recherche. Le consentement éclairé est à présent monnaie courante dans la pratique médicale éthique fondée sur l'autonomie et la sauvegarde de la santé et du bien-être. Actuellement, les militaires suivent des orientations civiles sur le consentement éclairé mais celles-ci peuvent ne pas être appropriées, les militaires devant mettre en balance la protection des personnes et les risques encourus, et ainsi obérer l'autonomie de ces personnes. Il reste à montrer comment ces risques sont quantifiés, qui décide si le risque est acceptable et si le consentement éclairé est nécessaire. Pour les civils, un individu compétent et autonome déciderait si le risque est acceptable dans les conditions du consentement éclairé ; mais pour les militaires, la perte partielle d'autonomie entraînée par le fait d'être membre d'une organisation dans laquelle on doit obéir aux ordres réglementaires rend le consentement éclairé difficile.

Ce mémoire définira les augmentations des capacités humaines, expliquera ce que sont les PCE (augmentations par la pharmacologie), et pour quelle raison un individu, ou les militaires, pourraient les employer. On donnera un bref aperçu des problèmes spécifiques concernant l'emploi des PCE dans les Armées, y compris la législation et la réglementation concernant la déontologie et la délivrance de médications exclusivement sur prescription, les effets que l'emploi des PCE pourrait avoir sur les carrières militaires et la chaîne de commandement, ainsi que la manière dont les utilisateurs des PCE pourrait être perçue par leurs collègues et par la société. Un aspect important de la vie militaire est le devoir des responsables de veiller au bien-être des subordonnés et ceci doit être pris en compte par ceux qui cautionnent des missions pour lesquelles l'emploi des PCE est considéré comme vital pour le succès de la mission. Les arguments pour ou contre le consentement éclairé dans les forces armées seront également exposés.

Le problème du consentement éclairé sera examiné en détail dans sa théorie et son histoire ; on évoquera les cas où les militaires ont connu le succès et l'échec vis-à-vis du consentement dans le passé. Toute substance doit faire l'objet d'une recherche approfondie avant d'être déclarée apte à être utilisée et cela requiert un degré d'exigence plus élevé concernant le consentement si l'on

---

5 Maxwell Mehlman, Patrick Lin et Keith Abney, Maxwell Mehlman, Patrick Lin, and Keith Abney, "Enhanced Warfighters: Risk, Ethics, and Policy" (« Soldats augmentés : risques, éthique et politique suivie »). Case Legal Studies Research Paper n° 2013–2 (2013), 4.

respecte les principes éthiques établis ; si l'expérience est menée par ou sur du personnel militaire faisant office de sujets de recherche, elle doit être approuvée par une commission d'éthique dédiée. Le présent mémoire précisera ce qui est demandé pour que le consentement soit « éclairé », et montrera que l'information n'est jamais entièrement connue des médecins qui souvent dissimulent leur manque de connaissances. La même analyse critique sera menée pour montrer jusqu'à quel point le consentement est « consensuel » dans les forces armées, dont le personnel doit obéir aux ordres et est donc soumis à la coercition.

La dernière partie de ce mémoire traitera du rôle des médecins militaires dans le processus du consentement et de la dualité unique de leur position, du fait que ceux-ci agissent à la fois comme praticiens et comme officiers militaires. Il sera proposé de donner la priorité au devoir éthique du médecin. Ce mémoire réunit des données concrètes et aboutit à une proposition de guide pour l'usage du consentement éclairé dans les Armées. On mettra l'accent sur la méthode, la façon de communiquer et les étapes de cette communication. Dans ce guide seront distingués le consentement au sens large du terme et le consentement éclairé pour l'usage des PCE en cours d'opération. Le but est d'obtenir un compromis théorique effectif pour maximiser l'information fournie et s'assurer lorsque cela est possible que l'usage des PCE est consensuel à quelques rares exceptions près. En vue de protéger au mieux les personnes elles-mêmes et la société vis-à-vis de soldats ayant été soumis aux PCE, les militaires doivent mettre en place une politique et une réglementation globales encadrant l'emploi desdites PCE (augmentation pharmacologique des capacités humaines).

CHAPITRE 1

Les augmentations pharmacologiques

Que sont les augmentations humaines et pharmacologiques ?

La définition des augmentations des capacités humaines selon Juengst est la suivante : « interventions dont le but est d'améliorer la forme ou le fonctionnement de l'être humain au-delà de ce qui est nécessaire à la sauvegarde ou au rétablissement de la santé »[1]. L'interprétation que fait Mehlman de cette définition exclut la vaccination, qui améliore les systèmes immunitaires pour sauvegarder la santé ; il regroupe tous les traitements médicaux contribuant à sauvegarder ou rétablir la santé[2]. Il existe une différence importante entre un médicament entrant dans le cadre d'un traitement et une substance utilisée en vue d'une augmentation, la société acceptant généralement un traitement dont l'objet est de combattre une maladie. La définition de Juengst laisse une zone grise dans les cas des traitements contre l'apparition d'une maladie future qui peut apparaître ou non, comme une colectomie totale pour prévenir la polyposis coli héréditaire, maladie qui est fortement susceptible d'entraîner un cancer de l'intestin[3]. Ceci peut difficilement être classé comme augmentation ou traitement car elle n'améliore que potentiellement le fonctionnement de l'organisme, et n'est pas strictement nécessaire à la sauvegarde de la santé.

Considérons des traitements qui peuvent être requis pour une condition médicale mais qui ont également des effets bénéfiques sur des personnes exemptes de maladies et considérées comme « normales ». L'érythropoïétine est employée pour traiter l'anémie mais a été utilisée par un coureur du Tour de France cycliste ayant un taux normal d'hémoglobine pour améliorer ses

1 Eric T. Juengst, "What Does Enhancement Mean?" (« *Que signifie augmentation ?* »), in: *Enhancing human traits: ethical and social implications*, éd. Eric Parens, Hastings Center Studies in Ethic Series (Washington D.C: Georgetown University Press, 2000), 29.

2 Maxwell Mehlman, Maxwell Mehlman, "Bioethics of Military Performance Enhancement" (« La bioéthique de l'augmentation des capacités militaires»), *Journal of the Royal Army Medical Corps*, 165, n° 4 (2019): 226.

3 McMillan Cancer Support, "Familial Adenomatous Polyposis (FAP)" (*La polyposis adénomateuse héréditaire*), Macmillan Cancer Support, "Familial Adenomatous Polyposis (FAP)," <https://www.macmillan.org.uk/cancer-information-and-support/worried-about-cancer/causes-and-risk-factors/familial-adenomatous-polyposis-fap,> (consulté le 6 avril 2020).

 | DOI:10.1163/9789004677746_013

performances[4]. Le patient a été traité tandis que le cycliste a été considéré comme dopé (augmenté). La différence fait porter l'attention sur le terme « normal », défini par Mehlman comme l'ensemble typique du fonctionnement chez l'être humain en tant qu'espèce par rapport à sa base de référence et à son « histoire » de santé[5]. Pour la concentration en hémoglobine, la fourchette se situe à 95 % ou 97,5 % d'une courbe normale de distribution générée par un groupe de population[6]. Néanmoins, les critères de normalité changent avec les époques, comme la taille et le poids des individus au cours du siècle dernier, et changeront certainement avec l'emploi des substances d'augmentation[7].

Mohamed a mis l'accent sur la difficulté qu'il y a à distinguer un traitement des effets d'augmentation en citant l'exemple de l'emploi de PCE contre le décalage horaire ou l'insomnie[8]. Le « médicament » utilisé traite-t-il les symptômes déjà présents, ou « augmente » -t-il le cerveau pour prévenir ces états ? On peut considérer de la même manière le cas des soldats soumis à des PCE pour combattre la fatigue causée par une opération et se demander si les PCE les ont remis dans leur état normal ou les ont « augmentés » au-delà de la normale. D'autres difficultés pour comprendre l'augmentation des capacités résident dans le fait qu'au cours des dernières décennies, la ligne de différenciation entre la bonne santé et la maladie est devenue plus floue et que de plus en plus d'interventions sont considérées comme des traitements[9]. Ce que l'on en conclut actuellement est que certaines PCE pourraient être considérées comme thérapie ou augmentation des capacités, bien que fondamentalement le problème du consentement reste le même pour les deux états.

De même, il est possible que quelques « augmentations » soient négatives, ou des « anti-augmentations, » comme l'emploi dans un cadre militaire d'une

---

4 Jacques Wilson, "Lance Armstrong's Doping Drugs – CNN" (« Les produits dopants de Lance Armstrong »), CNN, 18 janvier 2013. <https://edition.cnn.com/2013/01/15/health/armstrong-ped-explainer/index.html>, (consulté le 10 avril 2020).

5 Maxwell Mehlman, Patrick Lin et Keith Abney, "Enhanced Warfighters: Risk, Ethics, and Policy" (« Le soldat augmenté : risques, éthique et politiques »), Case Legal Studies Research Paper No. 2013–2, 14.

6 Ernest Beutler et Jill Waalen, "The Definition of Anemia: What Is the Lower Limit of Normal of the Blood Hemoglobin Concentration?" (« Définition de l'anémie : quelle est la limite inférieure de la concentration en hémoglobine ? ») *Blood* 107, n° 5 (2006): 1747.

7 S. Rosenbaum, "100 Years of Heights and Weights" (« 100 ans de tailles et de poids »), *Journal of the Royal Statistical Society,* Série A, 151, n° 2 (1988): 276–309.

8 Ahmed Dahir Mohamed, « Neuroethical Issues in : Pharmacological Cognitive Enhancement" (« Questions neuroéthiques dans l'augmentation cognitive pharmacologique »), WIRES Cognitive Science 5, n° 5 (2014) 538.

9 Mehlman, "Bioethics of Military Performance Enhancement" (*Bioéthique de l'augmentation des capacités dans les opérations militaires*), 226.

PCE pour abolir la mémoire de soldats affectés de troubles post-traumatiques[10]. Là encore, est-ce un traitement du mental ou son « augmentation » ? Si l'on ne fait pas la distinction entre la thérapie et l'augmentation des capacités, toute forme d'augmentation des capacités humaines pourrait devenir moralement acceptable[11]. Le présent mémoire se conformera à la définition de l'augmentation comme une amélioration de la personne, l'élevant à un niveau supérieur à la normale. Il mettra l'accent sur les substances pharmaceutiques comme étant un aspect de l'augmentation des capacités humaines, en excluant tout l'éventail des autres « augmentations » possibles comme la stimulation magnétique transcrânienne, les modifications génétiques et l'interaction être humain-ordinateur.

L'augmentation des capacités par la pharmacologie (PCE), pour ce qui est de ce mémoire, est définie comme l'administration de substances qui sont uniquement des médicaments prescrits par ordonnance (POM), et ne concerne pas celles acquises par des voies illicites ou sans ordonnance. Les procédures de contrôle pour les PCE (comme pour tous les médicaments) au Royaume-Uni sont mises en œuvre par la Medicine and Healthcare Products Regulatory Agency (MHRA) (Agence pour la réglementation des produits médicinaux et de santé). La MHRA autorise certains produits comme sûrs et classe certains produits comme étant « contrôlés » par une réglementation précise concernant leur utilisation normale et abusive[12]. Les médicaments prescrits par ordonnance (POM) ne peuvent être prescrits que par un docteur en médecine, bien qu'il existe une exemption à cette réglementation pour le milieu militaire, comme on le verra plus bas. Un médicament n'ayant pas fait l'objet d'un brevet peut être prescrit même s'il est marqué « non-indiqué » (« off-label »), mais

10 Mehlman, Lin et Abney, "Enhanced Warfighters: Risk, Ethics, and Policy" (« Le soldat augmenté : risques, éthique et politique suivie »), 15.

11 Allhoff *et al*, "Ethics of Human Enhancement: 25 Questions & Answers" (« Éthique de l'augmentation des capacités humaines : 25 questions et réponses »), 8.

12 Gouvernement du Royaume-Uni, – "About Us – Medicines and Healthcare Products Regulatory Agency" (« Agence pour la réglementation des médications et produits médicamenteux »), <https://www.gov.uk/government/organisations/medicines-and-healthcare-products-regulatory-agency/about#our-responsibilities>, *Misuse of Drugs Act 1971* (London: HMSO, 1971), <http://www.legislation.gov.uk/ukpga/1971/38/contents>, "The Controlled Drugs (Supervision of Management and Use) Regulations 2013. Information about the Regulations," 2013, (« Règlementation des médicaments soumis au contrôle (supervision de la gestion et de l'usage ») <https://assets.publishing.service.gov.uk/government/uploads/system/uploads/attachment_data/file/214915/15-02-2013-controlled-drugs-regulation-information.pdf> (consulté le 26 mars 2020).

le patient doit en être informé[13]. La majorité des PCE n'ont pas à l'origine été autorisés (listés) pour leurs propriétés d'augmentation et donc leur emploi est considéré comme non-indiqué (« off-label »), ce qui entraîne la nécessité d'en informer le patient. On présume que tout futur médicament créé serait soumis à la même réglementation.

On distingue deux grandes catégories de PCE, celles de caractère cognitif et celles modifiant les caractéristiques physiques. La cognition peut être définie comme étant le processus utilisé par l'être humain pour organiser l'information[14]. L'état de santé général, un régime équilibré et l'exercice physique régulier peuvent améliorer la cognition mais il existe un large éventail de substances affectant la chimie du cerveau, avec des effets positifs et négatifs[15]. Ces effets positifs peuvent être qualifiés d'augmentation cognitive, telle que la définit Sandberg : « l'amplification ou l'extension des capacités de base de l'intellect par l'amélioration ou l'augmentation des systèmes d'organisation de l'information interne ou externe »[16]. Les médicaments qui modifient la chimie du cerveau pourraient avoir des effets négatifs en altérant la perception que les soldats ont de leurs actions et des conséquences de leur comportement. La perte de toute liaison émotionnelle pourrait priver les forces armées du lien social et de la confiance qui sont actuellement instillés par leurs valeurs et leur code moral.

Parmi les substances bien connues agissant sur la cognition figure la nicotine, qui accroît la vigilance et les processus cognitifs[17], et la caféine qui élève le niveau de vigilance, particulièrement en cas de fatigue[18]. Cependant, le

13 Gouvernement du Royaume-Uni, "Off-Label or Unlicensed Use of Medicines: Prescribers' Responsibilities" (« Emploi des médicaments non listés : responsabilité des prescripteurs »), 2014 <https://www.gov.uk/drug-safety-update/off-label-or-unlicensed-use-of-medicines-prescribers-responsibilities>, (consulté le 4 mai 2020).

14 Nick Bostrom et Anders Sandberg, "Cognitive Enhancement: Methods, Ethics, Regulatory Challenges" (« Méthodes, éthique et problèmes de réglementation concernant l'augmentation cognitive »), *Science and Engineering Ethics* 15, n° 3 (2009); 312.

15 *Ibid.*, 314.

16 Sandberg et Bostrom, Sandberg and Bostrom, "Converging Cognitive Enhancements" (« Les augmentations cognitives convergentes »), 201.

17 Carol S. Myers *et al*, "Dose-Related Enhancement of Mood and Cognition in Smokers Administered Nicotine Nasal Spray" (« L'augmentation des humeurs et de la cognition chez les fumeurs auxquels on administre de la nicotine par spray nasal, selon la dose administrée »), *Neuropsychopharmacology* 33, n° 3 (2008): 594.

18 Tom McLellan, John A. Caldwell et Harris R Lieberman, "A Review of Caffeine's Effects on Cognitive, Physical and Occupational Performance" (« Étude des effets de la caféine sur les capacités cognitives, physiques et professionnelles »), *Neuroscience & Biobéhavioral Reviews* 71 (2016): 297.

présent mémoire emploie le sigle PCE pour désigner uniquement les substances qui peuvent être prescrites ; comme on peut se procurer de la nicotine et de la caféine sans ordonnance, elles n'entrent pas dans le champ de cette étude. Un exemple de PCE cognitive est le modafinil, médicament listé contre la narcolepsie, dans lequel on a constaté la propriété de maintenir la vigilance et d'améliorer la cognition[19]. Comme le modafinil peut augmenter la vigilance avec des effets secondaires minimes, il peut potentiellement « augmenter » un soldat par l'entremise d'une indication non prescrite[20]. Les amphétamines constituent un autre groupe de substances qui agissent comme stimulants et dont l'emploi a été approuvé par l'US Air Force pour des missions de longue durée[21]. Il existe des substances qui agissent sur la cognition et qui sont utilisées dans le traitement de troubles mentaux, telles que le propranolol, qui s'est avéré efficace dans le traitement des effets mémoriels provoqués par des troubles post-traumatiques (*post-traumatic stress disorder,* PTSD). Ces troubles PTSD reflètent un état bien connu des militaires, mais comme le propanolol a été utilisé dans ce cas comme traitement plus que comme augmentation des capacités, il n'entre pas dans le champ de cette étude[22].

Dans une perspective purement physique, il existe un certain nombre de PCE qui pourraient être utilisées pour « augmenter » un soldat, parmi lesquelles figurent les stéroïdes anabolisants, l'érythropoiétine (dopage sanguin), et les hormones de croissance[23]. Actuellement, ces substances sont interdites par les militaires, sauf si elles sont prescrites par un médecin pour une indication précise[24]. Intuitivement il semble que l'on souhaite un soldat « plus fort »

---

19 Kelli J. Westcott, "Modafinil, Sleep Deprivation, and Cognitive Function in Military and Medical Settings" (« Le modafinil, la privation de sommeil et la fonction cognitive dans les cadres militaire et médical »), *Military Medicine* 170, n (2005), 334.

20 *Ibid.*

21 John A. Caldwell et J. Lynn Caldwell, "Fatigue in Military Aviation: An Overview of U.S. Military-Approved Pharmacological Countermeasures" (« La fatigue chez les forces aéromobiles, étude des contremesures pharmacologiques approuvées par les militaires »), *Aviation, Space and Environmental Medicine* 76, n°7 (2005): C45.

22 Alain Brunet *et al,* "Reduction of PTSD Symptoms With Pre-Reactivation Propranolol Therapy: A Randomized Controlled Trial" (« Réduction des symptômes PTSD par une thérapie de pré-réactivation au propanolol : test randomisé »), *American Journal of Psychiatry* 175, n° 5 (2018): 427–33.

23 Karl E. Friedl, "U.S. Army Research on Pharmacological Enhancement of Soldier Performance: Stimulants, Anabolic Hormones, and Blood Doping" (« Recherches de l'Armée de Terre Britannique sur l'augmentation opérationnelle des soldats par voie pharmacologique : stimulants, hormones anabolisantes et dopage sanguin »), *The Journal of Strength & Conditioning Research* 29 (2015): S72.

24 Armée de Terre britannique, British Army, "People, Drugs and Supplements" (« Les personnes, les médicaments et les suppléments médicamenteux »), British Army, "People.

pour le combat rapproché, et l'Armée de Terre britannique a récemment élevé le niveau de condition physique requis[25]. D'autre part, l'importance de la force « brute » pour le personnel militaire au combat est peut-être perçue comme étant moins critique, puisque l'accès aux unités d'infanterie de première ligne est autorisé pour les femmes depuis 2018[26]. Incontestablement, un avantage réel apporté par les PCE sur les caractéristiques physiques serait d'augmenter l'énergie et l'endurance tout en réduisant la nécessité de se nourrir ; mais cela reste difficile car des suppléments nutritionnels sont requis pour concrétiser ces effets bénéfiques[27].

L'efficacité des PCE agissant sur les capacités physiques sera discutée plus bas, mais bien que de nombreux sujets sains prennent des substances PCE pour améliorer leur mémoire ou leur niveau de réactivité, l'étude que fait Maslen sur la littérature concernant la question montre que leur efficacité n'est pas démontrée ; il y a une augmentation limitée pour certaines tâches spécifiques, à des doses particulières, pour une partie des personnes concernées[28]. Il est intéressant de noter que la recherche n'a pas déterminé si les effets positifs des PCE améliorent les performances des systèmes d'armes habités ainsi que le bien-être des équipages[29]. D'autres questions à prendre en compte sont par

---

Drugs and Supplements," <https://www.army.mod.uk/people/join-well/drugs-and-supplements/>, (dernière consultation 30 mars 2020).

25 Armée de Terre britannique, "New Physical Employment Standards for the Army" (« Nouvelles normes physiques d'emploi pour l'Armée de Terre »), <https://www.army.mod.uk/physical-employment-standards/> (consulté le 6 mai 2020).

26 Lizzie Dearden, "Women Now Allowed to Apply for Royal Marines and All Other Frontline Military Roles, Defence Secretary Announces" (« Les femmes peuvent à présent candidater pour les Royal Marines et tout autre rôle militaire de contact, annonce le secrétaire à la Défense »), *The Independent*, 25 octobre 2018, <https://www.independent.co.uk/news/uk/home-news/women-soldiers-army-military-sas-defence-government-infantry-frontline-gavin-williamson-female-a8601371.html> (consulté le 2 avril 2020).

27 Joaquin Perez-Guisado et Philip M Jakeman, "Citrulline Malate Enhances Athletic Anaerobic Performance and Relieves Muscle Soreness" (*Le malate de citruline augmente les performances anaérobies athlétiques et soulage les douleurs musculaires*), *Journal of Strength and Conditioning Research* 24, n° (2010), 1222.

28 Hannah Maslen, Nadira Faulmüller et Julian Savulescu, "Pharmacological Cognitive Enhancement – How Neuroscientific Research Could Advance Ethical Debate" (« L'augmentation cognitive par la pharmacologie – comment la recherche neuroscientifique pourrait faire avancer le débat éthique »), *Frontiers in Systems Neuroscience* 8 (2014): 3.

29 Martin Meijer, "A Human Performance Perspective on the Ethical Use of Cogniceuticals: Commentary on 'Recommendations for the Ethical Use of Pharmacologic Fatigue Countermeasures in the U.S. Military'" (« Perspective de la performance humaine liée à la prise éthique de substances d'augmentation cognitive : commentaires sur les « recommandations concernant l'utilisation éthique de contremesures pour diminuer la

exemple : devrait-on utiliser les PCE de manière routinière ou seulement pour des missions précises, pour lesquelles leur non-utilisation pourrait entraîner des conséquences désastreuses ?

Pourquoi les PCE ont-elles une raison d'être actuellement ?

Discuter de l'utilisation de PCE dans le cadre militaire actuellement est pertinent, non seulement pour ajuster les discussions d'ordre éthique sur les avancées technologiques rapides, mais aussi pour la comparer à la place du sport dans ce débat, où il existe des problèmes semblables concernant la sécurité et la politique à suivre. En dépit des efforts accomplis pour éliminer les produits dopants du sport, leur utilisation reste très répandue du fait de l'attractivité du succès et de gains élevés, le risque de détection étant peu élevé et les sanctions minimes[30]. L'Agence Mondiale Antidopage (AMA) a déclaré l'utilisation des produits dopants illégale du fait du manque d'équité et d'égalité qu'elle créait si elle entraînait des performances augmentées, ou présentait un risque pour la santé, ou violait « l'esprit du sport »[31]. Parmi les PCE interdits par l'AMA, on distingue en gros deux catégories : les produits qui augmentent la force et ceux qui augmentent l'énergie[32]. De nombreux participants à des compétitions sportives ont bénéficié d'effets spectaculairement positifs après la prise de PCE pour prendre l'avantage, ce qui est exactement le même effet souhaité pour les militaires[33].

Savulescu prétend que le sport amène une discrimination à l'encontre des « génétiquement inaptes, » le gagnant est celui doté d'une combinaison de potentiels génétiques et d'un équilibre idéal entre sa psychologie, son

---

fatigue dans l'Armée américaine »), *Aviation, Space, and Environmental Medicine* 78, n° 5 (2007): B133.

30 J. Savulescu, B. Foffy et M. Clayton, "Why We Should Allow Performance Enhancing Drugs in Sport" (« Pourquoi l'utilisation de produits dopants dans le sport devrait être autorisée »), *British Journal of Medicine* 38, n° 6 (2004): 665.

31 Agence Mondiale Antidopage, *Code mondial antidopage*, (Montréal: Agence Mondiale Antidopage, 2015), 14, 30, « https://www.wada-ama.org/sites/default/files/resources/files/wada_anti-doping_code_2019_english_final_revised_v1_linked.pdf » (consulté le 12 mars 2020).

32 Lincoln Allison, "Faster, Stronger, Higher" (« Plus vite, plus fort, plus haut »), *The Guardian*, 9 août 2004, <https://www.theguardian.com/sport/2004/aug/09/athensolympics2004.olympicgames> (consulté le 1er janvier 2020).

33 Kate Harvey, "Sports Science and Medicine" (« La science et la médecine du sport »), The Nuffield Council on Bioethics, 2014, 5 <https://nuffieldbioethics.org/publications/sports-science-and-medicine> (consulté le 6 janvier 2020).

entraînement et son jugement. C'est pourquoi il souhaiterait que les compétiteurs soient autorisés à prendre des PCE pour égaliser les chances, éliminer l'inégalité génétique et l'écart financier entre les pays riches et les pays pauvres[34]. Les arguments contre ou en faveur des produits dopants se réfèrent à la justice et à l'égalité, contrairement aux militaires qui visent à éviter la justice et l'égalité en recherchant l'avantage sur l'adversaire. Un autre argument avancé par Mehlman est qu'un sportif « augmenté » ne profite pas à la société, alors que le fait d'augmenter les capacités du personnel militaire pour augmenter les chances de succès d'une mission à caractère national pourrait diminuer les risques encourus par la société entière[35]. Là où les deux opposants dans le débat sur le sport tombent d'accord, c'est que la santé et la sécurité de la personne l'emportent sur tout le reste[36]. Par contre, pour les militaires, la sécurité et la santé de l'unité ou même de la société l'emportent sur celles de l'individu.

Pourquoi les individus et les militaires prendraient-ils des substances pharmacologiques d'augmentation des capacités (PCE) ?

Les militaires pourraient souhaiter utiliser ces produits pour trois raisons : pour prendre l'avantage sur l'adversaire, pour être à la hauteur de ses capacités, ou dans le cas d'une opération de coalition avec d'autres nations. La possibilité d'augmenter les capacités humaines et de prendre l'avantage sur l'ennemi n'est pas une chose nouvelle. La guerre, au cours des siècles, a impliqué des combats frontaux et même avec la technologie moderne, c'est encore ce que l'on recherche comme on le voit dans la guerre contre le terrorisme et l'engagement du Royaume-Uni dans les conflits en Irak et en Afghanistan. Les Incas mâchaient au XVe siècle des feuilles de coca qui contenaient de la cocaïne et réduisaient la faim, la soif et la fatigue, tout en augmentant l'énergie et l'endurance[37]. Du rhum était distribué aux soldats et aux marins au XVIIe siècle

---

34 Savulescu, Foddyu, et Clayton, Savulescu, Foddy, and Clayton, "Why We Should Allow Performance Enhancing Drugs in Sport" (« Pourquoi les produits dopants devraient être autorisés dans le sport »), 667–8.

35 Mehlman, Lin et Abney, "Enhanced Warfighters: A Policy Framework" (« Le soldat augmenté : un cadre pour une politique »), 114.

36 Julian Savulescu, Leon Creaney et Anna Vondy, "Should Athletes Be Allowed to Use Performance Enhancing Drugs?" (« Doit-on autoriser les athlètes à utiliser des produits dopants ? ») *BMJ* (Critical Research Ed) 347 (20132): f6150.

37 L. Kamienski, Shooting Up: A History of Drugs in Warfare (« Le dopage : histoire des drogues dans la guerre »), (Oxford : Hurst, 2017), 46–47.

car on croyait que l'alcool en faisait de meilleurs combattants[38]. L'emploi de l'opium a eu des résultats mitigés : les soldats indiens y ont gagné en combativité et en efficacité au combat, alors que les Chinois ont subi des conséquences d'un abus d'opium suffisamment significatives pour affecter considérablement les capacités de leurs troupes[39].

À l'époque moderne, les amphétamines ont été utilisées pour améliorer l'énergie et maintenir la vigilance, comme les équipages des chars allemands qui prenaient du « Panzerschokolade » (chocolat du tankiste), et les pilotes de la RAF qui utilisaient la benzédrine[40]. La guerre menée par les États-Unis au Viêt-Nam a vu chez les soldats une consommation sans précédent de substances auto-prescrites psychoactives comme les amphétamines, la marijuana, le LSD et l'héroïne[41]. Des groupes armés irréguliers comme ISIS, les Talibans et Al-Qaïda ont utilisé des drogues psychoactives pour compenser leur manque de capacités militaires et en ont distribué comme récompense ou pour recruter des hommes, aussi bien que pour augmenter leurs capacités[42]. Les combattants de Daesh ont utilisé la « pilule jihadiste », produite surtout en Syrie, pour devenir intrépides et euphoriques[43].

Toutes les armées cherchent à obtenir l'avantage sur l'adversaire pour accroître les chances de succès de leur mission, que ce soit en faisant appel à la technologie, à l'entraînement ou à la doctrine ; un avantage dans le domaine cognitif en fait partie[44]. Ce point est devenu encore plus important depuis que le Royaume-Uni a réduit le nombre de recrues d'active au cours de la dernière décennie tout en maintenant les attentes. Bien que les plateformes modernes dédiées au combat emploient moins d'opérateurs et de personnel de maintenance, la conséquence en demeure un système surchargé et sous tension. L'impact est plus grand de par une résilience réduite du personnel, comme les médias l'ont souligné en indiquant qu'on prescrivait des antidépresseurs

38 *Ibid.*, 9.

39 *Ibid.*, 63.

40 *Ibid.*, 111, 117.

41 *Ibid.*, 188.

42 *Ibid.*, 233–235.

43 Mirren Gidda, "Drugs in War: What Is Captagon, the 'Jihad Pill' Used by Islamic State Militants?" (« Les drogues et la guerre : qu'est-ce que le Captagon, la « pilule jihadiste » utilisée par les combattants de l'État islamique ? »), *Newsweek*, 12 mai 2017 <https://www.newsweek.com/drugs-captagon-islamic-state-jihad-war-amphetamines-saudi-arabia-608233> (consulté le 26 mars 2020).

44 Michael B. Russo, "Recommendations for the Ethical Use of Pharmacologic Fatigue Countermeasures in the U.S. Military" (« Recommandations pour l'usage éthique de contremesures pharmacologiques pour combattre la fatigue dans l'armée américaine »), *Aviation, Space and Environmental Medicine* 78, n° 5 (2007): B125.

à un membre du personnel militaire sur treize depuis 2018, le taux de suicide étant en hausse[45]. Le manque de sommeil est également un problème pour les troupes, en opération ou hors opération, et ceci réduit leur fonctionnement cognitif, problème aggravé par la consommation de caféine et d'alcool[46]. Si la privation de sommeil détériore le jugement, augmente le risque d'erreur d'origine humaine et réduit la capacité d'innovation, il pourrait être impératif de donner des PCE aux soldats pour éviter de mauvaises prises de décision dues à une fatigue inévitable lors des opérations de combat[47].

En second lieu, toutes les armées modernes se font face à présent sur une base de parité technologique croissante dans un monde d'une fragilité elle aussi croissante[48]. Il faut accepter la perspective de voir les futurs adversaires fournir des PCE à leurs troupes pour amoindrir la fatigue, augmenter la force musculaire ou pour créer d'autres avantages dans le but de vaincre[49]. L'Armée de Terre américaine a approuvé l'usage de dextroamphétamine et l'US Air Force a approuvé le modafinil pour des pilotes et agents déterminés[50]. Les États-Unis disposent de spécialistes militaires de la recherche médicale cognitive qui développent et mettent à disposition des médicaments de pointe[51].

---

45 Sean Reymant, "Thousands of Soldiers on Antidepressants as They Battle Mental Health Issues, New Figures Reveal" (« Des milliers de soldats sous anti dépresseurs alors qu'ils luttent contre des problèmes mentaux, selon les dernières statistiques »), *The Mirror*, 28 juillet 2018.
<https://www.mirror.co.uk/news/uk-news/thousands-soldiers-antidepressants-battle-mental-12996613>; Ministry of Defence, "FOI2017/13417," 2018, <https://assets.publishing.service.gov.uk/government/uploads/system/uploads/attachment_data/file/691866/2017-13417.pdf> (consulté le 31 mars 2020).

46 Paul Scharre et Lauren Fish, "Human Performance Enhancement" (« L'augmentation des capacités humaines »), Center for a New American Security, 2018, 7, <https://www.cnas.org/publications/reports/human-performance-enhancement-1> (consulté le 6 janvier 2020).

47 Olav Kjellevold Olsen, Ståle Pallesen, and Eid Jarle, "The Impact of Partial Sleep Deprivation on Moral Reasoning in Military Officers" (« L'impact de privation partielle de sommeil sur le raisonnement chez les officiers »), *SLEEP* 33, n° 8 (2010): 1086.

48 Kenneth Ford et Clark Glymour, "The Enhanced Warfighter" (« Le soldat augmenté »), *Bulletin of the Atomic Scientists* 70, no. 1 (2014): 43.

49 *Ibid.*, 47.

50 Mary A. Kautz, Maria L. Thomas, et J. Lynn Caldwell, "Considerations of Pharmacology on Fitness for Duty in the Operational Environment" (« Considérations de la pharmacologie sur les capacités requises pour le service dans l'environnement opérationnel ») *Aviation, Space, and Environmental Medicine* 78, no. 5 (2007): B109.

51 Eric B. Schoomaker, "Military Medical Research on Cognitive Performance: The Warfighters Competitive Edge" (« La recherche médicale militaire sur les capacités cognitives : l'avantage des militaires sur l'aversaire »), *Aviation, Space, and Environmental Medicine* 78, no. 5 (2007): B4.

Ils s'intéressent déjà aux PCE qui améliorent la tolérance à la douleur ainsi qu'à l'oxygène encapsulé qui peut être stocké dans le corps pour augmenter les chances de survie pour les combattants blessés[52]. Il y a de fortes chances pour que d'autres acteurs étatiques et non-étatiques fassent la même chose, et par conséquent le Royaume-Uni doit faire de même pour égaliser les chances sur le champ de bataille[53].

En troisième lieu, les Armées britanniques pourraient avoir besoin de PCE pour travailler avec l'OTAN, l'ONU et d'autres forces de coalition au cas où quelques-unes ou toutes les autres nations utilisent des PCE. Il existe des risques inévitables dans le cas d'une disparité lorsque ce qui est éthiquement acceptable pour une nation peut être inacceptable pour une autre. Prenons le cas des Fijiens auxquels le chef d'une coalition occidentale avait interdit la consommation d'alcool mais pas celle de produire et de boire du kava, une substance qui contient des composés psychoactifs et qui agit sur la vision nocturne[54]. Qu'arrive-t-il si un soldat de la coalition qui a pris des PCE pour améliorer sa vigilance réagit à une situation d'urgence et a besoin du soutien d'un soldat britannique non « augmenté » qui est somnolent et incapable de réagir ?

Il existe un ensemble de raisons pour lesquelles un soldat peut faire usage de PCE. Schelle considère que la pression exercée par les autres soldats constitue un facteur d'influence important pour l'usage des PCE[55]. Il s'agit habituellement d'un processus positif, une personne étant plus susceptible de faire usage de PCE si ses amis et collègues en font autant, mais l'inverse est vrai aussi lorsqu'une forte désapprobation de la part des autres peut amoindrir la volonté de faire usage de PCE. Ces effets peuvent être multipliés par la pression sociale à l'extérieur du groupe d'amis proches. Une étude menée par des étudiants d'une université allemande a révélé que la volonté de prendre des PCE dépend de

52 James Patrey *et al.*, "Human Performance Enhancement for NATO Military Operations" (« Augmentation des capacités humaines pour les opérations militaires de l'OTAN »), (Science, Technology, and Ethics)," dans *NATO Research and Technology Organisation* (Virginia, USA: Office of Naval Research Warfighter Performance Department, 2009), 1, <https://apps.dtic.mil/dtic/tr/fulltext/u2/a562561.pdf> (consulté le 6 janvier 2020).

53 President's Council on Bioethics, *Beyond Therapy: Biotechnology and the Pursuit of Happiness*, Conseiller du Président sur la bioéthique (« Au delà de la thérapie : la biotechnologie et la poursuite du bonheur »), (New York: Regan Books, 2003), 136.

54 Russo, "Recommendations for the Ethical Use of Pharmacologic Fatigue Countermeasures in the U.S. Military" (« Recommandations pour l'usage éthique de contremesures pharmacologiques contre la fatigue chez les militaires américains »), B121.

55 Kimberly J. Schelle *et al.*, "Attitudes toward Pharmacological Cognitive Enhancement – a Review," (« Attitudes envers l'augmentation cognitive par voie pharmacologique – bilan »), *Frontiers in Systems Neuroscience* 8 (2014): 8.

l'attitude personnelle face au risque, de la prépondérance de l'influence exercée par les autres, du coût et des effets secondaires[56].

Les médias peuvent avoir une influence sur le fait de savoir si un individu peut faire usage de PCE en prenant plus clairement parti et en portant le problème à la connaissance du public. Une équipe de l'université de Cambridge a indiqué que 10 % des étudiants faisaient usage de substances comme le modafinil et la Ritaline pour améliorer leurs résultats universitaires ; ceci met en lumière les avantages et la normalité de cet usage[57]. Pourtant les effets secondaires sont connus, BBC News a même effectué un reportage sur le prix à payer par un étudiant pour les « pilules de l'intelligence », tout en soulignant l'illégalité de la vente de ces produits[58]. La société peut changer de perspective et d'attitude rapidement si les PCE sont normalisées par voie de presse, et l'usage des PCE peut être adopté si les médias multiplient les reportages[59].

Une autre raison de faire usage de PCE est l'automédication par choix de style de vie, pour faciliter la récupération après une séance de sport ou une activité physique quelconque, ou pour améliorer des performances physiques. De nombreux membres des forces armées utilisent déjà des « suppléments » qui vont des substances diététiques aux produits interdits ; c'est le cas de 38 % des recrues britanniques en formation selon une étude[60]. Il est étonnant que des soldats continuent à prendre des substances interdites malgré une politique de tolérance zéro[61]. Il existe des raisons spécifiques pour lesquelles des soldats prennent délibérément des PCE si l'on pense aux valeurs et à la philosophie inculquées aux militaires lorsqu'ils sont recrutés. Ils peuvent croire que

---

56 Sebastian Sattler *et al.*, "Evaluating the Drivers of and Obstacles to the Willingness to Use Cognitive Enhancement Drugs: The Influence of Drug Characteristics, Social Environment, and Personal Characteristics," (« Évaluation des facteurs favorisants et des obstacles concernant la volonté de faire usage des drogues d'augmentation cognitive : l'influence des caractéristiques des substances, de l'environnement social et des caractéristiques personnelles »), *Substance Abuse Treatment, Prevention, and Policy* 9, no. 1 (2014): 5.

57 Natasha Lennard, "One in Ten Takes Drugs to Study," *Varsity*, 6 mars 2009, <https://www.varsity.co.uk/news/1307> (consulté le mars 31, 2020).

58 BBC News, "Sussex University Students Illegally Buying 'Smart Pills,'" *BBC News*, 13 mars 2018, <https://www.bbc.co.uk/news/uk-england-43383717> (consulté le mars 31, 2020).

59 Adam Bear and Joshua Knobe, "Normality: Part Descriptive, Part Prescriptive," (« La normalité : mi-description, mi-prescription »), *Cognition* 167 (2017): 25.

60 Anna Casey *et al.*, "Supplement Use by UK-Based British Army Soldiers in Training," (« L'usage des compléments alimentaires ou autres par les soldats de l'Armée de Terre britannique en formation au Royaume-Uni »), *The British Journal of Nutrition* 112, no. 7 (2014): 1178–1180.

61 British Army, "People. Drugs and Supplements." Armée de Terre britannique, *Les drogues et autres « suppléments. »*

c'est une chose honorable, s'ils pensent qu'elles font partie d'un code moral, ou même ressentir un sentiment de culpabilité vis-à-vis de collègues qui sont déjà en opération. Un collègue peut, pour venger la mort d'un camarade au combat, prendre des PCE et augmenter ses capacités pour rechercher une occasion d'agression.

Enfin, il existe certaines activités professionnelles pour lesquelles les individus doivent se soumettre à certaines exigences, comme se laver les mains pour les chirurgiens avant d'opérer, ou les périodes de repos obligatoires pour les chauffeurs routiers[62]. Ce « contrat » professionnel dans lequel un individu consent à effectuer des actions spécifiques et à accepter certaines tâches est fondamentalement motivé par la préservation de leur santé et de leur sécurité. Donc les militaires pourraient déterminer une raison d'ordre professionnel pour que le personnel prenne des PCE de la même manière que l'US Air Force fait prendre des stimulants à ses pilotes pour des missions de longue durée. Cependant il est peu probable que cette démarche soit adoptée pour la majorité des PCE, pour lesquels la limite entre les risques et les avantages n'est pas clairement définie.

Quelles sont les préoccupations des militaires concernant l'usage des PCE (augmentation des capacités par voie pharmacologique) ?

Il existe un certain nombre de questions concernant l'usage des PCE dans les Armées : questions d'ordre juridique, politique, opérationnel, mais aussi des questions sur les relations civilo-militaires et le consentement éclairé. Les forces britanniques doivent respecter à la fois les règlements militaires et la législation, en notant que « Pour que les Forces Armées puissent opérer efficacement, il faut nécessairement maintenir la discipline personnelle et celle qui est imposée »[63]. Si des PCE sont illégales dans la vie civile ou interdites dans le cadre militaire, elles ne pourront pas être autoprescrites ; si elles sont autorisées, on doit mettre en place une politique pour encadrer leur usage.

Interdire les PCE ou limiter leur accès pourrait entraîner un accroissement du marché noir et conduire à une dégradation de la sécurité. C'est ce qui est

62 Maslen, Faulmüller, and Savulescu, "Pharmacological Cognitive Enhancement – How Neuroscientific Research Could Advance Ethical Debate" (« L'augmentation cognitive par voie pharmacologique – comment la recherche neuroscientifique pourrait faire avancer le débat éthique »).

63 Royaume-Uni, ministère de la Défense JSP 830: The Manual of Service Law (Londres: HMSO, 2016), 1-1-3. (JSP 830 *Manuel de Discipline Générale dans les Armées*).

arrivé avec le Viagra, ce qui a obligé la MHRA (Agence pour la réglementation des produits médicinaux et de santé) à le changer de catégorie : à l'origine « produit prescrit sur ordonnance », il est devenu « produit accessible sans ordonnance »[64]. D'autres études sur la sûreté et l'efficacité donneront confiance aux consommateurs dans l'usage des PCE, et le fait de légaliser les PCE permettra de les développer tout en les rendant ainsi moins chers et plus sûrs[65]. Les militaires devraient s'inspirer de la recommandation de Scharre, c'est-à-dire instaurer une politique très précise, examiner chaque PCE au cas par cas et étudier son efficacité, sa sûreté et son utilité[66]. De plus, l'usage des PCE dans la recherche ou en opération doit être basé sur le volontariat.

Le programme 17 de la réglementation médicale du Royaume-Uni autorise les Forces Armées à fournir et administrer des médicaments aux soldats en se passant d'une ordonnance officielle[67]. Le but de cette exemption est de protéger les troupes dans les environnements où aucun médecin n'est disponible. Tout traitement devrait – idéalement – être prescrit par un auxiliaire sanitaire (« medic »)[68] qui a été déclaré compétent par un médecin ; s'il n'y a pas de personnel ayant une certaine compétence médicale, l'autorisation doit être obtenue par l'entremise d'une communication avec un médecin si cela est possible. Qu'est-ce qui empêche le chef d'une unité déployée d'ordonner à ses auxiliaires sanitaires de prescrire des PCE, ou d'ordonner au soldat de se les administrer tout comme on prend des comprimés de fentanyl ?[69] Même si l'on

---

64 Sabrina Barr, "Viagra Now Available over the Counter without Prescription in UK" (« Le Viagra maintenant disponible sans ordonnance au Royaume-Uni »), *The Independent*, le 27 mars 2018, <https://www.independent.co.uk/life-style/health-and-families/viagra-buy-without-prescription-over-counter-uk-pharmacies-male-impotence-erectile-dysfunction-a8275461.html> (consulté le 3 avril 2020).

65 Bostrom et Sandberg, "Cognitive Enhancement: Methods, Ethics, Regulatory Challenges" (« L'augmentation des capacités cognitives : méthodes, éthique, problèmes de réglementation »), 333.

66 Scharre et Fish, "Human Performance Enhancement," (*L'augmentation des capacités humaines*), 3.

67 Royaume-Uni, "The Human Medicines Regulations 2012," (« La réglementation en matière de médication humaine »), Pub. L. No. 1916, Pro-gramme 17 (2012), Pt. 2, 10, Pt. 5, 17, <http://www.legislation.gov.uk/uksi/2012/1916/schedule/17/made> (consulté le 6 avril 2020).

68 « Medic » est un terme qui désigne un « technicien » médical en zone de combat de l'Armée de Terre Britannique et des autres Armées (de l'Air, etc.). Ils sont formés pour diagnostiquer, prescrire et gérer les urgences médicales mais ne dépendent pas d'un organisme national de réglementation.

69 Équipe NRBC (guerre nucléaire, radiologique, biologique et chimique), *2017DIN04-165. FentanylLozenge800Micrograms(OTFC)Single-IntroductionintoServiceasSelfAdministered Operational Analgesia.* (« Comprimé fentazyl 800 microgrammes : introduction dans les

se trouve dans un cadre légal, il doit y avoir une autorité responsable dans ce cas de figure pour assurer la sécurité et la protection du soldat.

Dans une perspective opérationnelle et de commandement, les éléments de coercition et d'insubordination seront discutés dans la partie traitant du consentement éclairé, mais l'usage des PCE a d'autres impacts potentiels. La carrière d'un soldat serait-elle accélérée si, en prenant des PCE, il se voyait dès lors confier des missions plus importantes ? Le même facteur pourrait affecter sa rémunération, sa promotion et l'attribution de récompenses et de médailles. La cohésion et le moral d'une unité sont vitaux pour le succès d'une mission grâce à la communication, au travail d'équipe et à une philosophie morale partagée. Tout ceci resterait-il inchangé entre les soldats « augmentés » et les autres ? Cela pourrait-il entraîner les soldats « non-augmentés » dans un scénario de type « eux c'est eux, nous c'est nous » et les amener à se sentir des soldats de deuxième catégorie ou des laissés pour compte ? Plus important : une mission pourrait être annulée si ceux qui l'entreprennent ne sont pas « augmentés ».

Les soldats représentent la société et ses valeurs, et l'on compte sur eux pour protéger la société tout en respectant les droits humains et les lois humanitaires internationales[70]. Le Royaume-Uni a un contrat moral intitulé « Armed Forces Covenant » (AFC), qui reconnaît que les soldats placent les besoins du service au-dessus des leurs, ce qui potentiellement peut amener le sacrifice de leur vie, et que la société doit s'assurer qu'ils sont traités avec équité ; ainsi est établie une relation « gagnant – gagnant » entre les militaires et la société[71]. Ce contrat (ou convention) (« covenant ») établit un cadre définissant un devoir de protection envers le personnel militaire ayant accepté une discipline imposée et par conséquent une réduction de son autonomie ; aussi, le public n'approuverait pas l'usage des PCE s'il était considéré comme peu sûr ou injuste. Ce devoir de protection a été considéré comme si important que le gouvernement a invité les autres services à mettre à jour leurs responsabilités légales et morales et pas seulement à réitérer leurs valeurs, normes et philosophie morale[72].

armées comme analgésique opérationnel auto-administré »), (Bristol, ministère de la Défense, 2017).

70 Armée de Terre Britannique, *Values and Standards of the British Army, AC 64649* (« Valeurs et normes de l'Armée de Terre Britannique »), (Andover : état-major de l'Armée de Terre, 2018), 25.

71 Helen McCartney, "The Military Covenant and the Civil–Military Contract in Britain" (« La convention militaire et le contrat civilo-militaire en Grande-Bretagne »), *International Affairs* 86, no. 2 (2010): 413.

72 Commission de la Défense de la Chambre des Communes, *Duty of Care* (« Devoir de diligence ») *2004–05. Volume I. HC63-I* (Londres: The Stationery Office Limited, 2005), 5.

CHAPITRE 2

Le consentement éclairé

Théorie du consentement éclairé (« informed consent, IC »)

Avant d'examiner en détail les questions relevant du consentement éclairé dans le milieu militaire, il n'est pas inutile de comprendre son évolution. Le XXe siècle a connu un certain nombre d'événements fondamentaux qui ont donné forme au développement du consentement éclairé (IC) ; le premier est apparu lors de la Seconde Guerre mondiale, lorsque les nazis ont utilisé des prisonniers des camps de concentration comme cobayes pour effectuer des expériences cruelles, contre leur volonté. Après les procès qui s'ensuivirent, au cours desquels des médecins durent répondre de leurs actes, le Code de Nuremberg a été rédigé en 1947, lequel énumérait dix principes explicites concernant l'expérimentation médicale sur les êtres humains et interdisait les expériences sur les prisonniers[1]. Le premier principe était l'obtention d'un consentement éclairé (IC) volontaire de la part du sujet[2]. L'année suivante, les Nations-Unies rédigèrent une Déclaration des Droits Humains en réponse aux actions inhumaines perpétrées par les nazis à une grande échelle, dont l'article 5 stipulait que personne ne devait être soumis à des traitements cruels ou inhumains[3].

La Déclaration d'Helsinki (1964), rédigée par l'Association Médicale Mondiale, promulgua les principes éthiques pour la recherche sur les êtres humains ou les données et restes humains identifiables, en distinguant les procédures thérapeutiques et non-thérapeutiques[4]. Elle a défini le devoir

---

1 "The Nuremberg Code (1947)" (« Le Code de Nuremberg »), *British Medical Journal* 313, no. 7070 (1996): 1448.

2 Michael Gross, *Military Medical Research Ethics: Investigational Drugs, Clinical Trials and Enhancement* (« L'éthique dans la recherche médicale militaire : recherche sur les médicaments, tests cliniques et augmentation des capacités humaines »), dans: Ana S. Iltis and Douglas MacKay (ed), (Oxford: Oxford University Press, 2019), 2.

3 United Nations, "Universal Declaration of Human Rights" (*Déclaration Universelle des Droits Humains*), 1948, <https://www.un.org/en/universal-declaration-human-rights/> (consulté le 9 janvier 2020).

4 Association Médicale Mondiale, "Ethical Principles for Medical Research Involving Human Subjects" (« Principes éthiques pour la recherche médicale impliquant des sujets humains »), WMA Declaration d'Helsinki, 2018, <https://www.wma.net/policies-post/wma-declaration-of-helsinki-ethical-principles-for-medical-research-involving-human-subjects/>, (consulté le 7 avril 2020).

 | DOI:10.1163/9789004677746_014

fondamental des médecins comme étant celui de promouvoir la santé et de protéger le droit des patients dans le cadre de la recherche, le médecin devant être tenu pour responsable sur ces deux points. Les directives précisent que les risques de toute étude ne doivent pas dépasser les avantages recherchés et que l'on doit obtenir l'aval de la Commission d'Éthique pour la Recherche ; le consentement éclairé volontaire du patient est essentiel, et on doit rester attentif à la relation médecin-patient. La déclaration indique que s'il n'est pas prouvé qu'une intervention sera efficace, elle peut tout de même être exécutée, à condition que le patient ait donné son consentement éclairé et que le médecin juge que l'intervention sauvera la vie du patient, rétablira sa santé ou soulagera ses souffrances.

Le Rapport Belmont fut publié en 1979 et se voulait être une tentative de résumer l'état de l'éthique telle qu'elle existait à cette date[5]. Ce rapport définit trois principes de base concernant les personnes, les effets bénéfiques et la justice[6]. Le « respect de la personne » signifie traiter les individus comme personnes autonomes et douées de libre-arbitre, tout en protégeant ceux qui sont considérés comme vulnérables. Les « effets bénéfiques » signifient fondamentalement éviter de nuire et maximiser les bienfaits tout en minimisant les effets néfastes possibles dans le traitement d'un patient. En dernier lieu, la « justice » signifie l'équité, de manière à ce que toute une société partage les bienfaits de la recherche ainsi que ses contraintes.

Nuremberg, Helsinki et Belmont étaient tous axés sur l'éthique de la recherche et la nécessité du consentement volontaire. Le concept du consentement éclairé (IC) concernant les questions médicales est apparu dans les années 50, préconisant d'accorder une plus grande importance à la compréhension du patient qu'à la simple déclaration du médecin. Avant les années 50, tout consentement impliquait d'éviter au maximum toute déclaration pouvant déstabiliser le patient[7]. L'affaire Salgo en 1957 donna son nom au concept de « informed concept » (IC) : un homme fut frappé de paralysie suite à une intervention médicale routinière. Le cas fut qualifié de « blessure occasionnée

5 Commission Nationale pour la protection des êtres humains soumis à la recherche biomédicale et comportementale, "The Belmont Report: Ethical Principles and Guidelines for the Protection of Human Subjects of Research," (« Le Rapport Belmont : principes et directives éthiques pour la protection des êtres humains soumis à des expériences médicales »), 1979, <https://www.hhs.gov/ohrp/sites/default/files/the-belmont-report-508c_FINAL.pdf>, (consulté le 8 janvier 2020).

6 *Ibid.*, 4.

7 Tom L. Beauchamp, "Informed Consent: Its History, Meaning, and Present Challenges" (« Le consentement éclairé : son histoire, sa signification et les défis actuels »), *Cambridge Quarterly of Healthcare Ethics* 20, no. 4 (2011): 515.

involontairement, » le jugement stipulant qu'il y avait obligation de déclarer les risques et les choix de traitement[8]. Quelques années plus tard, l'affaire Natanson alla plus loin en qualifiant l'absence de consentement éclairé d'acte de négligence de la part du médecin et non plus de blessure involontaire ; cette position n'a pas évolué depuis[9]. En 1972, trois affaires différentes aux USA à des décisions qui privilégiaient le consentement du patient, ce qui signifiait que le patient devait être suffisamment informé pour lui permettre de faire un choix intelligent[10]. Cela déplut aux médecins, qui pensèrent que l'obligation qui leur était faite de délivrer ces informations serait trop onéreuse, et même incompatible avec des soins satisfaisants.

S'inspirant du passé, l'IC est basé sur le respect de l'autonomie et l'autodétermination du patient. Le terme « autonomie » vient du grec « auto, » et « nomos » qui signifie « règle » ou « loi. »[11] L'IC est une autorisation autonome donnée par l'individu pour permettre à un professionnel de santé d'exécuter un acte médical sur sa personne, uniquement si l'individu est compétent et libre de tout contrôle exercé par d'autres personnes. Berg a défini l'IC comme étant ce qui « se réfère à la réglementation légale qui prescrit des règles de conduite aux médecins et autres professionnels de santé dans leur interaction avec les patients »[12]. Les deux parties doivent s'engager à ce que le patient dispose du droit à l'IC et à ce que le médecin ait le devoir ou l'obligation de s'y conformer[13]. Le consentement éclairé (IC) peut aussi être envisagé en termes de règle institutionnelle et de politique à suivre ; ainsi, dans le cas des soins de santé, si les règles établies par le National Health Service (Service National de Santé britannique) concernant le consentement sont respectées, celui-ci est considéré comme valide et éclairé[14].

Au cours de ces 50 dernières années, le consentement éclairé a constitué la pratique médicale acceptable d'un point de vue éthique sur la base des valeurs que sont l'autonomie et le bien-être individuel ; actuellement, on

---

8 R. R. Faden, T. L. Beauchamp, et N. M. P. King, *A History and Theory of Informed Consent* (« Histoire et théorie du consentement éclairé »), (New York: Oxford University Press, 1986), 125.

9 *Ibid.*, 129.

10 *Ibid.*, 132.

11 J. W. Berg *et al.*, *Informed Consent: Legal Theory and Clinical Practice* (« Le consentement éclairé : théorie juridique et pratique clinique »), (New York: Oxford University Press, 2001), 15.

12 *Ibid.*, 3.

13 *Ibid.*, 14.

14 Beauchamp, *Informed Consent: Its History, Meaning, and Present Challenges* (« Le consentement éclairé : histoire, signification et défis actuels »), 518.

met davantage l'accent sur une prise de décision commune entre médecin et patient. Comme Berg l'a décrit, l'IC implique des actes formels avec des connotations juridiques, qui nécessitent souvent une documentation, comme pour les actes chirurgicaux. Pour ces actes formels, il est entendu que les deux parties doivent avoir une pleine compréhension des avantages de cette « transaction » ainsi que des effets négatifs éventuels, le patient devant faire confiance au professionnel de santé. De nombreux domaines en dehors de la médecine sont revêtus d'un formalisme croissant et sont souvent considérés de la même manière que la protection du consommateur ou l'étiquette en petits caractères qui accompagne un produit ou un service. Fondamentalement, il semble être le promoteur de la formalité et un consentement écrit constitue une protection des acteurs contre les accusations, les contentieux et les compensations[15].

En résumé, pour que l'IC soit valable dans le domaine des soins de santé, une personne doit respecter les quatre critères suivants :

1. Être mentalement fiable, ce qui potentiellement exclut les personnes vulnérables, inconscientes ou ayant atteint un âge très avancé.
2. Comprendre les risques, les avantages et les autres choix possibles, y compris celui de ne rien faire, avec la possibilité de poser des questions.
3. Avoir la possibilité de revenir sur sa décision n'importe quand.
4. Ne pas se trouver sous la contrainte.

Tout ceci paraît simple et clair mais Corrigan discute ce qu'il considère comme un modèle « éthique vide » dans lequel toute personne autonome et suffisamment informée, et ayant le temps de « digérer » ces informations, prendra la décision d'accepter un traitement ou non. Ceci implique des normes universelles mais fait l'impasse sur les différences culturelles[16]. La capacité de chacun à comprendre exigera une quantité d'informations et de temps variable, ce qui implique que le processus de l'IC devra être adapté à chaque individu.

Les problèmes posés par le consentement éclairé dans le contexte militaire

Dans le passé, les armées avaient aligné leur doctrine IC sur celle des civils, et l'avaient contournée dans certaines circonstances, avec des conséquences

15 O. O'Neill, "Some Limits of Informed Consent" (« Des limites au consentement éclairé »), *Journal of Medical Ethics* 29, no. 1 (2003): 4.

16 Oonagh Corrigan, "Empty Ethics: The Problem with Informed Consent" (« Un vide éthique : le problème posé par le consentement éclairé »), *Sociology of Health & Illness* 25, no. 3 (2003): 770.

néfastes, renonçant au devoir de diligence envers les soldats. La déclaration de Nuremberg prescrit que le principe fondamental est que le consentement volontaire et éclairé du patient est absolument crucial[17]. En dépit de ce principe, le Royaume-Uni et les États-Unis ont pratiqué des expériences sur des personnels militaires sans leur consentement au cours de la Guerre froide, les exposant à des radiations, à des agents chimiques et au LSD[18]. Plus récemment, le département de la Défense des États-Unis a obtenu une dérogation de la Food and Drug Administration (FDA) concernant le consentement pour administrer de la pyridostigmine et des vaccins contre la toxine botulinique à des personnes participant à l'opération Desert Storm[19]. Les raisons invoquées pour cette dérogation étaient qu'il était impossible d'obtenir un consentement éclairé de la part de plus de 500.000 soldats, et que l'on ne pouvait pas les exposer au danger[20]. Le vaccin, mais pas la pyridostigmine, fut finalement administré sur la base du volontariat, l'argument étant « l'expérimentation » contre la « protection » des troupes. La pyridostigmine a été considérée comme sûre après des décennies d'expérimentation, avec l'utilisation de plus fortes doses pour traiter la myasthénie grave, alors que le vaccin a fait l'objet d'investigations pour prouver son efficacité[21].

Il y a donc un dangereux précédent de cas où l'IC a pu faire l'objet d'une dérogation au profit de la Défense. Cependant, pour qu'une telle dérogation soit valide, des conditions rigoureuses doivent être respectées :

> Pour faciliter le succès de la mission militaire, la préservation de la santé de l'individu ainsi que la sécurité des autres personnels, il faut qu'un traitement particulier soit assuré au profit d'un groupe spécifique de

---

17 Gross, *Military Medical Research Ethics: Investigational Drugs, Clinical Trials and Enhancement*, 2. (« L'éthique de la recherche médicale militaire : les substances faisant l'objet de recherches, les tests cliniques et l'augmentation des capacités »).

18 George J. Annas, "Changing the Consent Rules for Desert Storm" (« Le changement de la réglementation du consentement lors de l'Opération Desert Storm »), *New England Journal of Medicine* 326, no. 11 (12 mars 1992): 771, Adam Lusher, "The Bizarre True Story of When the UK Military Tested LSD on Royal Marines" (« L'histoire bizarre mais véridique des tests au LSD pratiqués par l'Armée britannique sur les Royal Marines »), *The Independent,* 24 mai 2018, « https://www.independent.co.uk/news/uk/home-news/lsd-video-porton-down-chemical-weapons-experiments-trials-uk-military-army-marines-sixties-acid-a8366906.html » (consulté le 29 avril 2020).

19 Joel Martin Schofer, "Violations of Informed Consent During War" (« Violation du consentement éclairé en temps de guerre »), *JAMA* 281, no. 17 (1999): 1657.

20 George J. Annas, "Changing the Consent Rules for Desert Storm" (« Le changement de la réglementation du consentement lors de l'Opération Desert Storm »), 770.

21 *Ibid.,* 772.

> militaires, sans tenir compte de ce que pourraient être les préférences personnelles d'un quelconque individu pour une absence de traitement ou pour tout autre traitement[22].

Ceux qui refuseraient les drogues devraient soit quitter le théâtre des opérations sans pouvoir accomplir leurs obligations militaires, soit rester sans protection, ce qui les exposerait aux risques, exposerait leurs camarades à un risque accru, et réduirait les chances de succès de la mission[23]. L'affaire des drogues non approuvées par la FDA et administrées de force par les militaires américains fit l'objet d'un procès qui fut perdu même en appel ; le Code de Nuremberg ne fut pas cité une seule fois, l'usage de la pyridostigmine fut justifié de par son utilisation comme traitement[24].

En 2002, deux pilotes revenant sur le Koweït après un exercice d'entraînement sur une zone lointaine en Afghanistan, prirent par erreur un tir réel pour une activité des insurgés ennemis et tuèrent quatre pilotes canadiens, tragédie due au tir fratricide. Au cours du procès qui s'ensuivit, la défense avança que les pilotes avaient été forcés de prendre de la Dexedrine, ce qui avait dégradé leurs capacités et entraîné leur tir accidentel. La mise en accusation fut rejetée, et bien que la substance médicamenteuse ne fût pas mise en cause, le cas mit en lumière le problème de l'absence de consentement éclairé pour la prise d'une substance prescrite[25]. La Dexedrine a-t-elle affecté leurs capacités mentales ou influencé leur aptitude à contrôler leur comportement, ou s'agit-il simplement

---

22 Richard A. Rettig, "Military Use of Drugs Not Yet Approved by the FDA for CW/BW Defense: Lessons from the Gulf War," (« L'usage militaire des drogues qui ne sont pas encore approuvées par la FDA (Food and Drug Administration) pour la guerre chimique et biologique : enseignements de la guerre du Golfe »), (Santa Monica: RAND Corporation, 1999), XII.

23 Richard A. Rettig, "Waiving Informed Consent: Military Use of Non-FDA-Approved Drugs in Combat" (« Les dérogations pour le consentement éclairé : l'usage militaire de drogues non approuvées par la FDA dans les opérations de combat »), (Santa Monica: RAND Corporation, 2000), <https://www.rand.org/pubs/research_briefs/RB7534.html> (consulté le 30 avril 2020).

24 George J. Annas, "Protecting Soldiers from Friendly Fire: The Consent Requirement for Using Investigational Drugs and Vaccines in Combat" (« La protection des soldats contre les tirs fratricides : la nécessité du consentement pour l'utilisation des drogues et des vaccins expértimentaux dans les opérations de combat »), *American Journal of Law & Medicine* 24, no. 2/3 (1998): 249.

25 Lauren R. Robbins, "Refusing to Be All That You Can Be: Regulating against Forced Cognitive Enhancement in the Military" (« Le refus d'être tout ce que l'on peut être : la règlementation contre l'augmentation forcée des capacités cognitives dans les Armées »), in: *Military Medical Ethics for the 21st Century,* ed. M. L. Gross et D. Carrick, "Military and Defence Ethics," (Farnham: Ashgate Publishing Limited, 2013), 127.

d'une erreur du pilote, ce qui fut la conclusion de la commission d'enquête ?[26] Les soldats américains n'ont pas le droit de refuser un traitement médical qui les rend aptes au combat ou leur permet de réintégrer le service actif[27]. Par conséquent, la Dexedrine fut-elle utilisée comme « traitement, » ou était-elle nécessaire pour les rendre aptes au combat ? La réglementation de l'Armée américaine stipule qu'« un membre de l'Armée de Terre en service actif ou en cours d'entraînement devra habituellement être soumis aux soins médicaux nécessaires pour protéger sa vie, soulager des souffrances inutiles, ou pour protéger ou sauvegarder la santé des autres. »[28] La question fondamentale est de savoir si la prise de PCE constitue une norme des « soins médicaux » pour « protéger ou sauvegarder la vie des autres. »

À la suite des violations passées des droits et de l'éthique de personnels militaires, et du fait du danger de voir la Défense obtenir des dérogations pour éviter l'IC, Mehlman a adapté les principes de Belmont pour les militaires. Les effets bénéfiques obtenus, le respect des personnes et la justice ont changé pour devenir la proportionnalité, le paternalisme et l'équité[29]. En premier lieu, la proportionnalité a trait à l'imposition d'un risque médical à des soldats uniquement si cela est nécessaire pour une opération justifiée, où ce risque est proportionnel aux avantages militaires obtenus. Deuxièmement, le paternalisme intervient en cas d'autonomie réduite et d'un devoir d'obéir qui restreint les capacités d'un soldat à refuser son consentement. Par conséquent, un chef militaire doit s'assurer que les risques biomédicaux imposés sont proportionnés et doit maintenir l'intimité, la dignité et la confidentialité[30]. Enfin, l'équité

---

26 Oliver Burkeman and Richard Norton-Taylor, "US Pilots Blame Drug for Friendly Fire Deaths" (« Des pilotes américains expliquent les morts occasionnés par un feu fratricide par la prise de produits médicamenteux »), *The Guardian,* 4 janvier 2003, <https://www.theguardian.com/world/2003/jan/04/afghanistan.richardnortontaylor> (consulté le 27 mars 2020).

27 Annas, "Protecting Soldiers from Friendly Fire: The Consent Requirement for Using Investigational Drugs and Vaccines in Combat" (« Protection des soldats contre les tirs fratricides : la nécessité du consentement pour l'usage de substances ou de vaccins expérimentaux »), 250.

28 Stephen E. Deardorff, "Informed Consent, Termination of Medical Treatment, and the Federal Tort Claims Act--A New Proposal for the Military Health Care System" (« Le consentement éclairé, la cessation du traitement médical, et le Federal Tort Claims – une nouvelle proposition pour le système de santé des Armées »), *Military Law Review*, No. 115, janvier 1987 : 68.

29 Maxwell J. Mehlman and Stephanie Corley, "A Framework for Military Bioethics" (« Un cadre pour la bioéthique militaire »), *Journal of Military Ethics* 13, no. 4 (2014): 337.

30 Michael L. Gross, *Bioethics and Armed Conflict. Moral Dilemmas of Medicine and War* (« La bioéthique et les conflits armés. Dilemmes moraux de la médecine et de la guerre »), (Cambridge: MIT Press, 2006), 45.

est un domaine difficile pour les chefs militaires qui peuvent être amenés à gérer l'imposition d'un risque biomédical sur une partie de leurs subordonnés, tout en s'assurant que tout se passe sans discrimination, sans que la décision soit vécue comme une punition[31].

Bien que les principes de Belmont aient été élaborés dans le but de guider la recherche, les principes de Mehlman adaptés au milieu militaire stipulent ce que signifie « devoir de diligence » : le terme recouvre toutes les responsabilités morales et juridiques, allant des blessures à la sécurité au travail. Le devoir de diligence est un concept important, une responsabilité de tous les personnels militaires ayant un grade supérieur au simple soldat et responsables ou encadrant leurs subordonnés d'un grade inférieur[32]. Lorsque de nouvelles recrues s'engagent dans les forces armées, elles perdent un certain niveau d'autonomie, et comprennent qu'elles peuvent recevoir l'ordre de se trouver dans une situation mettant leur vie en péril[33]. Le soldat nouvellement recruté consent implicitement à effectuer un ensemble d'activités permettant d'atteindre des objectifs militaires légitimes, sachant que l'institution a le devoir de diligence de minimiser les risques. Un soldat accepte l'utilisation d'armes nouvelles et un entraînement en constante évolution : cela peut-il être comparé à de nouveaux médicaments avec consentement tacite pour la prise de PCE ? Il est universellement admis que les militaires peuvent participer à une guerre impliquant un risque pour leur vie, mais il est moins connu que l'usage de PCE est possible. Néanmoins, ce qui est connu varie toujours avec le temps, et si l'usage des PCE se banalisait, le consentement tacite pourrait devenir légitime.

La chaîne de commandement militaire est responsable de la minimisation des risques et doit garantir le devoir de diligence, en partie assuré pour le Royaume-Uni par le Competent Medical Authority (CMA). Le CMA est un médecin militaire haut gradé qui a donné son aval aux aspects médicaux d'un plan de déploiement, en toute responsabilité. Cependant, qui détient la responsabilité ultime ? Cet organisme est-il indépendant, et est-il habilité à empêcher les militaires de se compromettre pour atteindre leur but ?[34] Comme

---

31 Mehlman and Corley, "A Framework for Military Bioethics," (« Un cadre pour la bioéthique militaire »), 339–340.

32 House of Commons Defence Committee, *Duty of Care*, Third Report of Session (« Commission de la Défense de la Chambre des Communes, Devoir de diligence, troisième rapport de la session »), 2004–05. Volume I. HC 63-I,29.

33 William J. FitzPatrick and Lee L. Zwanziger, "Defending Against Biochemical Warfare" (« La défense contre la guerre biochimique »), *The Journal of Philosophy, Science & Law* 3, no. 2 (2003): 9.

34 Jessica Wolfendale and Steve Clarke, "Paternalism, Consent, and the Use of Experimental Drugs in the Military" (« Le paternalisme, le consentement et l'usage de drogues

les PCE sont classés comme des médicaments, les Defence Medical Services (DMS) (Services Médicaux des Armées) seraient cette autorité militaire et son Général de Corps d'Armée (trois étoiles au RU), qui en est le directeur général, en détient la pleine responsabilité[35]. Heureusement, il existe des inspections externes indépendantes, complétées par la Care Quality Commission (commission pour la qualité des soins), qui peut engager des poursuites contre les DMS si les normes médicales ne sont pas appliquées, par exemple si des personnes subissent des préjudices ou si elles sont placées dans des situations dangereuses[36].

Est-il acceptable que des militaires violent le processus de consentement et adoptent une posture paternaliste s'ils croient que ceci va dans le sens du devoir de diligence ? Le paternalisme a été défini comme « l'immixtion d'un État ou d'un individu sur un autre individu sans son consentement, expliqué ou motivé en prétendant que l'individu sur lequel on interfère s'en portera mieux ou sera protégé contre tout préjudice »[37]. Les politiques paternalistes limitent les choix des individus mais sont permises si l'autorité considère qu'elles sont dans l'intérêt ultime de l'individu[38]. Bien que la médecine se soit éloignée des attitudes paternalistes, celles-ci restent dominantes dans les Armées aujourd'hui et des dérogations peuvent être accordées au processus de consentement si un individu, en privilégiant ses propres inclinations, met sa vie en danger ainsi que celle des autres[39] ; il faut souligner à ce propos que la santé d'un soldat peut affecter ceux qui l'entourent[40]. Si des dérogations sont accordées pour les PCE, cela fait-il de l'individu un cobaye, et cela fait-il que la drogue va tomber dans la catégorie « expérimentale » ou « en cours

---

expérimentales dans les Armées »), *The Journal of Medicine and Philosophy: A Forum for Bioethics and Philosophy of Medicine* 33, no. 4 (2008): 347.

35 United Kingdom. HM Government, "Defence Medical Services" (*Services de Santé de la Défense*) <https://www.gov.uk/government/groups/defence-medical-services> (consulté le 1er mai 2020).

36 Care Quality Commission, "Defence Medical Services" (Commission pour la qualité de la diligence, « Les Services de Santé des Armées »), 2019, <https://www.cqc.org.uk/what-we-do/services-we-regulate/defence-medical-services,> (consulté le 9 avril 2020).

37 Gerald Dworkin, "Paternalism" ed. Edward N. Zalta, The Stanford Encyclopedia of Philosophy (Stanford: Metaphysics Research Lab, Stanford University, 2019), <https://plato.stanford.edu/entries/paternalism/>, (consulté le 8 janvier 2020).

38 Wolfendale and Clarke, "Paternalism, Consent, and the Use of Experimental Drugs in the Military" (« Le paternalisme, le consentement et l'usage de drogues expérimentales dans les Armées »), 339.

39 *Ibid.*, 341.

40 Edmund G. Howe and Edward D. Martin, *Treating the Troops* (« Traitement médical des troupes »), Hastings Center Report 21, no. 2 (1991): 23.

de recherche », avec pour conséquence l'obtention d'un niveau supérieur de consentement ? La confiance envers les responsables doit être maintenue, le devoir de diligence devant présider à la prise de décision si le processus de consentement fait l'objet d'une dérogation, comme ce fut le cas pour la pyridostigmine et l'usage de drogues expérimentales au combat[41].

Le concept de « consentement anticipé » définit le cas dans lequel la personne ne peut pas donner son consentement à cause d'une perte temporaire de ses pleines capacités, comme une injection de ComboPen, l'antidote nécessaire en cas d'incapacité due à un agent neurotoxique[42]. Cela pourrait être en cohérence avec les PCE, par exemple la mise à disposition de substances combattant la fatigue à un moment critique où l'on n'a pas le temps de discuter longuement. Cependant, cela ressemble plus à un traitement qu'à une augmentation des capacités. Certains domaines de la vie militaire qui pourraient exiger le consentement anticipé pourraient être incorporés dans un système de consentement plus large, plus général et moins spécifique[43]. Les situations dans lesquels les soldats pourraient être amenés à donner leur consentement seraient esquissées, ce qui permettrait une certaine souplesse et fournirait une base de références. Ce type de consentement pourrait être initié au recrutement, reconduit chaque année ou à l'occasion de nouveaux développements ou d'avancées scientifiques[44]. L'avantage qu'aurait un consentement au sens large du terme, reconduit chaque année, est que la répétition et l'accumulation des informations aboutissent à une plus grande compréhension. Mais le risque est que cela devienne juste un dossier de plus à signer et que la compréhension de sa portée soit limitée[45].

Concernant l'usage des PCE, au vu du problème exposé, il semblerait logique que l'on évite d'accorder des dérogations, et si possible que l'on adopte le système du consentement plus large et la procédure du consentement éclairé.

41 Wolfendale and Clarke, "Paternalism, Consent, and the Use of Experimental Drugs in the Military" (« Le paternalisme, le consentement et l'usage de drogues expérimentales dans les Armées »), 345.

42 iMedi.co.uk, "Autoject (Combopen) Nerve Agent Antidote (« Antidote Autoject contre les agents neurotoxiques »), L4a1," 2009, <https://imedi.co.uk/autoject-combopen-nerve-agent-antidote-l4a1> (consulté le 30 avril 2020).

43 Gert Helgesson, "In Defense of Broad Consent" (« Pour préconiser le consentement au sens large du terme »), *Cambridge Quarterly of Healthcare Ethics* 21, no. 1 (2012): 40.

44 Rettig, *Military Use of Drugs Not Yet Approved by the FDA for CW/BW Defense: Lessons from the Gulf War* (« L'usage militaire des drogues non encore approuvées par la FDA pour la guerre chimique et biologique : enseignements de la Guerre du Golfe »), ch. 4.

45 FitzPatrick and Zwanziger, "Defending Against Biochemical Warfare" (« La défense contre la guerre biochimique »), 15.

Cependant, O'Neill exprime son désaccord avec la procédure du consentement éclairé : il pense que ceux qui l'encouragent avancent des arguments peu convaincants et des allégations exagérées, citant l'exemple de trop nombreuses exceptions pour l'IC dans la pratique médicale, comme le cas des personnes qui ont un mental perturbé, qui sont inconscientes ou sous contrainte comme les prisonniers[46]. Il décrit également une « opacité du consentement » lorsqu'un individu consent à un certain acte sans comprendre que celui-ci pourrait entraîner une autre action qui serait nécessaire[47]. Cette opacité a été mise en lumière par l'Hôpital des enfants malades Alder Hey, où des organes d'enfants ont été prélevés après leur mort. Les parents avaient consenti à ce que des tissus soient utilisés pour la recherche mais n'auraient pas donné leur consentement pour que des organes soient prélevés, même si les organes sont effectivement constitués de tissus[48]. Les décideurs devraient donc introduire ou resserrer les procédures de l'IC pour mieux protéger le bien-être des patients et leur capacité à faire un choix éclairé[49].

L'importance du consentement éclairé (IC) pour la recherche militaire

Le consentement éclairé dans le cadre de la recherche biomédicale nécessite un niveau élevé de consentement pour éviter aux patients et volontaires sains d'être exploités et de subir des préjudices, comme le définissent la Déclaration d'Helsinki et les principes de Belmont. Les seules exceptions dans le domaine civil pour lesquelles l'IC n'est pas requis pour la recherche sont les cas d'études rétrospectives et dictées par l'urgence[50]. Pour les États-Unis, le Defense Appropriation Act peut accorder des dérogations au consentement si les patients profitent directement de la recherche, si celle-ci contribue au développement d'un produit médical nécessaire aux militaires et si elle respecte

46 O'Neill, "Some Limits of Informed Consent," (Quelques limites au consentement éclairé), 4.

47 *Ibid.*, 6.

48 Clare Dyer, "Consent Needed For Organ Retention, BMA Says" (« Le consentement est nécessaire pour la rétention d'organes, déclare la BMA (Association Médicale Britannique »), *British Medical Journal* 321, no. 7269 (2000): 1098.

49 Corrigan, "Empty Ethics: The Problem with Informed Consent," (« Un vide éthique : le problème du consentement éclairé »), 769.

50 Gross, "Military Medical Research Ethics: Investigational Drugs" (« L'éthique de la recherche médicale : les drogues expérimentales »), *Clinical Trials and Enhancement* (« Tests et augmentation cliniques »), 6.

les lois et la réglementation normales[51]. Depuis 2002, aucune dérogation n'a été accordée, mais Gross pense que pour améliorer la recherche médicale militaire, la réglementation actuelle doit être exploitée, faire l'objet de dérogations et doit élargir le champ de la recherche médicale civile aux objectifs militaires[52].

Pour éviter aux soldats britanniques d'être exploités, le ministère de la Défense dispose de sa propre commission d'éthique pour la recherche (MODREC), composée d'experts et d'intervenants indépendants[53]. Le rôle de ces derniers est crucial pour promouvoir, en dehors de toute influence militaire, la protection de la sécurité des personnes participant à la recherche, et pour éviter une « culture du commandement »[54]. Le MODREC a publié ses principes, qui « protègent et soutiennent les intérêts des participants en décrivant une conduite scientifique et éthique rigoureuse, ainsi qu'une gestion équilibrée, basée sur la certification de la recherche impliquant des êtres humains. »[55] Ces principes s'alignent sur les principes d'éthique nationaux et internationaux qui stipulent que les droits des sujets faisant l'objet de tests « prévalent sur les intérêts de la science et de la société. »[56] Sur le consentement éclairé, le MODREC indique de manière explicite qu'un soldat peut refuser de participer à tout projet de recherche, que l'information fournie doit apparaître sous un format adéquat et qu'elle doit être proportionnelle au ratio

51 John McManus *et al.*, "Informed Consent and Ethical Issues in Military Medical Research" (« Le consentement éclairé et les problèmes éthiques dans la recherche médicale »), *Academic Emergency Medicine*, 12, no. 11 (2005): 1123.

52 Gross, *Military Medical Research Ethics: Investigational Drugs, Clinical Trials and Enhancement* (« L'éthique de la recherche médicale militaire : les drogues expérimentales, tests cliniques et augmentation »), 7.

53 United Kingdom. Ministry of Defence, "Ministry of Defence Research Ethics Committee" (« Royaume-Uni, ministère de la Défense, Commission d'Éthique de la Recherche du ministère de la Défense »), <https://www.gov.uk/government/groups/ministry-of-defence-research-ethics-committees#guidance-documents> (consulté le 9 janvier 2020).

54 United Kingdom. Ministry of Defence, JSP 536. "Governance of Research Involving Human Participants. Part 1: Directive," 3me ed. (« Royaume-Uni, ministère de la Défense, gouvernance de la recherche impliquant des participants humains, 1e partie, directives »). (London: HMSO, 2020), 5–5; Mehlman, Lin, and Abney, "Enhanced Warfighters: A Policy Framework." (« Cadre pour une politique concernant le soldat augmenté »), 115.

55 United Kingdom. Ministry of Defence, JSP 536. "Governance of Research Involving Human Participants" Part 1: Directive (« Royaume-Uni, ministère de la Défense, gouvernance de la recherche impliquant des participants humains, 1e partie, directives »), 1–1.

56 United Kingdom, "The Medicines for Human Use (Clinical Trials) Regulations" (« Les médicaments pour l'usage humain (tests cliniques), règlementation »), Pub. L. No. 1031, Schedule 1, pt. 2, para. 3, (2004), <http://www.legislation.gov.uk/uksi/2004/1031/schedule/1/part/2/paragraph/3/made#text%3Dinformed consent> (consulté le 1er janvier 2020).

risque/effets bénéfiques donné par l'analyse[57]. La proportionnalité signifie que si les risques sont élevés ou si les substances impliquées dans le traitement dévient des normes, beaucoup plus d'informations doivent être données pour favoriser la proportionnalité définie par les principes de Belmont adaptés par Mehlman.

La personne concernée doit disposer d'un « laps de temps raisonnable » pour décider si elle va s'impliquer ; cette décision ne doit pas intervenir le jour même où elle reçoit l'information[58]. Corrigan a découvert à partir de ses propres recherches que les personnes soumises aux expériences ne comprenaient pas toutes les informations reçues, ni ce qui faisait l'objet de l'expérience, ni si cette dernière impliquait un traitement actif[59]. Les raisons invoquées étaient la confiance en les experts médicaux, et le fait que les médecins feraient passer l'intérêt des personnes avant toute autre chose[60]. La manière dont les personnes perçoivent la recherche médicale varie selon leurs antécédents et leurs références culturelles[61]. Même l'intitulé du travail de recherche affecte les perceptions ; par exemple, le terme « expérience » est moins bien reçu et le terme « étude » est plus populaire[62]. Il serait intéressant de savoir pourquoi les personnes donnent leur consentement pour la recherche ; la courte étude de Corrigan a montré que plus de 96 % des personnes donnent leur consentement pour des compensations financières, quelques-unes pour contenter leur médecin[63]. Ses conclusions étaient que le processus IC, isolément, aboutissait à un « vide éthique, » dans lequel les principes de l'IC ne tenaient pas compte du contexte social[64].

Faden a prétendu que toute recherche ne nécessitait pas d'IC, particulièrement pour la recherche d'efficacité comparée. Il pense que celle-ci « surprotège » les patients lorsqu'elle a peu d'effet sur ce qui leur importe le plus, mais qu'ils sont sous-protégés contre les erreurs, et que la gestion devient trop

57 United Kingdom. Ministry of Defence, JSP 536. "Governance of Research Involving Human Participants." Part 1: Directive, (Royaume-Uni, ministère de la Défense, « Gouvernance de la recherche impliquant des participants humains » 1e partie, directives).

58 *Ibid.*

59 Corrigan, "Empty Ethics: The Problem with Informed Consent" (« Un vide éthique : le problème du consentement éclairé »), 774–775.

60 *Ibid.*, 778–780.

61 *Ibid.*, 777.

62 Ruth R. Faden, *Advisory Committee on Human Radiation Experiments* (« Commission consultative pour les expériences sur les radiations impliquant des humains »), Final report (Washington DC: U.S. Government Printing Office, 1995), 734.

63 Corrigan, "Empty Ethics: The Problem with Informed Consent," (« Un vide éthique : le problème du consentement éclairé »), 782–784.

64 *Ibid.*, 787.

lourde lorsque la recherche est appelée à réduire ces problèmes[65]. Si une institution avait une vision partagée de l'apprentissage continu pour améliorer les soins aux patients dans une transparence totale, alors le simple fait d'informer les patients d'une étude qui leur donne la possibilité de refuser serait éthiquement acceptable. Ceci ne peut fonctionner que s'il existe des possibilités comparables de traitement, et non si les risques et l'incertitude sont plus grands, ou si le manque d'information est plus important[66]. La détermination de ce qui constitue le moindre risque pour les tests randomisés est définie comme ce que l'on appelle un équilibre clinique, tombant dans la catégorie des normes actuelles pour les soins médicaux[67].

Dans le cadre de la recherche, il est également pertinent de poser le dilemme entre le rôle prépondérant des impératifs militaires et le maintien de l'autonomie du patient. Le succès de la mission pour atteindre un objectif militaire peut prévaloir sur les droits individuels d'un soldat, et selon les termes employés par Gross, « *la médecine militaire n'est pas exclusivement centrée sur le patient. Sa mission est plutôt de maintenir la préparation des forces.* »[68] Comme les PCE seraient employées sans prescription sur des volontaires militaires sains, il est probable qu'aucune procédure judiciaire ne passe par une commission d'éthique, selon un auteur néerlandais[69]. Les PCE ne sont pas encore entrées dans les normes de la médication et constituent potentiellement un risque élevé, ce qui implique un plein consentement pour la recherche. Le Royaume-Uni ne devrait pas suivre les États-Unis en accordant des dérogations pour l'IC, mais respecter une éthique de recherche reconnue afin d'acquérir des connaissances qui pourraient mieux protéger les soldats en opération, comme le devoir de diligence. Ce faisant, les militaires devraient suivre le conseil de

65 Ruth R. Faden, Tom L. Beauchamp, and Nancy E. Kass, "Informed Consent, Comparative Effectiveness, and Learning Health Care" (« Le consentement éclairé, l'efficacité comparée, et l'apprentissage des actes médicaux »), *New England Journal of Medicine* 370, no. 8 (2014) : 766.

66 *Ibid.*, 767.

67 Marilyn C. Morris and Robert M. Nelson, "Randomized, Controlled Trials as Minimal Risk: An Ethical Analysis," (« Les tests randomisés comme risque minimum : analyse éthique »), *Critical Care Medicine* 35, no. 3 (2007): 943.

68 Gross, *Military Medical Research Ethics: Investigational Drugs,* (« L'éthique de la recherche médicale : les drogues expérimentales »), Clinical Trials and Enhancement (Tests et augmentation cliniques), 4.

69 D. O. E. Gebhardt, "Off-Label Administration of Drugs to Healthy Military Personnel. Dubious Ethics of Preventive Measures" (« L'usage de médicaments sans presription aux personnels militaires sains. L'éthique contestable des mesures préventives »), *Journal of Medical Ethics* 31, no. 5 (2005): 268.

Mehlman, selon lequel une période prolongée de tests rigoureux est nécessaire pour tout PCE, qui devrait être introduit seulement progressivement[70].

70 Mehlman, Lin, et Abney, "Enhanced Warfighters: Risk, Ethics, and Policy" (« Le soldat augmenté : risques, éthique et politique suivie »), 65.

CHAPITRE 3

L'avenir du consentement éclairé

Dans quelle mesure le consentement éclairé est-il « éclairé » et « consensuel » ?

Afin de s'assurer qu'un soldat est vraiment informé, les effets positifs souhaités, les effets indésirables et les risques doivent être connus et explicités au soldat d'une manière compréhensible. Le risque principal concernant les PCE est leurs effets secondaires, variables selon les médicaments. Les PCE agissant sur les qualités physiques, comme les stéroïdes anabolisants, peuvent causer des dommages irréparables au foie et les hormones de croissance peuvent provoquer une perte de la vue et un diabète[1]. Des stimulants comme les amphétamines provoquent l'agitation, la nervosité, la somnolence, l'irritabilité et des nausées[2]. Le modafinil peut causer des maux de tête, des troubles gastro-intestinaux, des troubles du sommeil, des dépressions et des tendances suicidaires ; ces troubles sont considérés comme si graves que l'Agence Européenne du Médicament a conclu que l'on ne devait pas les prescrire pour de nombreuses pathologies, comme les troubles du sommeil dus au travail de nuit[3].

Les risques et les effets positifs doivent être quantifiés quand c'est possible pour faciliter la prise de décision. Par exemple, le médicament A peut entraîner une augmentation cognitive pour 20 % des patients, mais 1 % des patients se suicident. Ceci mène au dilemme suivant : qui détermine si le rapport risque/effet positif est trop haut ? Le CMA (Autorité Médicale Compétente), le chef opérationnel ou le soldat ? Ceci ajouté au risque non déterminé de mort ou de blessure à la suite d'une mission et à la question de savoir si le soldat était « augmenté » ou non, rend l'analyse difficile. Ce que l'on sait est qu'une probabilité d'effets secondaires diminue la volonté de prendre des PCE[4], et bien que

1 U.S. Anti-Doping Agency, "Effects of Performance-Enhancing Drugs," (Agence antidopage américaine, (« Effets des substances d'augmentation des performances »), <https://www.usada.org/athletes/substances/effects-of-performance-enhancing-drugs/> (consulté le 8 mai 2020).

2 Scharre et Fish, "Human Performance Enhancement." (« L'augmentation des performances humaines »), 8.

3 European Medicines Agency, "Modafinil" (Agence Européenne du Médicament, « Le modafinil »), 2010 <https://www.ema.europa.eu/en/medicines/human/referrals/modafinil>.

4 Sattler *et al.*, "Evaluating the Drivers of and Obstacles to the Willingness to Use Cognitive Enhancement Drugs: The Influence of Drug Characteristics, Social Environment, and

 | DOI:10.1163/9789004677746_015

la tolérance des effets secondaires soit un problème individuel, collectivement il pourrait impacter le succès de la mission. Tout le monde pense que l'autonomie de chaque individu peut prévaloir sur des risques médicaux mineurs ; selon Bostrom, les personnes les plus à même de déterminer si les effets positifs valent la peine de courir ces risques ne sont pas forcément des experts médicaux[5].

La compréhension des informations est un aspect crucial du consentement éclairé (IC), chaque personne ayant une perception et une compréhension différentes, surtout en ce qui concerne les risques statistiques. La capacité de compréhension d'un soldat peut être limitée du fait de son niveau d'alphabétisation : l'Armée de Terre a récemment recruté des soldats ayant une capacité de lecture de celle d'un enfant de cinq ans, et presque 40 % en tout ont la capacité de lire et de compter d'un enfant de onze ans[6]. Par conséquent, un jeune soldat ne peut être considéré comme informé si les limites de la compréhension entraînent le fait que fondamentalement ils ne comprennent pas ce à quoi ils donnent leur consentement.

Les PCE doivent être réversibles, de manière à ce que les effets d'augmentation et les risques associés disparaissent lorsqu'elles ne sont plus utiles, lorsque l'on revient de mission ou lorsque l'on quitte l'Armée. Cependant, les PCE qui agissent sur les processus cognitifs ont normalement des effets irréversibles, du fait de la complexité des processus neurologiques et de l'adaptation des cellules cérébrales à une chimie neurologique altérée. Ceci pose problème si des militaires sont obligés de prendre des médicaments sans possibilité de choix. Si la PCE n'est pas réversible, elle aura un impact sur la société dans laquelle va évoluer une personne « augmentée. »[7] Plus de la moitié de la population

---

Personal Characteristics" (« Évaluation du rôle moteur et des obstacles à la volonté de faire usage de substances d'augmentation cognitive : l'influence des caractéristiques des produits, de l'environnement social, et des caractéristiques personnelles »), 9.

5 Bostrom and Sandberg, "Cognitive Enhancement: Methods, Ethics, Regulatory Challenges" (« L'augmentation des capacités cognitives : méthodes, éthique, problèmes de règlementation »), 323.

6 Neil Sears, "Army Signs up Recruits with a Reading Age as Young as FIVE in Desperate Bid to Boost Troop Numbers" (« L'Armée de Terre recrute des jeunes dont le niveau de lecture peut être aussi bas que celui d'un enfant de cinq ans, dans une démarche désespérée visant à gonfler ses effectifs »), *The Daily Mail*, 5 avril 2020, <https://www.dailymail.co.uk/news/article-8190009/Army-signs-recruits-reading-age-young-FIVE-desperate-bid-boost-troop-numbers.html>; Katherine Sellgren, "Almost 40 % of Army Recruits Have Reading Age of 11, MPs Warn" (« Presque 40 % des recrues de l'Armée de Terre ont le niveau de lecture d'un enfant de onze ans, préviennent les Membres du Parlement »), *BBC News*, 18 juillet, 2013, <https://www.bbc.co.uk/news/education-23346693> (consulté le 1er mai 2020).

7 Allhoff *et al.*, "Ethics of Human Enhancement: 25 Questions & Answers" (« L'éthique de l'augmentation des capacités humaines : 25 questions et réponses »), 15.

croit que les PCE donnent un avantage injuste aux utilisateurs, indépendamment du fait de savoir si cela constitue une tricherie[8]. Cependant, un usage plus répandu des PCE pourrait être bénéfique pour la société, une productivité accrue amenant une réduction de la pauvreté[9]. Buchanan va même plus loin, en prédisant un effet spectaculairement bénéfique pour la société et l'économie en général du fait de l'augmentation des capacités[10].

D'autres questions ont trait au risque de dépendance et d'abus ; une étude nationale publiée en 2006 révèle que 13 % des personnes prenant des stimulants comme des amphétamines entrent dans les critères de dépendance ou d'abus qui peuvent avoir un impact sur la société[11]. Des conséquences non voulues des PCE peuvent affecter les individus, réduisant les capacités de ceux qui sont déjà très performants dans un domaine particulier, comme on le constate avec les amphétamines agissant sur la créativité[12]. Et si la conception des PCE devenait une technologie de la « boule noire » qui mettrait fin à la civilisation ?[13] Considérons une PCE sur les capacités cognitives qui changerait fondamentalement le comportement de l'usager, si bien que celui-ci deviendrait plus enclin à la violence et à la destruction après plusieurs années d'utilisation. Si tout le mécanisme des actions et des effets secondaires n'est pas compris, s'agit-il de consentement éclairé ? Cependant, malgré les progrès de la science, une compréhension complète de la manière dont agissent les PCE et de leurs effets secondaires ne sera jamais possible et par conséquent, les informations fournies ne peuvent être que celles qui sont connues au départ, en en admettant toutes les lacunes et toutes les limitations.

Katz pense que les médecins privilégient la longévité par rapport à la qualité de la vie, et que ce devrait être la médecine et non le droit qui devrait

8 Schelle *et al.*, "Attitudes toward Pharmacological Cognitive Enhancement – a Review" (« Attitudes envers l'augmentation cognitive par voie pharmacologique : bilan »), 10.

9 Mohamed, "Neuroethical Issues in: Pharmacological Cognitive Enhancement" (« Problèmes neuroéthiques de l'augmentation cognitive par voie pharmacologique »), 537.

10 A. E. Buchanan, *Beyond Humanity?: The Ethics of Biomedical Enhancement* (« Au-delà de l'humain ? L'éthique de l'augmentation des capacités par voie biomédicale »), (Oxford: OUP Oxford, 2011), 45.

11 Larry A. Kroutil *et al.*, "Nonmedical Use of Prescription Stimulants in the United States" (« L'usage non-médical des stimulants sur ordonnance aux États-Unis »), *Drug and Alcohol Dependence* 84, no. 2 (2006): 140.

12 Martha J. Farah *et al.*, "When We Enhance Cognition with Adderall, Do We Sacrifice Creativity? A Preliminary Study" (« Lorsque nous augmentons les facultés cognitives avec l'Aderall, sacrifions-nous la créativité ? Étude préliminaire »), *Psychopharmacology* 202, no. 1 (2009): 541.

13 Nick Bostrom, "The Vulnerable World Hypothesis" (« L'hypothèse du monde vulnérable »), *Global Policy* 10, no. 4 (2019): 455.

formuler la doctrine de l'IC, en privilégiant les explications par rapport au consentement[14]. La réalité est que les médecins formulent leurs déclarations de manière à éviter toute responsabilité pénale pour des non-déclarations présumées[15]. Comment les soldats peuvent-ils être informés sur les PCE lorsque les médecins sont mal à l'aise en admettant leur ignorance des effets bénéfiques et des risques, les alternatives au traitement, ou lorsqu'ils présentent ces informations sous un format facilement « digérable » par les patients ?[16] Katz juge que la garantie ultime est de privilégier l'autonomie, alors que les avantages présumés pourraient réduire une personne à une maladie ou à une étiquette, à être moins attentive et à augmenter les chances de voir le médecin prendre la décision pour le compte du patient[17]. Sa conclusion est que les médecins doivent reconnaître les limites de leurs connaissances scientifiques et éventuellement leur ignorance, adopter une politique de décision commune et permettre au patient d'avoir le mot de la fin[18].

Comme ils renoncent à une partie de leur autonomie lorsqu'ils s'engagent dans l'Armée, il se peut que les soldats soient « informés » de la nécessité de consommer des PCE en faisant l'impasse sur l'aspect « consentement »[19]. Pour s'assurer que l'usage des PCE est soumis au consentement du soldat, le principe de Belmont concernant le respect de la personne est crucial lorsque les recrues peuvent être considérées comme une catégorie vulnérable, susceptible d'être sous influence quand il s'agit d'obéir aux instructions de la chaîne de commandement. Comme on l'a vu précédemment, la camaraderie dans une unité augmente la pression exercée par le groupe sur l'individu pour que ce dernier se conforme à un ensemble de valeurs communes, et ceci peut l'inciter à prendre des PCE contre ce que dit sa conscience. Si un soldat reçoit l'ordre direct de prendre une PCE, il doit obéir si cet ordre est réglementaire. Cependant, obéir à tous les ordres réglementaires ne se justifie pas toujours car dans certains cas, ces ordres peuvent être supplantés par la nécessité de se

14 Jay Katz, "Informed Consent – Must It Remain a Fairy Tale" (« Le consentement éclairé doit-il rester un conte de fées ? »), *Journal of Contemporary Health Law and Policy* 10 (1994): 71.

15 *Ibid.*, 77.

16 *Ibid.*, 80–83.

17 *Ibid.*, 85.

18 *Ibid.*, 90–91.

19 Robbins, "Refusing to Be All That You Can Be: Regulating against Forced Cognitive Enhancement in the Military" (« Le refus d'être tout ce que vous pouvez être : pour réglementer l'augmentation cognitive forcée dans les Armées »), 148.

conformer à d'autres réglementations, comme la Convention de Genève, ou le Droit des Conflits Armés[20].

Les humains intelligents sont en mesure de faire des choix de manière autonome, mais qu'en est-il si une mesure particulière profite à toute une unité ? Existe-t-il des cas où le sacrifice de l'autonomie personnelle est acceptable pour favoriser la sécurité et donc la santé du groupe dans son ensemble ? Pellegrino soutient que oui dans une optique préventive, lorsque le tissu social implique que les individus « renoncent à l'autonomie pour en tirer certains avantages », et que l'absolu « intérêt personnel est incompatible avec la vie dans une communauté civilisée »[21]. On peut citer des exemples comme le port obligatoire du casque de moto pour réduire les blessures à la tête en cas d'accident, ou le port de la ceinture de sécurité en voiture pour réduire les traumatismes multiples. Il faut noter que les mesures préventives les plus effectives sont celles qui ont été imposées par la loi plutôt que par une restriction des choix[22]. Il existe une similitude entre renoncer à une partie de son autonomie en s'engageant dans l'Armée et le port réglementaire du gilet pare-balles ou des uniformes ignifuges.

En suivant la ligne de la prévention, si l'usage des PCE améliore la santé et la sécurité individuelles et collectives, le consentement doit être forcé et non sollicité. Annas est d'une opinion différente : il pense que l'on ne devrait pas obliger les soldats à prendre des médicaments sur prescription et que l'on ne devrait pas forcer les médecins militaires à les prescrire[23]. Si un soldat refuse une PCE, cela le rend-il inapte à participer aux opérations, et potentiellement à limiter ses choix de carrière future ? Si un soldat refuse un traitement médical qui préserve sa santé ou celle des autres en service actif, cela peut être considéré comme une infraction à la discipline[24]. Le refus d'autres types de traitement médical oblige à en référer à une commission médicale pour déterminer

20 United Kingdom. Development Concepts and Doctrine Centre, JSP 383. *The Joint Service Manual of the Law of Armed Conflict* (« Royaume-Uni, Centre de Doctrine et de Développement des Concepts : Manuel interarmées du Droit des Conflits Armés ») (Shrivenham: DCDC, 2004), 13–14, 21–26.

21 Edmund D. Pellegrino, "Autonomy and Coercion in Disease Prevention and Health Promotion" (« L'autonomie et la coercition dans la prévention des maladies et la promotion de la santé »), *Theoretical Medicine* 5, no. 1 (1984): 88.

22 *Ibid.*, 90.

23 Catherine L. Annas and George J. Annas, "Enhancing the Fighting Force: Medical Research on American Soldiers" (« Augmenter les forces combattantes : la recherche médicale sur les soldats américains »), *Journal of Contemporary Health Law and Policy* 25, no. 2 (2009): 308.

24 Annas, "Changing the Consent Rules for Desert Storm" (« Le changement des règles du consentement pour l'Opération Tempête du Désert »), 772.

si le refus est raisonnable ou non[25]. La commission détermine si le traitement médical est nécessaire pour protéger la santé du soldat, celle des autres, ou s'il lui permet d'accomplir ses tâches correctement. S'il est décidé que le traitement médical est nécessaire, le soldat est soumis à une procédure disciplinaire ou administrative ; dans ce dernier cas il est révoqué du service[26]. Robbins considère que le soldat est responsable : celui-ci doit avoir le droit de refuser sans que cela affecte sa liberté[27]. Si un soldat refuse avant d'être déployé, une autre personne peut prendre sa place, mais un refus sur le champ de bataille mettrait ses camarades en danger. À l'évidence, on doit mettre en œuvre une politique énonçant la réglementation et les orientations concernant les PCE ; elle doit incorporer une approche consensuelle lorsque c'est possible, et éviter les situations critiques de refus durant les conflits.

Comme les PCE sont des substances qui doivent faire l'objet de prescription par un docteur en médecine, un médecin militaire peut-il décider que les effets positifs des PCE sur un individu ou une équipe partant en mission peuvent éviter la nécessité du consentement, indépendamment du problème de l'information ? Ceci nous amène à la question de savoir si les médecins militaires sont des docteurs, des officiers, ou les deux, et quel statut prévaut sur l'autre. Pour Annas, la réponse est claire : le médecin militaire doit être « d'abord, en dernier ressort, et toujours » médecin[28]. L'éthique médicale doit rester inchangée pour un médecin, qu'il soit civil ou militaire, en temps de paix ou de guerre, mais il existe des exemples dans l'histoire qui visiblement ont justifié des variations dans les obligations éthiques du domaine médical. La pénicilline fut donnée en priorité durant la Seconde Guerre mondiale aux troupes souffrant de maladies sexuellement transmissibles plutôt qu'aux blessés, car ces troupes retourneraient en première ligne plus rapidement ; plus récemment, on a suggéré de prescrire des psychorégulateurs (stabilisateurs d'humeur) pour s'assurer que les soldats restent ou reviennent sur les théâtres d'opérations en Iraq et en Afghanistan[29].

---

25 Robbins, "Refusing to Be All That You Can Be: Regulating against Forced Cognitive Enhancement in the Military" (« Le refus d'être tout ce que l'on peut être : la règlementation contre l'augmentation forcée des capacités cognitives dans les Armées »), 129.

26 *Ibid.*, 130.

27 Robbins, "Refusing to Be All That You Can Be: Regulating against Forced Cognitive Enhancement in the Military," (« Le refus d'être tout ce que l'on peut être : la règlementation contre l'augmentation forcée des capacités cognitives dans les Armées »), 134.

28 George J. Annas, "Military Medical Ethics – Physician First, Last, Always" (« L'éthique médicale militaire – médecin d'abord, en dernier ressort, et toujours »), *New England Journal of Medicine* 359, no. 11 (2008): 1090.

29 *Ibid.*, 1088.

Les rôles antagonistes de médecin et de soldat sont source d'un dilemme de double allégeance pour chacune de ces deux professions. Ce problème peut être facilement résolu si les directives internationales sont suivies, comme celles de l'Association Médicale Mondiale qui préconise qu'au cours d'un conflit armé, les médecins aient une obligation prioritaire vis-à-vis du patient, et celles de la Convention de Genève qui spécifient qu'un traitement médical doit être administré pour des raisons médicales et être conforme à l'éthique médicale[30]. Ces deux recueils de directives comportent des lacunes potentielles ; les PCE ne constituent pas des traitements administrés pour des raisons médicales et les obligations prioritaires envers les patients peuvent en fait devenir l'usage forcé des PCE pour leur protection. Cependant, un sujet de préoccupation apparaît si les nécessités militaires exigent l'usage forcé de PCE, prévalant sur les principes et l'éthique des médecins, ce qui ouvre la voie à des abus potentiels[31].

Un médecin est responsable envers la société où il vit, et cette responsabilité est déterminée à la fois par sa profession et par des structures de réglementation indépendantes[32]. Pour un médecin militaire, cela comprend des réglementations fixées par le Conseil Médical Général (General Medical Council), le collège professionnel de la spécialité médicale et l'Armée (Terre, etc.) qui l'emploie[33]. Il n'existe pas de dispositif bien défini pour résoudre tous les conflits entre ces différentes structures de

30 Daniel Messelken et Hans Ulrich Baer, "Hovering Between Roles: Military Medical Ethics," (« Hésitation entre deux rôles : l'éthique militaire et l'éthique médicale »), in: *Military Medical Ethics for the 21st Century* (« Ethique Médicale Militaire pour le 21e Siècle »), ed. M. L. Gross et D. Carrick, "Military and Defence Ethics," (Farnham: Ashgate Publishing Limited, 2013), 268.

31 *Ibid.*, 270.

32 Dan W. Brock, "Conscientious Refusal by Physicians and Pharmacists: Who Is Obligated to Do What, and Why?" (« Le refus par objection de conscience de la part des médecins et des pharmaciens : qui est tenu de faire quoi, et pourquoi ? »), *Theoretical Medicine and Bioethics* 29, no. 3 (2008): 193.

33 Des exemples de ces réglementations sont: General Medical Council (Conseil Médical Général), "Good Medical Practice" (« La bonne pratique médicale »), 2019, <https://www.gmc-uk.org/ethical-guidance/ethical-guidance-for-doctors/good-medical-practice>, The Royal College of Anaesthetists (Association Royale des Anesthésistes), "Guidelines for the Provision of Anaesthetic Services," (« Directives pour la prestation de services d'anesthésie »), 2020, <https://www.rcoa.ac.uk/safety-standards-quality/guidance-resources/guidelines-provision-anaesthetic-services>; United Kingdom. Ministry of Defence (ministère de la Défense du Royaume-Uni), "The Queen's Regulations for the Army 1975," (« Réglements de la Couronne pour l'Armée de Terre »), AC13206, (London: Ministry of Defence, 2019), <https://assets.publishing.service.gov.uk/government/uploads/system/uploads/attachment_data/file/826092/The_Queen_s_Regulations_for_the_Army_1975.pdf> (consulté le 6 avril 2020).

réglementation[34]. Le médecin militaire est-il d'abord un officier militaire qui doit obéir et donner des ordres réglementaires, ou un docteur dont le premier souci est l'intérêt du patient ? Cantor a préconisé que les médecins devaient accomplir leurs tâches indépendamment de leurs convictions, mais cet avis visait à combattre l'objection de conscience, et impliquait que le devoir du médecin devait prévaloir sur tout le reste[35]. Les procès de Nuremberg ont prouvé que faire quelque chose pour obéir à un ordre à l'encontre de votre code de moralité ne constituait pas un argument de défense[36]. À l'inverse, Mehlman ne pense pas que les médecins militaires respectant une éthique médicale et un devoir moral puissent contourner leurs obligations militaires ; il pense qu'ils doivent expliciter les risques médicaux aux décideurs et résister fermement aux intentions de leurs supérieurs hiérarchiques[37].

Les médecins sont censés pratiquer des actes médicaux qui vont dans le sens de l'amélioration et du rétablissement de la santé, et ne sont pas tenus de rendre des services non-médicaux. Ceci est la thèse de Gamble, qui souligne que « Les soldats s'engageant volontairement dans les Armées ne peuvent être forcés de faire tout ce qui fait partie de leurs compétences, et on peut dire la même chose des médecins. »[38] Si le fait de prescrire une PCE apporte un résultat positif sur la santé, cela constituerait un acte médical. Mais s'il est prescrit en l'absence de symptômes ou de pathologie, pour des raisons dictées par des besoins d'ordre militaire, cela constitue un acte socio-clinique, comme le définit Gamble, accompli pour répondre à désirs d'ordre social, comme la chirurgie esthétique[39]. Ce mémoire a défini les PCE comme « augmentation des capacités » et non comme « traitement », et donc les prescrire est un acte

34 Nathan K. Gamble et Michal Pruski, "Medical Acts and Conscientious Objection: What Can a Physician Be Compelled to Do?" (« Les actes médicaux et l'objection de conscience : que peut être obligé de faire un médecin ? »), *The New Bioethics* 25, no. 3 (2019): 263.

35 Julie D. Cantor, "Conscientious Objection Gone Awry – Restoring Selfless Professionalism in Medicine" (L'objection de conscience tourne mal – rétablir le professionalisme altruiste en médecine), *New England Journal of Medicine* 360, no. 15 (2009): 1485.

36 Harvard Law School Library (Bibliothèque de la faculté de droit de Harvard), "Nuremberg – Transcript Viewer – Transcript for NMT 1: Medical Case" (« Nuremberg – transcription officielle – transcription pour NMT1 : cas médical »), Nuremberg Trials Project (« Rapport sur les Procès de Nuremberg »), 2016, <http://nuremberg.law.harvard.edu/transcripts/1-transcript-for-nmt-1-medical-case?seq=2586> (consulté le 11 mars 2020).

37 Mehlman and Corley, "A Framework for Military Bioethics"(« Cadre pour une bioéthique militaire »), 345.

38 Gamble and Pruski, "Medical Acts and Conscientious Objection: What Can a Physician Be Compelled to Do?" (« L'acte médical et l'objection de conscience : que peut être obligé de faire un médecin ? »), 268.

39 *Ibid.*, 275.

socio-clinique, Gamble pense que les médecins militaires ne doivent pas être « obligés » de suivre cette voie.

Actuellement, il n'existe aucune politique écrite concernant la question de savoir si un médecin militaire peut recevoir l'ordre réglementaire d'administrer un médicament si ceci est considéré comme contraire à l'éthique médicale. Une exception pourrait être le cas où cela serait considéré comme une thérapie dans l'urgence des combats. Cette dérive éthique peut entraîner des effets néfastes pour le patient, comme l'illustre la prise d'un agent coagulant pour lui sauver la vie en cas de polytraumatisme, prescrit effectivement par des supérieurs hiérarchiques médicaux alors que les recherches n'ont pas établi complètement ses effets. Des recherches ultérieures ont montré que l'usage de cet agent entraînait des décès « inutiles » et que même à l'époque où cela se faisait, les médecins s'en préoccupaient à l'hôpital en temps de guerre à Bagdad en 2006. « Je trouve inquiétant que des effets négatifs aient affecté des soldats par la pratique de thérapies – par excès de zèle – dont l'efficacité n'était pas avérée »[40]. L'impact de ce problème est amplifié lorsqu'en dépit du fait qu'un soldat doit accepter les traitements médicaux normalisés ou faire l'objet de mesures disciplinaires, il n'est pas obligé d'accepter des interventions qui ne sont pas reconnues par la profession médicale comme procédures normalisées[41]. De même que pour les situations impliquant des PCE, l'usage de l'agent coagulant n'était pas une procédure normalisée et n'aurait dû être adopté que sous consentement éclairé ou, s'il était adopté sans consentement dans l'urgence, uniquement dans le cadre d'une analyse connue et acceptée des effets positifs et négatifs.

Un consentement éclairé effectif dans le contexte militaire

La dernière partie de ce mémoire étudiera les aspects pratiques du consentement éclairé dans les Armées, pour indiquer quand et comment il doit être obtenu pour maximiser les composantes « information » et « consentement, »

40 Robert Little, "Army Medicine: Untested in Battle," (« La médecine dans l'Armée de Terre n'a pas fait l'objet de tests en opérations de combat »), *The Baltimore Sun*, 29 mars 2009, <https://www.baltimoresun.com/news/nation-world/bal-te.militarymed29mar29-story.html> (consulté le 30 mars 2020).

41 J. Annas, "Protecting Soldiers from Friendly Fire: The Consent Requirement for Using Investigational Drugs and Vaccines in Combat" (« La protection des soldats contre les tirs fratricides : la nécessité du consentement pour l'utilisation des drogues et des vaccins expértimentaux dans les opérations de combat »), 257.

et le cadre de la politique concernant l'IC. Le consentement éclairé (IC) doit être étayé par une communication effective entre l'informateur et la personne devant donner son consentement. Au cours de la guerre du Golfe (1991), la vaccination contre l'anthrax n'était pas obligatoire, mais pratiquée sous réserve d'un consentement tacite[42]. Les anciens combattants ont plus tard signalé une dégradation de leur état de santé que nombre d'entre eux mettaient sur le compte de cette vaccination ; ceci eut pour conséquence une crainte et une méfiance envers l'institution militaire. Pour prévenir ce problème dans le cadre de la guerre d'Iraq de 2003, on a fait usage du consentement explicite, en parallèle avec un programme d'information exposé par écrit, verbalement et par vidéo. Un délai de réflexion a été permis avant la signature de la déclaration de consentement pour étayer le processus IC[43]. En dépit de cela, plus de la moitié des militaires britanniques ont refusé le vaccin contre l'anthrax[44]. Une étude portant sur les troupes déployées durant la guerre d'Iraq en 2003 a révélé que leur souci concernant la vaccination avait pour cause sa sûreté, son efficacité et le problème du consentement[45]. Malgré toute l'information et la communication, le problème n'a pas été perçu de façon équilibrée et les inquiétudes concernant son efficacité et ses séquelles sur la santé n'ont pas été dissipées[46]. Les inquiétudes sur le fait de savoir pourquoi la vaccination était à présent volontaire et soumise à l'IC, alors que précédemment elle était obligatoire, entraînèrent une perte de confiance envers le ministère de la Défense, dont on a cru qu'il dissimulait les effets négatifs du vaccin. La conclusion a été que l'IC pouvait être souhaitable sur des bases éthiques ou juridiques, mais pouvait ne pas donner les effets positifs attendus[47]. Par conséquent, une

---

42 Dominic Murphy *et al.*, "UK Armed Forces Responses to an Informed Consent Policy for Anthrax Vaccination: A Paradoxical Effect?" (« Les réactions des troupes du Royaume-Uni face à une politique du consentement éclairé pour la vaccination contre l'anthrax : un effet paradoxal ? »), *Vaccine* 24, no. 16 (2006): 3109.

43 *Ibid.*, 3110.

44 Cathel Kerr, "Anthrax Vaccine Gets Cold Shoulder from Troops" (« Le vaccin contre l'anthrax mal perçu par les troupes »), *Canadian Medical Association Journal* 168, no. 10 (2003): 1308.

45 Dominic Murphy *et al.*, "UK Armed Forces Responses to an Informed Consent Policy for Anthrax Vaccination: A Paradoxical Effect?" (« Les réactions des troupes du Royaume-Uni face à une politique du consentement éclairé pour la vaccination contre l'anthrax : un effet paradoxal ? »), *Vaccine* 24, no. 16 (2006): 3110.

46 Dominic Murphy, Neil Greenberg, and Duncan Bland, "Health Concerns in UK Armed Forces Personnel" (« Les inquiétudes sur la santé parmi les personnels des forces armées britanniques »), *Journal of the Royal Society of Medicine* 102, no. 4 (2009): 144.

47 Murphy *et al.*, "UK Armed Forces Responses to an Informed Consent Policy for Anthrax Vaccination: A Paradoxical Effect?" (« Les réactions des troupes du Royaume-Uni face

politique du consentement éclairé pour les PCE qui augmente l'inquiétude et en réduit l'usage n'atteindra pas ses buts.

La méthode de communication pour l'IC est cruciale, pour confirmer que la personne est informée, en particulier pour la compréhension du risque, et que son consentement est libre. Des enseignements peuvent être tirés sur la manière dont les autorités publiques de santé diffusent l'information concernant les risques domaine dans lequel les buts de la communication sont globalement de présenter l'information de telle manière qu'elle doit être comprise et utilisable, ce qui permet aux personnes de porter un jugement sur les risques, et d'être assistées activement par les informateurs[48]. Nicholson a souligné que les risques doivent être discutés de vive voix, en employant un langage commun, un ton empathique, avec ce qu'il faut de compétence et de franchise[49]. Il a également noté qu'une tenue vestimentaire plus informelle favorisait une communication effective. Ceci pourrait constituer un point important pour les militaires, du fait de l'évidente différence entre les grades lorsqu'ils portent l'uniforme, et le degré de coercition que cela peut impliquer.

L'Organisation Mondiale de la Santé a noté des changements dans la perception de l'information par le public, avec moins de confiance en ce que disent les experts et les autorités, et une tendance à consulter des sources sur internet et les réseaux sociaux pour obtenir des conseils. La préférence va à des histoires reflétant des opinions plutôt que des données de référence[50]. Le point principal est d'établir la confiance, et il est heureux que les médecins soient ceux qui bénéficient le plus de la confiance du public[51] ; ce sont donc eux qui doivent donner l'information, et non les fonctionnaires du ministère de la Défense qui ne sont pas médecins. Le fait de surcharger l'information peut aller à l'encontre de la compréhension ; par conséquent, l'information doit être donnée en de multiples occasions, chacune devant transmettre quelques messages et faits cruciaux qui s'ajoutent logiquement à ceux énoncés auparavant.

à une politique du consentement éclairé pour la vaccination contre l'anthrax : un effet paradoxal ? »), 3113.

48 P. J. Nicholson, "Communicating Health Risk" (« La communicatiuon des risques médicaux »), *Occupational Medicine* 49, no. 4 (1999): 253.

49 *Ibid.*, 254.

50 World Health Organisation, "An Introduction to Risk Communication" (Organisation Mondiale de la Santé, *Introduction à la communication concernant le risque*), 1, <https://www.who.int/risk-communication/introduction-to-risk-communication.pdf?ua=1>, (consulté le 12 mars 2020).

51 Nicholson, "Communicating Health Risk," (« La communication des risques de santé »), 254.

Avec le temps, de nouvelles informations apparaîtront inévitablement, celles-ci devant être données le plus tôt possible pour maintenir le consentement éclairé[52].

Pour les soldats se lançant dans une carrière militaire, il devrait exister à la fois un consentement général et un consentement éclairé pour l'usage futur des PCE. Le consentement général seul pourrait être l'objet d'une exploitation abusive, comme ce fut le cas pour la tribu indienne Havasupai, qui signa un contrat de consentement général pour la recherche sur le diabète ; celui-ci fut élargi à d'autres fins, pour lesquelles ces personnes auraient refusé de signer si elles avaient été mises au courant[53]. Cette tribu fut considérée comme une population vulnérable, pouvant peut-être être comparée aux nouvelles recrues militaires. Le consentement général serait amélioré s'il existait des limites approximatives définissant ce qu'il englobe, mais cela placerait la responsabilité du devoir de diligence auprès de la chaîne de commandement. Cependant, comme point de départ, le consentement général pour un usage potentiel futur des PCE doit être mis en place pour tout soldat nouvellement recruté, avec la possibilité de se désengager et de quitter l'Armée à ce stade. Ce processus de consentement général devrait être renouvelé à l'occasion de chaque promotion, et à chaque fois que le soldat renouvelle son contrat avec les Armées. Cette répétition permettrait d'en équilibrer la fréquence et d'éviter qu'il devienne simplement une case à cocher, et permettrait de mettre à jour les informations à mesure qu'elles deviennent disponibles. Et surtout, cela tiendrait compte du fait qu'un individu mûrit en passant de l'état de recrue à celui de soldat entraîné, et que par sa progression de carrière, il acquiert l'expérience de la vie et l'expérience militaire qui modifient sa compréhension et son attitude face au risque[54].

Le processus complet du consentement éclairé doit être effectué lorsque le soldat rejoint une unité qui utilise des PCE pour que ses missions réussissent et il doit être réitéré dans la mesure où il doit faire partie de la mise en condition opérationnelle. Ce sont deux moments qui permettent de refuser l'usage des PCE, la mise en condition constituant la dernière occasion où ce refus peut survenir. Une fois que l'unité a été déployée dans un environnement

52 Mahmood Adil, "Risk Communication in Healthcare: An Overview," (« La communication du risque en matière médicale : bilan »), *Journal of Communication in Healthcare* 1, no. 4 (2008): 365.

53 Beauchamp, "Informed Consent: Its History, Meaning, and Present Challenges," (« Le consentement éclairé : son histoire, sa signification, et les défis actuels »), 521.

54 Thomas Dohmen *et al.*, "Risk Attitudes across the Life Course" (« Les attitudes face au risque dans les différentes périodes de la vie »), *The Economic Journal* 127, no. 605 (2017): F114.

opérationnel où les PCE ont été jugés indispensables au succès de la mission, un des membres qui n'a pas été « augmenté » peut accroître le risque pour lui-même et pour l'unité, et devenir un handicap. Dans ce cas, on pourra ne pas tenir compte du refus du consentement et forcer le soldat à utiliser le PCE. Si des soldats sont recrutés pour la recherche, pour éviter qu'ils se fassent exploiter, une procédure IC plus complète reste obligatoire, conformément au rapport Belmont et à l'approbation du MODREC (commission d'éthique pour la recherche).

Pour éviter toute sorte de coercition et pour entretenir la confiance, les informations concernant le consentement éclairé (IC) doivent être données dans un environnement propice par un médecin formé à la communication du risque, connaissant bien les PCE, idéalement dans une tenue civile et sans la présence de supérieurs hiérarchiques[55]. On doit encourager les questions et l'information doit être donnée par tous les supports médiatiques possibles ; on peut utiliser un recueil des questions fréquemment posées et de leurs réponses, qui soit facilement accessible sur internet et intranet Défense. En collaborant avec la chaîne de commandement, les soldats pourraient même récupérer une autonomie partielle en contrôlant le timing et la méthode d'utilisation des PCE.

Doit-il y avoir un formulaire de consentement à signer pour les PCE, alors que le consentement tacite est employé pour la prescription d'autres substances ?[56] Un consentement signé n'implique pas forcément le consentement éclairé, ni que toutes les explications concernant les risques et les effets positifs connus ont été fournies, ni qu'un minimum de données a été exposé. Toute information communiquée par le médecin doit être fidèle à ses directives professionnelles. Cependant, comme on l'a vu plus haut, les médecins font souvent l'impasse sur les domaines où leurs connaissances sont limitées ou sur lesquels on connaît peu de chose, et ce problème doit être résolu. Néanmoins, un formulaire de consentement signé constitue un document prouvant qu'il y a eu un entretien. Il pourrait mettre en relief les domaines d'information qui ont été évoqués et il protège le médecin militaire en constituant la base d'une défense juridique dans le cas d'une plainte déposée[57]. Tout compte fait, un formulaire de consentement éclairé signé devrait être utilisé pour les soldats qui

55 McManus *et al.*, "Informed Consent and Ethical Issues in Military Medical Research" (« Le consentement éclairé et les questions éthiques dans la recherche médicale militaire »), 1122.

56 Beauchamp, "Informed Consent: Its History, Meaning, and Present Challenges" (« Le consentement éclairé : histoire, signification, défis actuels »), 517.

57 *Ibid.*, 519.

acceptent les PCE, pour des raisons de transparence et de responsabilité, et être conservé précieusement comme faisant partie de leur dossier médical.

Indéniablement, une politique doit être mise en œuvre concernant l'usage des PCE, englobant toutes les implications juridiques, comme la question de savoir qui est responsable au cas où un mauvais dosage est effectué. Est-ce le médecin, l'individu, le chef militaire ou le fabricant ? Maslen a fait remarquer qu'une telle politique ne peut être informée et éthique que lorsque les effets bénéfiques et tous les risques liés à l'augmentation des capacités sont connus[58]. Comme cette information ne peut jamais être complètement connue, la base de toute politique lorsque l'on fait usage de CPE doit englober les quatre composantes d'une prise de décision éthique telles que définies par l'US Army Aeromedical Research Laboratory (Laboratoire de l'Armée de Terre Américaine pour la Recherche Aéromédicale)[59] :

1. L'usage est volontaire.
2. Le médicament est sûr pour l'utilisation voulue.
3. Le dosage et l'utilisation sont cohérents avec sa fonction.
4. Les agents alternatifs non-pharmacologiques ont été complètement explorés.

Ceux-ci s'alignent sur les principes de Belmont, adaptés par Mehlman (la proportionnalité, le paternalisme et l'équité) et sur le cadre hybride qu'il a publié auparavant, traitant des problèmes plus larges de transparence envers le public et de la responsabilité des autorités qui doivent prendre des décisions dictées par la nécessité[60].

---

58 Maslen, Faulmüller, et Savulescu, "Pharmacological Cognitive Enhancement – How Neuroscientific Research Could Advance Ethical Debate" (« L'augmentation des capacités par voie pharmacologique – comment la recherche neuroscientifique peut faire avancer le débat éthique »), 8.

59 Scharre and Fish, "Human Performance Enhancement" (« L'augmentation des capacités humaines »), 10.

60 Mehlman, Lin, et Abney, "Enhanced Warfighters: Risk, Ethics, and Policy" (« Le soldat augmenté : risques, éthique et politique à suivre »), 75–76.

Conclusion

Aujourd'hui, il est déjà possible d'augmenter les capacités humaines et le Royaume-Uni devra prendre en compte l'usage des PCE, soit dans une approche positive qui investit dans cette technologie, soit en y étant forcé pour être à même de contrer des adversaires dans des conflits. Cette question mérite d'être examinée dès à présent en période de paix relative car en temps de guerre ou de conflit, il est beaucoup plus difficile de lui consacrer un débat aussi rationnel et rigoureux. Quelle que soit la direction que prendra le Royaume-Uni, il paraît raisonnable de suivre les conseils qu'Annas donne aux médecins militaires et de s'efforcer de mettre en œuvre une politique dénuée d'équivoque, basée sur une éthique traditionnelle dans laquelle l'intérêt du patient passe avant tout[1]. Les PCE ne devraient pas être considérés comme un traitement médical mais comme un ensemble de drogues disponibles uniquement sur prescription d'un docteur en médecine, qui augmentent les capacités d'un soldat au-delà de ses capacités normales.

L'auteur de ce mémoire est d'accord avec Gross lorsqu'il dit : « L'éthique médicale militaire ne fait que *permettre* le consentement éclairé »[2]. Par conséquent, l'usage des PCE dans les Armées nécessitera un processus IC pour protéger un individu qui, contrairement à ses homologues civils, a renoncé à une partie de son autonomie lorsqu'il est devenu militaire, et qui subit l'influence de ses camarades ainsi qu'une coercition (volontaire ou non) de la part des chefs. Ce processus n'a pas prévalu dans les Armées dans le passé et des soldats se sont fait exploiter, avec des effets négatifs réels et potentiels ; donc un processus IC modifié, adapté à partir des procédures civiles actuelles, est nécessaire.

Le consentement ne peut être considéré comme « éclairé » que lorsque les risques, les effets bénéfiques et la durée de ces effets sont communiqués d'une manière adaptée aux capacités intellectuelles du patient et qu'on s'est assuré qu'ils ont été bien compris. Ces informations devront en grande partie être tirées d'études récentes. Comme les auteurs de cette recherche seront probablement des militaires, le consentement éclairé pour les PCE tel que défini

1 George J. Annas, "Protecting Soldiers from Friendly Fire: The Consent Requirement for Using Investigational Drugs and Vaccines in Combat" (« La protection des soldats contre les tirs fratricides : la nécessité du consentement pour l'utilisation des drogues et des vaccins expértimentaux dans les opérations de combat »), *American Journal of Law & Medicine* 24, no. 2/3 (1998): 275.

2 Gross, "Bioethics and Armed Conflict. Moral Dilemmas of Medicine and War," (« La bioéthique et les conflits armés. Les dilemmes moraux de la médecine et la guerre »), 107.

 | DOI:10.1163/9789004677746_016

dans le rapport Belmont doit être respecté, et approuvé par le MODREC, qui protège les droits des personnels. Lorsque ces informations manquent, les médecins doivent entretenir la confiance en faisant preuve d'honnêteté et en admettant toute lacune ou limitation.

Afin de s'assurer que l'usage des PCE reste basé sur le consentement, la possibilité de refus doit être autorisée sans menace d'ordre disciplinaire, et les effets négatifs sur la carrière doivent être minimisés. Même si le consentement a été donné auparavant, le refus de prendre des PCE à n'importe quel moment avant le déploiement doit être accepté sans préjudice. Néanmoins, une fois que la mission a été lancée, l'ordre peut être donné de prendre des PCE. La justification de cette utilisation sans consentement serait que l'intérêt de l'unité, de la mission ou du pays passe avant celui de l'individu[3]. Les difficultés se situent au niveau des conséquences non voulues des PCE, qui peuvent rester inconnues durant de nombreuses années ; qui décide que les risques des PCE sont jugés essentiels pour le succès de la mission, et qu'ils l'emportent sur les effets bénéfiques ?

Le processus du consentement éclairé pour l'usage des PCE doit être étayé par une politique et une tournure d'esprit acceptées selon lesquelles l'IC est un processus évolutif et non définitif. Ce processus devrait débuter par un consentement général lors de l'engagement dans la vie militaire, et réitéré à l'occasion de chaque promotion et de renouvellement de contrat, ou lorsque de nouvelles informations importantes apparaissent. Ce consentement doit être étendu pour devenir plein consentement comme on l'a défini dans ce mémoire lorsque le soldat rejoint une unité dont les missions sont susceptibles de requérir des PCE, et aussi à l'occasion de la mise en condition avant déploiement. L'IC, mais non le consentement général, doit s'accompagner d'une signature ; la transmission des informations doit être faite par un médecin militaire qui a été formé à la communication du risque, dans un environnement fait pour minimiser tout sentiment de hiérarchie, donc en facilitant l'approche consensuelle et en évitant la coercition. L'information de fond doit être rendue librement accessible sur internet par toutes formes de communication médiatique. Si cette méthode d'IC est suivie dans les Armées, elle protégera au mieux les personnes prenant des PCE en assurant un équilibre entre la proportionnalité, le paternalisme et l'équité. Elle protégera également les médecins militaires délivrant les prescriptions contre l'éventualité de la négligence et protégera les chefs par la transparence et la responsabilité.

3 Mehlman, Lin, et Abney, "Enhanced Warfighters: Risk, Ethics, and Policy" (« Le soldat augmenté : risques, éthique et politique à suivre »), 58.

Bibliographie

Adil, Mahmood. "Risk Communication in Healthcare: An Overview." *Journal of Communication in Healthcare* 1, no. 4 (2008): 363–72. DOI: 10.1179/cih.2008.1.4.363.

Advisory Committee on Human Radiation Experiments. "Executive Summary and Guide to Final Report," 1995. <https://www.osti.gov/opennet/servlets/purl/120931/120931.pdf> (visité le 9 janvier, 2020).

Allhoff, Fritz, Lin Patrick, Moor James, et Weckert John. "Ethics of Human Enhancement: 25 Questions & Answers." *Studies in Ethics, Law, and Technology* 4, no. 1 (2010) 1–39. DOI: 10.2202/1941-6008.1110.

Allison, Lincoln. "Faster, Stronger, Higher." *The Guardian*, le 9 aout, 2004. <https://www.theguardian.com/sport/2004/aug/09/athensolympics2004.olympicgames> (visité le 1ier avril, 2020).

Annas, Catherine L., et George J. Annas, "Enhancing the Fighting Force: Medical Research on American Soldiers," *Journal of Contemporary Health Law and Policy* 25, no. 2 (2009): 283–308.

Annas, George J. "Changing the Consent Rules for Desert Storm." *New England Journal of Medicine* 326, no. 11 (1992): 770–73. DOI: 10.1056/NEJM199203123261117.

Annas, George J. "Military Medical Ethics – Physician First, Last, Always," *New England Journal of Medicine* 359, no. 11 (2008): 1087–90. DOI: 10.1056/NEJMp0805975.

Annas, George J. "Protecting Soldiers from Friendly Fire: The Consent Requirement for Using Investigational Drugs and Vaccines in Combat," *American Journal of Law & Medicine* 24, no. 2/3 (1998): 245–60.

Barr, Sabrina. "Viagra Now Available over the Counter without Prescription in UK," *The Independent*, le 27 mars, 2018. <https://www.independent.co.uk/life-style/health-and-families/viagra-buy-without-prescription-over-counter-uk-pharmacies-male-impotence-erectile-dysfunction-a8275461.html> (visité le 3 avril, 2020).

BBC News. "Sussex University Students Illegally Buying 'Smart Pills.'" *BBC News*, le 13 mars, 2018. <https://www.bbc.co.uk/news/uk-england-43383717> (visité le 31 mars, 2020).

Bear, Adam, et Joshua Knobe. "Normality: Part Descriptive, Part Prescriptive." *Cognition* 167 (2017): 25–37. DOI: <https://doi.org/10.1016/j.cognition.2016.10.024>.

Beauchamp, Tom L. "Informed Consent: Its History, Meaning, and Present Challenges," *Cambridge Quarterly of Healthcare Ethics* 20, no. 4 (2011): 515–523. DOI: 10.1017/S0963180111000259.

Berg, J. W., P. S. Appelbaum, C. W. Lidz, et L.S. Parker. *Informed Consent: Legal Theory and Clinical Practice*. 2me ed. (New York: Oxford University Press, 2001).

Beutler, Ernest, and Jill Waalen. "The Definition of Anemia: What Is the Lower Limit of Normal of the Blood Hemoglobin Concentration?" *Blood* 107, no. 5 (March 2006): 1747–50. DOI: 10.1182/blood-2005-07-3046.

Bostrom, Nick. "The Vulnerable World Hypothesis." *Global Policy* 10, no. 4 (2019): 455–76. DOI: 10.1111/1758-5899.12718.

Bostrom, Nick, and Anders Sandberg. "Cognitive Enhancement: Methods, Ethics, Regulatory Challenges," *Science and Engineering Ethics* 15, no. 3 (2009): 311–41. DOI: 10.1007/s11948-009-9142-5.

British Army. "New Physical Employment Standards for the Army," <https://www.army.mod.uk/physical-employment-standards/> (visité le 6 mai 2020).

British Army. "People. Drugs and Supplements." <https://www.army.mod.uk/people/join-well/drugs-and-supplements/> (visité le 30 mars, 2020).

British Army. *Values and Standards of the British Army*. AC *64649*, Andover: Army Headquarters, 2018, <https://www.army.mod.uk/media/5219/20180910-values_standards_2018_final.pdf> (visité le 26 mars, 2020).

British Medical Journal. "The Nuremberg Code (1947)." *British Medical Journal* 313, no. 7070 (1996): 1448. DOI: 10.1136/bmj.313.7070.1448.

Brock, Dan W. "Conscientious Refusal by Physicians and Pharmacists: Who Is Obligated to Do What, and Why?" *Theoretical Medicine and Bioethics* 29, no. 3 (2008): 187–200. DOI: 10.1007/s11017-008-9076-y.

Brunet, Alain, Daniel Saumier, Aihua Liu, David L Streiner, Jacques Tremblay, et Roger K Pitman. "Reduction of PTSD Symptoms With Pre-Reactivation Propranolol Therapy: A Randomized Controlled Trial," *American Journal of Psychiatry* 175, no. 5 (janvier 12, 2018): 427–33. DOI: 10.1176/appi.ajp.2017.17050481.

Buchanan, A. E. *Beyond Humanity?: The Ethics of Biomedical Enhancement*, (Oxford: OUP Oxford, 2011).

Burkeman, Oliver, et Richard Norton-Taylor. "US Pilots Blame Drug for Friendly Fire Deaths." *The Guardian*, le janvier 4, 2003, <https://www.theguardian.com/world/2003/jan/04/afghanistan.richardnortontaylor> (visité le 27 mars, 2020).

Caldwell, John A., and J. Lynn Caldwell. "Fatigue in Military Aviation: An Overview of U.S. Military-Approved Pharmacological Countermeasures." *Aviation, Space, and Environmental Medicine* 76, no. 7 (2005): C39–51.

Cantor, Julie D. "Conscientious Objection Gone Awry – Restoring Selfless Professionalism in Medicine." *New England Journal of Medicine* 360, no. 15 (2009): 1484–85. DOI: 10.1056/NEJMp0902019.

Care Quality Commission. "Defence Medical Services," 2019. <https://www.cqc.org.uk/what-we-do/services-we-regulate/defence-medical-services> (visité le 9 2020).

Carrick, D., P. M. L. Gross, P. J. Connelly, P. G. Lucas, et P.P. Robinson. *Military Medical Ethics for the 21st Century*, Military and Defence Ethics. (Ashgate Publishing Limited, 2013).

Casey, Anna, Jason Hughes, Rachel M Izard, and Julie P Greeves. "Supplement Use by UK-Based British Army Soldiers in Training." *The British Journal of Nutrition* 112, no. 7 (2014): 1175–84. DOI: 10.1017/S0007114514001597.

CBRN Delivery Team. *2017DIN04-165. Fentanyl Lozenge 800 Micrograms (OTFC) Single – Introduction into Service as Self Administered Operational Analgesia.* (Bristol: Ministry of Defence, 2017).

Corrigan, Oonagh. "Empty Ethics: The Problem with Informed Consent." *Sociology of Health & Illness* 25, no. 3 (2003): 768–92.

Dearden, Lizzie. "Women Now Allowed to Apply for Royal Marines and All Other Frontline Military Roles, Defence Secretary Announces," *The Independent*, le 25 octobre, 2018, <https://www.independent.co.uk/news/uk/home-news/women-soldiers-army-military-sas-defence-government-infantry-frontline-gavin-williamson-female-a8601371.html> (visité le 2 avril, 2020).

Deardorff, Stephen E. "Informed Consent, Termination of Medical Treatment, and the Federal Tort Claims Act--A New Proposal for the Military Health Care System," *Military Law Review* 115, no. Winter (1987): 1–120.

Dohmen, Thomas, Armin Falk, Bart H H Golsteyn, David Huffman, et Uwe Sunde. "Risk Attitudes across the Life Course." *The Economic Journal* 127, no. 605 (2017): F95–116. DOI: 10.1111/ecoj.12322.

Drabiak-Syed, Katherine. "Reining In the Pharmacological Enhancement Train: We Should Remain Vigilant about Regulatory Standards for Prescribing Controlled Substances," *The Journal of Law, Medicine & Ethics* 39, no. 2 (2011): 272–79. DOI: 10.1111/j.1748-720X.2011.00596.x.

Dunne, T. "Liberalism," in *The Globalisation of World Politics. An Introduction to World Politics*, édité par John Baylis, Steve Smith, et Patricia Owens, 102–13. (Oxford: Oxford University Press, 2011).

Dworkin, Gerald. "Paternalism," édité par Edward N. Zalta, *The Stanford Encyclopedia of Philosophy*. Stanford: Metaphysics Research Lab, Stanford University, 2019. <https://plato.stanford.edu/entries/paternalism/> (visité le 8 janvier, 2020).

Dyer, Clare. "Consent Needed For Organ Retention, BMA Says." *British Medical Journal* 321, no. 7269 (2000): 1098.

European Medicines Agency. "Modafinil," 2010. <https://www.ema.europa.eu/en/medicines/human/referrals/modafinil> (visité le 31 mars, 2020).

Faden, R. R., T. L. Beauchamp, et N. M. P. King. *A History and Theory of Informed Consent*, (New York: Oxford University Press, 1986).

Faden, Ruth R. *Advisory Committee on Human Radiation Experiments. Final Report.* (Washington DC: U.S. Government Printing Office, 1995).

Faden, Ruth R., Tom L. Beauchamp, et Nancy E. Kass. "Informed Consent, Comparative Effectiveness, and Learning Health Care." *New England Journal of Medicine* 370, no. 8 (2014): 766–68. DOI: 10.1056/NEJMhle1313674.

Farah, Martha J., Caroline Haimm, Geena Sankoorikal, et Anjan Chatterjee. "When We Enhance Cognition with Adderall, Do We Sacrifice Creativity? A Preliminary Study," *Psychopharmacology* 202, no. 1 (2009): 541–47. DOI: 10.1007/s00213-008-1369-3.

FitzPatrick, William J., et Lee L. Zwanziger. "Defending Against Biochemical Warfare." *The Journal of Philosophy, Science & Law* 3, no. 2 (2003): 1–19, DOI: 10.5840/jpsl2003323.

Ford, Kenneth, et Clark Glymour. "The Enhanced Warfighter." *Bulletin of the Atomic Scientists* 70, no. 1 (2014): 43–53.

Friedl, Karl E. "U.S. Army Research on Pharmacological Enhancement of Soldier Performance: Stimulants, Anabolic Hormones, and Blood Doping," *The Journal of Strength & Conditioning Research* 29 (2015): S71–76.

Galliott, J., and M Lotz. *Super Soldiers: The Ethical, Legal and Social Implications. Emerging Technologies, Ethics and International Affairs*. (Farnham: Taylor & Francis, 2016).

Gamble, Nathan K., and Michal Pruski. "Medical Acts and Conscientious Objection: What Can a Physician Be Compelled to Do?" *The New Bioethics* 25, no. 3 (2019): 262–82. DOI: 10.1080/20502877.2019.1649871.

Gebhardt, D. O. E. "Off-Label Administration of Drugs to Healthy Military Personnel. Dubious Ethics of Preventive Measures." *Journal of Medical Ethics* 31, no. 5 (2005): 268. DOI: 10.1136/jme.2004.008821.

General Medical Council. "Good Medical Practice," 2019. <https://www.gmc-uk.org/ethical-guidance/ethical-guidance-for-doctors/good-medical-practice> (visité le 6 avril, 2020).

Gidda, Mirren. "Drugs in War: What Is Captagon, the 'Jihad Pill' Used by Islamic State Militants?" *Newsweek*, May 12, 2017, <https://www.newsweek.com/drugs-captagon-islamic-state-jihad-war-amphetamines-saudi-arabia-608233> (visité le 26 mars, 2020).

Gross, Michael. *Military Medical Research Ethics: Investigational Drugs, Clinical Trials and Enhancement*. (Oxford: Oxford University Press, 2019).

Gross, Michael L. *Bioethics and Armed Conflict. Moral Dilemmas of Medicine and War*. (Cambridge: MIT Press, 2006).

Harvard Law School Library. "Nuremberg – Transcript Viewer – Transcript for NMT 1: Medical Case," *Nuremberg Trials Project*, 2016. <http://nuremberg.law.harvard.edu/transcripts/1-transcript-for-nmt-1-medical-case?seq=2586> (visité le 11 mars, 2020).

Harvey, Kate. "Sports Science and Medicine." *The Nuffield Council on Bioethics*, 2014, <https://nuffieldbioethics.org/publications/sports-science-and-medicine> (visité le 6 janvier, 2020).

Helgesson, Gert. "In Defense of Broad Consent." *Cambridge Quarterly of Healthcare Ethics* 21, no. 1 (2012): 40–50. DOI: 10.1017/S096318011100048X.

House of Commons Defence Committee. *Duty of Care. Third Report of Session 2004–05. Volume I. HC 63-I*. (London: The Stationery Office Limited, 2005).

Howe, Edmund G., et Edward D. Martin. "Treating the Troops." *Hastings Center Report* 21, no. 2 (1991): 21–24. DOI: 10.2307/3562332.

iMedi.co.uk. "Autoject (Combopen) Nerve Agent Antidote L4a1," 2009. <https://imedi.co.uk/autoject-combopen-nerve-agent-antidote-l4a1> (visité le 30 avril, 2020).

JASON. JSR-07-625. "Human Performance." Virginia, USA, 2008, <https://fas.org/irp/agency/dod/jason/human.pdf> (visité le 9 avril 2020).

Juengst, Eric T. "What Does Enhancement Mean?" in: *Enhancing Human Traits: Ethical and Social Implications*, édité par Eric Parens, 29–47. "Hastings Center Studies in Ethics Series." (Washington DC: Georgetown University Press, 2000).

Kamienski, L. *Shooting Up: A History of Drugs in Warfare*, (Oxford: Hurst, 2017).

Kamm, Frances M. "Is There a Problem With Enhancement?" *The American Journal of Bioethics* 5, no. 3 (2005): 5–14. DOI: 10.1080/15265160590945101.

Katz, Jay. "Informed Consent – Must It Remain a Fairy Tale." *Journal of Contemporary Health Law and Policy* 10 (1994): 69–92.

Katz, J., et A. M. Capron. *The Silent World of Doctor and Patient.* (Baltimore: Johns Hopkins University Press, 2002).

Kautz, Mary A., Maria L. Thomas, et J. Lynn Caldwell. "Considerations of Pharmacology on Fitness for Duty in the Operational Environment." *Aviation, Space, and Environmental Medicine* 78, no. 5 (2007): B107–12.

Kerr, Cathel. "Anthrax Vaccine Gets Cold Shoulder from Troops." *Canadian Medical Association Journal* 168, no. 10 (2003): 1308.

Kroutil, Larry A., David L. Van Brunt, Mindy A. Herman-Stahl, David C. Heller, Robert M. Bray, et Michael A. Penne. "Nonmedical Use of Prescription Stimulants in the United States," *Drug and Alcohol Dependence* 84, no. 2 (2006): 135–43.

Lennard, Natasha. "One in Ten Takes Drugs to Study." *Varsity*. March 6, 2009, <https://www.varsity.co.uk/news/1307> (visité le 31 mars, 2020).

Little, Robert. "Army Medicine: Untested in Battle." *The Bal-timore Sun*, mars 29, 2009. <https://www.baltimoresun.com/news/nation-world/bal-te.militarymed29mar29-story.html> (visité le 30 mars, 2020).

Lusher, Adam. "The Bizarre True Story of When the UK Military Tested LSD on Royal Marines." *The Independent*. le 24 mai 2018. <https://www.independent.co.uk/news/uk/home-news/lsd-video-porton-down-chemical-weapons-experiments-trials-uk-military-army-marines-sixties-acid-a8366906.html> (visité le 29 avril, 2020).

Maheshwari, Nidhi, et Vineeth V Kumar. *Military Psychology: Concepts, Trends and Interventions*, (New Delhi, India: Sage Publications Pvt. Ltd, 2016).

Maslen, Hannah, Nadira Faulmüller, et Julian Savulescu. "Pharmacological Cognitive Enhancement – How Neuroscientific Research Could Advance Ethical Debate," *Frontiers in Systems Neuroscience* 8 (2014): 1–12. DOI: 10.3389/fnsys.2014.00107.

McCartney, Helen. "The Military Covenant and the Civil–Military Contract in Britain," *International Affairs* 86, no. 2 (2010): 411–28. DOI: 10.1111/j.1468-2346.2010.00889.x.

McLellan, Tom M., John A. Caldwell, et Harris R. Lieberman. "A Review of Caffeine's Effects on Cognitive, Physical and Occupational Performance." *Neuroscience &*

Biobehavioral Reviews 71 (2016): 294–312. DOI: <https://doi.org/10.1016/j.neubiorev.2016.09.001>.

McManus, John, Sumeru G. Mehta, Annette R. McClinton, Robert A. De Lorenzo, et Toney W. Baskin. "Informed Consent and Ethical Issues in Military Medical Research." *Academic Emergency Medicine* 12, no. 11 (2005): 1120–26. DOI: 10.1197/j.aem.2005.05.037.

Mehlman, Maxwell. "Bioethics of Military Performance Enhancement," *Journal of the Royal Army Medical Corps* 165, no. 4 (2019): 226–231. DOI: 10.1136/jramc-2018-001130.

Mehlman, Maxwell J. et Stephanie Corley. "A Framework for Military Bioethics." *Journal of Military Ethics* 13, no. 4 (2014): 331–49. DOI: 10.1080/15027570.2014.992214.

Mehlman, Maxwell J., Patrick Lin, et Keith Abney. "Enhanced Warfighters: A Policy Framework," in: *Military Medical Ethics for the 21st Century*, édité par M.L. Gross et D. Carrick, 113–26, "Military and Defence Ethics," (Farnham: Ashgate Publishing Limited, 2013).

Mehlman, Maxwell, Patrick Lin, et Keith Abney. "Enhanced Warfighters: Risk, Ethics, and Policy." *Case Legal Studies Research Paper No. 2013–2*. (Elsevier BV), le 18 janvier 2013. DOI: 10.2139/ssrn.2202982.

Meijer, Marten. "A Human Performance Perspective on the Ethical Use of Cogniceuticals: Commentary on 'Recommendations for the Ethical Use of Pharmacologic Fatigue Countermeasures in the U.S. Military.'" *Aviation, Space, and Environmental Medicine* 78, no. 5 (2007): B131–33.

Messelken, Daniel, et Hans Ulrich Baer. "Hovering Between Roles: Military Medical Ethics," in: *Military Medical Ethics for the 21st Century*, édité par M.L. Gross et D. Carrick, 261–77. "Military and Defence Ethics," (Farnham: Ashgate Publishing Limited, 2013).

Mohamed, Ahmed Dahir. "Neuroethical Issues in Pharmacological Cognitive Enhancement." *WIREs Cognitive Science* 5, no. 5 (2014): 533–49. DOI: 10.1002/wcs.1306.

Morris, Marilyn C., et Robert M. Nelson. "Randomized, Controlled Trials as Minimal Risk: An Ethical Analysis," *Critical Care Medicine* 35, no. 3 (2007): 940–44.

Murphy, Dominic, Christopher Dandeker, Oded Horn, Matthew Hotopf, Lisa Hull, Margaret Jones, Theresa Marteau, Roberto Rona, et Simon Wessely. "UK Armed Forces Responses to an Informed Consent Policy for Anthrax Vaccination: A Paradoxical Effect?" *Vaccine* 24, no. 16 (2006): 3109–14. DOI: 10.1016/j.vaccine.2006.01.043.

Murphy, Dominic, Neil Greenberg, et Duncan Bland. "Health Concerns in UK Armed Forces Personnel." *Journal of the Royal Society of Medicine* 102, no. 4 (2009): 143–47. DOI: 10.1258/jrsm.2009.080387.

Myers, Carol S., Richard C. Taylor, Eric T. Moolchan, et Stephen J. Heishman. "Dose-Related Enhancement of Mood and Cognition in Smokers Administered Nicotine

Nasal Spray." *Neuropsychopharmacology* 33, no. 3 (2008): 588–98. DOI: 10.1038/sj.npp.1301425.

Newlands, Emma. "'They Even Gave Us Oranges on One Occasion': Human Experimentation in the British Army During the Second World War." *War & Society* 32, no. 1 (2013): 19–63. DOI: 10.1179/0729247312Z.00000000016.

Nicholson, P. J. "Communicating Health Risk." *Occupational Medicine* 49, no. 4 (1999): 253–56. DOI: 10.1093/occmed/49.4.253.

O'Neill, O. "Some Limits of Informed Consent." *Journal of Medical Ethics* 29, no. 1 (2003): 4–7. DOI: 10.1136/jme.29.1.4.

Olsen, Olav Kjellevold, Ståle Pallesen, et Eid Jarle. "The Impact of Partial Sleep Deprivation on Moral Reasoning in Military Officers," *Sleep* 33, no. 8 (2010): 1086–90. DOI: 10.1093/sleep/33.8.1086.

Parens, E. *Enhancing Human Traits: Ethical and Social Implications*. Hastings Center Studies in Ethics Series. (Washington DC: Georgetown University Press, 2000).

Patrey, James, Judith Lytle, William Sobotka, GeorgiAnna Sheppard, et Susan R. Kayar. "Human Performance Enhancement for NATO Military Operations (Science, Technology, and Ethics)," in: *NATO Research and Technology Organisation*, 1–7. Virginia, USA: Office of Naval Research Warfighter Performance Department, 2009 <https://apps.dtic.mil/dtic/tr/fulltext/u2/a562561.pdf> (visité le 6 janvier, 2020).

Pellegrino, Edmund D. "Autonomy and Coercion in Disease Prevention and Health Promotion." *Theoretical Medicine* 5, no. 1 (1984): 83–91. DOI: 10.1007/BF00489248.

Pérez-Guisado, Joaquín, and Philip M Jakeman, "Citrulline Malate Enhances Athletic Anaerobic Performance and Relieves Muscle Soreness," *The Journal of Strength & Conditioning Research* 24, no. 5 (2010): 1215–22.

President's Council on Bioethics. *Beyond Therapy: Biotechnology and the Pursuit of Happiness*. (New York: Regan Books, 2003).

Rayment, Sean. "Thousands of Soldiers on Antidepressants as They Battle Mental Health Issues, New Figures Reveal," *The Mirror*, July 28, 2018. <https://www.mirror.co.uk/news/uk-news/thousands-soldiers-antidepressants-battle-mental-12996613> (visité le 31 mars, 2020).

Rettig, Richard. *Waiving Informed Consent: Military Use of Non-FDA-Approved Drugs in Combat*. Santa Monica: RAND Corporation, 2000. DOI: 10.7249/rb7534 (visité le 30 avril, 2020).

Rettig, Richard A. "Military Use of Drugs Not Yet Approved by the FDA for CW/BW Defense: Lessons from the Gulf War." Santa Monica: RAND Corporation, 1999. <https://www.rand.org/pubs/monograph_reports/MR1018z9.html> (visité le 11 mars, 2020).

Robbins, Lauren R. "Refusing to Be All That You Can Be: Regulating against Forced Cognitive Enhancement in the Military," in: *Military Medical Ethics for the 21st Century*, edited by M.L. Gross et D. Carrick, 127–38. Military and Defence Ethics. (Farnham: Ashgate Publishing Limited, 2013).

Rosenbaum, S. "100 Years of Heights and Weights." *Journal of the Royal Statistical Society. Series A (Statistics in Society)* 151, no. 2 (1988): 276–309. DOI: 10.2307/2982758.

Russo, Michael B. "Recommendations for the Ethical Use of Pharmacologic Fatigue Countermeasures in the U.S. Military." *Aviation, Space, and Environmental Medicine* 78, no. 5 (2007): B119–27.

Sandberg, Anders, and Nick Bostrom. "Converging Cognitive Enhancements." *Annals New York Academy of Sciences* 1093 (2006): 201–27. DOI: 10.1196/annals.1382.015.

Sattler, Sebastian, Guido Mehlkop, Peter Graeff, et Carsten Sauer. "Evaluating the Drivers of and Obstacles to the Willingness to Use Cognitive Enhancement Drugs: The Influence of Drug Characteristics, Social Environment, and Personal Characteristics." *Substance Abuse Treatment, Prevention, and Policy* 9, no. 1 (2014): 1–14. DOI: 10.1186/1747-597X-9-8.

Savulescu, Julian. "Conscientious Objection in Medicine." *BMJ* 332, no. 7536 (2006): 294–97. DOI: 10.1136/bmj.332.7536.294.

Savulescu, J., et N Bostrom. *Human Enhancement.* (Oxford: OUP Oxford, 2009).

Savulescu, J., B. Foddy, et M. Clayton. "Why We Should Allow Performance Enhancing Drugs in Sport." *British Journal of Sports Medicine* 38, no. 6 (2004): 666–670. DOI: 10.1136/bjsm.2003.005249.

Savulescu, Julian, Leon Creaney, et Anna Vondy. "Should Athletes Be Allowed to Use Performance Enhancing Drugs?" *BMJ (Clinical Research Ed.)* 347 (2013): f6150. DOI: 10.1136/bmj.f6150.

Scharre, Paul, et Lauren Fish. "Human Performance Enhancement." *Center for a New American Security*, 2018. <https://www.cnas.org/publications/reports/human-performance-enhancement-1> (visité le 6 janvier 6, 2020).

Schelle, Kimberly J., Nadira Faulmüller, Lucius Caviola, et Miles Hewstone. "Attitudes toward Pharmacological Cognitive Enhancement – a Review." *Frontiers in Systems Neuroscience* 8 (2014): 1–14. DOI: 10.3389/fnsys.2014.00053.

Schofer, Joel Martin. "Violations of Informed Consent During War." *JAMA* 281, no. 17 (mai 5, 1999): 1657.

Schoomaker, Eric B. "Military Medical Research on Cognitive Performance: The Warfighters Competitive Edge." *Aviation, Space, and Environmental Medicine* 78, no. 5 (2007): B4–6.

Sears, Neil. "Army Signs up Recruits with a Reading Age as Young as FIVE in Desperate Bid to Boost Troop Numbers." *The Daily Mail,* le 5 avril 2020. <https://www.dailymail.co.uk/news/article-8190009/Army-signs-recruits-reading-age-young-FIVE-desperate-bid-boost-troop-numbers.html> (visité le 1ier mai, 2020).

Sellgren, Katherine. "Almost 40% of Army Recruits Have Reading Age of 11, MPs Warn." *BBC News*, le 18 juillet 2013. <https://www.bbc.co.uk/news/education-23346693> (visité le 1ier mai, 2020).

Support, Macmillan Cancer. "Familial Adenomatous Polyposis (FAP)." <https://www.macmillan.org.uk/cancer-information-and-support/worried-about-cancer/causes-and-risk-factors/familial-adenomatous-polyposis-fap> (visité le 6 avril, 2020).

The National Commission for the Protection of Human Subjects of Biomedical and Behavioural Research. "The Belmont Report: Ethical Principles and Guidelines for the Protection of Human Subjects of Research," 1979. <https://www.hhs.gov/ohrp/sites/default/files/the-belmont-report-508c_FINAL.pdf> (visité le 8 janvier, 2020).

The Royal College of Anaesthetists. "Guidelines for the Provision of Anaesthetic Services," 2020. <https://www.rcoa.ac.uk/safety-standards-quality/guidance-resources/guidelines-provision-anaesthetic-services> (visité le 6 avril, 2020).

U.S. Anti-Doping Agency. "Effects of Performance-Enhancing Drugs." <https://www.usada.org/athletes/substances/effects-of-performance-enhancing-drugs/> (visité le 8 mai 2020).

United Kingdom. Department of Health. "About Us – Medicines and Healthcare Products Regulatory Agency." <https://www.gov.uk/government/organisations/medicines-and-healthcare-products-regulatory-agency/about#our-responsibilities> (visité le 26 mars, 2020).

United Kingdom. Department of Health. "The Controlled Drugs (Supervision of Management and Use) Regulations 2013. Information about the Regulations," 2013. <https://assets.publishing.service.gov.uk/government/uploads/system/uploads/attachment_data/file/214915/15-02-2013-controlled-drugs-regulation-information.pdf> (visitié le 26 mars, 2020).

United Kingdom. Development Concepts and Doctrine Centre. *JSP 383. The Joint Service Manual of the Law of Armed Conflict*. Shrivenham: DCDC, 2004.

United Kingdom. HM Government. "Defence Medical Services." <https://www.gov.uk/government/groups/defence-medical-services> (visité le 18 mai, 2020).

United Kingdom. HM Government. "Off-Label or Unlicensed Use of Medicines: Prescribers' Responsibilities," 2014. <https://www.gov.uk/drug-safety-update/off-label-or-unlicensed-use-of-medicines-prescribers-responsibilities> (visité le 4 mai, 2020).

United Kingdom. HM Government. "Misuse of Drugs Act 1971," 1971. <http://www.legislation.gov.uk/ukpga/1971/38/contents> (visité le 26 mars, 2020).

United Kingdom. Ministry of Defence. "FOI2017/13417," 2018. <https://assets.publishing.service.gov.uk/government/uploads/system/uploads/attachment_data/file/691866/2017-13417.pdf> (visité le 31 mars, 2020).

United Kingdom. Ministry of Defence. *JSP 536. Governance of Research Involving Human Participants. Part 1: Directive*. 3ième ed. (London: HMSO, 2020).

United Kingdom. Ministry of Defence. *JSP 830: The Manual of Service Law*. (London: HMSO, 2016).

United Kingdom. Ministry of Defence. *The Queen's Regulations for the Army 1975. AC13206*. (London: Ministry of Defence, 2019).

United Kingdom. Ministry of Defence. "Ministry of Defence Research Ethics Committee." <https://www.gov.uk/government/groups/ministry-of-defence-research-ethics-committees#guidance-documents> (visité le 9 janvier, 2020).

United Kingdom. The Human Medicines Regulations 2012, Pub. L. No. 1916, Schedule 17 (2012). <http://www.legislation.gov.uk/uksi/2012/1916/schedule/17/made> (visité le 6 avril 6, 2020).

United Kingdom. The Medicines for Human Use (Clinical Trials) Regulations, Pub. L. No. 1031, Schedule 1 (2004). <http://www.legislation.gov.uk/uksi/2004/1031/schedule/1/part/2/paragraph/3/made#text%3Dinformed%consent> (visité le 1ier janvier, 2020).

United Nations. "Universal Declaration of Human Rights," 1948. <https://www.un.org/en/universal-declaration-human-rights/> (visité le 9 janvier, 2020).

Wamberg, Jacob, Mads Rosendahl Thomsen, et Kasper Lippert-Rasmussen. *The Posthuman Condition : Ethics, Aesthetics and Politics of Biotechnological Challenges*. (Aarhus, Denmark: Aarhus University Press, 2012).

Westcott, Kelli J. "Modafinil, Sleep Deprivation, and Cognitive Function in Military and Medical Settings." *Military Medicine* 170, no. 4 (2005): 333–35. DOI: 10.7205/MILMED.170.4.333.

Wilson, Jacque. "Lance Armstrong's Doping Drugs – CNN." *CNN*, 18 janvier 18, 2013. <https://edition.cnn.com/2013/01/15/health/armstrong-ped-explainer/index.html> (visité le 12 avril, 2020).

Wolfendale, Jessica. "Performance-Enhancing Technologies and Moral Responsibility in the Military." *The American Journal of Bioethics* 8, no. 2 (2008): 28–38. DOI: 10.1080/15265160802014969.

Wolfendale, Jessica, et Steve Clarke. "Paternalism, Consent, and the Use of Experimental Drugs in the Military." *The Journal of Medicine and Philosophy: A Forum for Bioethics and Philosophy of Medicine* 33, no. 4 (2008): 337–55. DOI: 10.1093/jmp/jhn014.

World Anti-Doping Agency. "World Anti-Doping Code." Montreal: World Anti-Doping Agency, 2015. <https://www.wada-ama.org/sites/default/files/resources/files/wada_anti-doping_code_2019_english_final_revised_v1_linked.pdf> (visité le 12 mars, 2020).

World Health Organisation. "An Introduction to Risk Communication." (visité le 12 mars, 2020). <https://www.who.int/risk-communication/introduction-to-risk-communication.pdf?ua=1>.

World Medical Association. "Ethical Principles for Medical Research Involving Human Subjects." *WMA Declaration of Helsinki*, 2018. <https://www.wma.net/policies-post/wma-declaration-of-helsinki-ethical-principles-for-medical-research-involving-human-subjects/> (visité le 9 janvier, 2020).